AQA Human Biology

AS

Exclusively endorsed by AQA

'UG'

Pauline Lowrie

Nelson Thornes

Published in 2008 by:
Nelson Thornes Ltd
Delta Place
27 Bath Road
CHELTENHAM
GL53 7TH
United Kingdom

08 09 10 11 12 / 10 9 8 7 6 5 4 3 2

A catalogue record for this book is available from the British Library

ISBN 978 0 7487 8277 2

Cover photograph by Getty Images/LWA/Dann Tardif

Illustrations include artwork drawn by Barking Dog Art and GreenGate Publishing

Page make-up by GreenGate Publishing, Kent

Printed and bound in Great Britain by Scotprint

Loughborough
COLLEGE est 1909

Photograph Acknowledgements

The authors and publisher are grateful to the following for permission to reproduce photographs and other copyright material in this book.

Alamy: Alex Segre p 15; Blend Images p 186 (right); Corbis Premium RF p 168 (right & left); David Cook, www.blueshiftstudios.co.uk p 86 (top); David Wall p 209 (top); Digital Vision p 186 (bottom left); Edward Moss p 74; Holger Ehlers p 186 (middle left); Martin Jenkinson p 67; Mary Evans Picture Library p 70; Nik Taylor p 3; Peter Arnold, Inc. p 100; Phototake Inc. p 56 (left), p 73; Robert Estall photo agency p 209 (bottom); **BBC:** p 172; **Cells Alive, Jim Sullivan:** p 71 (top left); **Corbis:** p 203; Ashley Cooper p 36; Jeffrey L. Rotman p 9; Stephen Morrison p 109 (top); **Corel 127 (NT):** p 148 (top); **Corel 473 (NT):** p 174; **Corel 766 (NT):** p 206 (left & right); **Digital Vision 17 (NT):** p 4, p 14; **Digital Vision CP (NT):** p 5 (top), p 5 (bottom); **Getty Images:** LWA/Dann Tardif p viii; **iStock:** p 13; **Mark Beech:** p 27 (chromatogram); **Photodisc 6 (NT):** p 206 (top); **Photodisc 54 (NT):** p 159 (right); **photolibrary.com:** p 55; **Science Photo Library:** p 119 (top right); Alfred Pasieka p 56 (right), p 68; Anatomical Travelogue p 84; Anthony Cooper p 148 (bottom); A. Barrington Brown p 119 (bottom); Biology Media p 57 (top); Biophoto Associates p 61, p 107; BSIP, Mendil p 60 (left); Charles D. Winters p 27; Craig Lovell/AgstockUSA p 204 (right); Colin Cuthbert p 34, p 91; Cordelia Molloy p 35 (bottom); CRNI p 66, p 99; Dr M. A. Ansary p 88; D. Phillips p 42; Dr Tony Brain p 35 (middle); Dr P. Marazzi p 86 (bottom), p 140, p 129; Eye of Science p 35 (top), p 66, p 197; GustoImages p 17; ISM p 77 (top); James King-Holmes p 204 (left); Jason Kelvin p 188 (left); J.C. Revy p 30; Jerry Mason p 168 (left); John Reader p 166, p 177; Lauren Shear p 145; Louise Murray p 188 (right); Mark Clarke p 11 (top); Michael W. Tweedie p 156 (top & bottom); Neil Borden p 97; Paul Rapson p 11 (bottom); Paul Zahl p 159 (left); Prof. G Gimenez-Martin p 139 (all); R. Umesh Chandran p 109 (bottom); Science Source p 119 (top left), p 77 (bottom); Simon Fraser/RVI, Newcastle-Upon-Tyne p 60 (right), p 104; Sovereign, ISM p 101; St. Mary's Hospital Medical School p 71 (bottom left); Steve Gschmeissner p 57 (bottom), p 59, p 82; Tom McHugh p 117; Zephyr p 69.

Every effort has been made to trace and contact all copyright holders and we apologise if any have been overlooked. The publisher will be pleased to make the necessary arrangements at the first opportunity.

Contents

AQA introduction

Nelson Thornes and AQA

Nelson Thornes has worked in collaboration with AQA to ensure that this book offers you the best support for your AS level course and helps you to prepare for your exams. The partnership means that you can be confident that the range of learning, teaching and assessment practice materials has been checked by the senior examining team at AQA before formal approval, and is closely matched to the requirements of your specification.

Blended learning

Printed and electronic resources are blended. This means that links between the topics and activities between the book and the electronic resources, help you to work in the way that best suits you, and enable extra support to be provided online. For example, you can test yourself online, and feedback from the test will direct you back to the relevant parts of the book.

Electronic resources are available in a simple-to-use online platform called Nelson Thornes *learning space*. If your school or college has a licence to use the service, you will be given a password through which you can access the materials through any internet connection.

Icons in this book indicate where there is material online related to that topic. The following icons are used:

Learning activity

These resources include a variety of interactive and non-interactive activities to support your learning:

- Animations
- Simulations
- Maths skills
- Key diagrams
- Glossary

Progress tracking

These resources include a variety of tests that you can use to check your knowledge on particular topics (Test yourself) and a range of resources that enable you to analyse and understand examination questions (On your marks...). You will also find the answers to the examination-style questions online.

Research support

These resources include WebQuests, in which you are assigned a task and provided with a range of web links to use as source material for research.

These are designed as Extension resources to stretch you and broaden your learning, in order for you to attain the highest possible marks in your exams.

Web links

Our online resources feature a list of recommended weblinks, spilt by chapter. This will give you a head start, helping you to navigate to the best websites that will aid your learning and understanding of the topics in your course.

How science works

These resources are a mixture of interactive and non-interactive activities to help you learn the skills required for success in this new area of the specification.

Practical

This icon signals where there is a relevant practical activity to be undertaken, and support is provided online.

When you see an icon, go to Nelson Thornes *learning space* at www.nelsonthornes.com/aqagce, enter your access details and select your course. The materials are arranged in the same order as the topics in the book, so you can easily find the resources you need.

How to use this book

This book covers the specification for your course and is arranged in a sequence approved by AQA.

The textbook will cover all three of the Assessment Objectives required in your AQA A Level Human Biology course.

The main text of the book will cover AO1 – Knowledge and understanding. This consists of the main factual content of the specification. The other Assessment Objectives (AO2 – Application of knowledge and understanding and AO3 – How science works) make up around 50% of the assessment weighting of the specification, and as such will be covered in the textbook in the form of the feature 'Applications and How science works' (see below). You will **not** be asked to recall the information given under these headings for the purpose of examinations.

The book content is divided into the two theory units of the AQA Human Biology AS specification; Unit 1 – The body and its diseases and Unit 2 – Humans – their origins and adaptations. Units are then further divided into chapters, and then topics, making the content clear and easy to use.

Unit openers give you a summary of the content you will be covering, and a recap of ideas from GCSE that you will need.

The features in this book include:

Learning objectives

At the beginning of each section you will find a list of learning objectives that contain targets linked to the requirements of the specification. The relevant specification reference is also provided.

Key terms

Terms that you will need to be able to define and understand are highlighted in bold blue type within the text, e.g. **mitosis**. You can look up these terms in the glossary on page 216.

Hint

Hints to aid your understanding of the content.

Link

Links highlight any key areas where sections relate to one another.

Applications and How science works

These features may cover either or both of the assessment objectives AO2 – Application of knowledge and understanding and AO3 – How science works, both key parts of the new specification.

As with the specification, these objectives are integrated throughout the content of the book. This feature highlights opportunities to apply your knowledge and understanding and draws out aspects of 'How science works' as they occur within topics, so that it is always relevant to what you are studying. The ideas provided in these features intend to teach you the skills you will need to tackle this part of the course, and give you experience that you can draw upon in the examination. You will not be examined on the exact information provided in this book with relation to the Application and How science works features.

For more information, see 'How science works' on page 1 for more detail.

Summary questions

Short questions that test your understanding of the subject and allow you to apply the knowledge and skills you have acquired to different scenarios. Answers are supplied at the back of the book. These answers are more than just a mark scheme. They often include exaplanations of the answers to aid learning and understanding. These answers are not exhaustive and there may be acceptable alternatives.

Examiner's tip

Hints from AQA examiners to help you with your studies and to prepare you for your exam.

AQA Examination-style questions

Questions from past AQA papers that are in the general style that you can expect in your exam. These occur at the end of each chapter to give practice in examination-style questions for a particular topic. They also occur at the end of each unit; the questions here may cover any of the content of the unit.

Answers to these questions are supplied online.

AQA examination questions are reproduced by permission of the Assessment and Qualifications Alliance.

Nelson Thornes is responsible for the solution(s) given and they may not constitute the only possible solution(s).

Web links in the book

Because Nelson Thornes is not responsible for third party content online, there may be some changes to this material that are beyond our control. In order for us to ensure that the links referred to in the book are as up-to-date and stable as possible, the web sites provided are usually homepages with supporting instructions on how to reach the relevant pages if necessary.

Please let us know at **webadmin@nelsonthornes.com** if you find a link that doesn't work and we will do our best to correct this at reprint, or to list an alternative site.

Studying AS Human Biology

Welcome to Human Biology at AS level.

This book aims to make your study of human biology successful and interesting.

The book is written to cover the content of the AS course for the AQA specification. Each chapter in the book corresponds exactly to the subdivisions of each unit of the specification.

AS course structure (% of total AS marks is shown in brackets)

Unit 1 The body and its diseases
(40%) Chapters 1-6

Unit 2 Humans – their origins and adaptations
(40%) Chapters 7-11

Unit 3 Investigative and Practical skills
(20%) Online resources

Using the book

You will find that the AS course builds on the skills and understanding you developed in your GCSE course. New ideas are presented in the book in a careful step by step manner to enable you to develop a firm understanding of concepts and ideas. Human Biology at AS level will require you to describe and explain facts and processes in detail and with accuracy. However, the course is also about developing skills so that you can apply what you have learned. Examination papers will test skills such as interpreting new information, analysing experimental data, and evaluating information. In the AQA specification you will see sections which begin 'candidates should be able to ....' These are the sections which set out the skills you will need to develop to achieve success. You will find 'Application and How science works' features in the book. These features present relevant and challenging information which will enable you to develop these skills. The factual content of these sections is **not** required for examination purposes.

The AQA specification also emphasises how scientists work and how their work affects people in their everyday lives. For example, information is often presented in newspapers and on TV on science issues such as the possible side-effects of vaccines or drugs. Such reports may even contain conflicting evidence. The validity of evidence and the accuracy of conclusions is constantly questioned by scientists. Information in the text and in the accompanying resources will enable you to analyse evidence and data and to evaluate the way scientists obtain new evidence.

Checking your progress

You will find questions at the end of each chapter so that you can check your progress as you complete each section. Each chapter represents a manageable amount of learning so that you do not try to achieve too much too quickly. At the end of each unit there are questions written by AQA examiners in the same style that you will meet in examinations.

Investigative and practical skills

There are two routes for the assessment of Investigative and Practical Skills:

Either, **Route T**: Practical Skills Assessment (PSA) + Investigative Skills Assignment (ISA), which will be marked by your teacher.

Or, **Route X**: Practical Skills Verification (PSV) (assessed by your teacher) + Externally Marked Practical Assessment (EMPA), which is set and marked by an external AQA appointed examiner.

Both routes form 20% of the total AS assessment and will involve carrying out practical work, collecting and processing data, and then using the data to answer questions in a written test. The resources which accompany the book provide examples of investigations so that you can develop your practical and investigative skills as you progress through the topics in Units 1 and 2.

The book and accompanying resources provides a wealth of material specifically written for your AS biology course. As well as helping you to achieve success, you should find the resources interesting and challenging.

How science works

You have already gained some skills through the 'How science works' component of your GCSE course. As you progress through your AS Human Biology course, you will develop your scientific skills further and learn about important new ideas and applications through the 'How science works' component of your A level course. These skills are a key part of how every scientist works. Scientists use them to probe and test new theories and applications in whatever field of work they are working in. Now you will develop them further and gain new skills as you progress through the course.

'How science works' is developed in this book through relevant features in the main content of the book and are highlighted accordingly. The 'How science works' features in this book will help you to develop the relevant 'How science works' skills necessary for examination purposes but more importantly these features should give you a thorough grasp of how scientists work, as well as a deeper awareness of how science is used to improve the quality of life for everyone.

When carrying out their work scientists:

- Use theories, models and ideas to develop scientific explanations and make progress when validated evidence is found that supports a new theory or model.

- Use their knowledge and understanding when observing objects or events, in defining a problem and when questioning the explanations of themselves or of other scientists

- Make observations that lead to explanations in the form of hypotheses. In turn hypotheses lead to predictions that can be tested experimentally.

- Carry out experimental and investigative activities that involves making accurate measurements, and recording measurements methodically.

- Analyse and interpret data to look for patterns and trends, to provide evidence and identify relationships.

- Evaluate methodology, evidence and data, and resolve conflicting evidence.

- Appreciate that if evidence is reliable and reproducible and does not support a theory, the theory must be modified or replaced with a different theory.

- Communicate the findings of their research to provide opportunity for other scientists to replicate and further test their work.

- Evaluate, and report on the risks associated with new technology and developments.

- Consider ethical issues in the treatment of humans, other organisms and effects on the environment.

- Appreciate the role of the scientific community in validating findings and developments .

- Appreciate how society in general uses science to inform decision making.

UNIT
1
The body and its diseases

Chapters in this unit

The human body is composed of many different cell types. To maintain a healthy body, humans need to eat a balanced diet. Chapter 1 explores what a 'balanced diet' means and the food groups involved in human nutrition. We also look at some topical issues regarding diet, such as food labelling, and vitamin supplements. Food groups contain a variety of different molecules that come from cells of other living organisms. You will learn about these molecules and how they are digested using enzymes.

Enzymes act as catalysts in the body. In Chapter 2 you will find out how enzymes work, how they are affected by different factors and their uses in medicine. You will also learn about the medical problems caused when the body does not make a particular enzyme properly.

Humans also need to exchange gases with their surroundings. In Chapter 3 you will learn how the lungs are adapted for efficient gas exchange, and gases are transported around the body in the blood to cells. The structure of cells is described. Cystic fibrosis results from an inherited disorder of cell membranes. People with cystic fibrosis have difficulties with gas exchange and in absorbing digested food. You will learn more about this disease and learn how the symptoms of cystic fibrosis arise and how they can be treated.

Diseases, such as tuberculosis, may also result from infection by microorganisms. This is a bacterial infection and is treated by antibiotics. HIV/AIDS is a viral disease. Issues such as antibiotic resistance are explored further in Chapter 4. How the body fights infection is explored in Chapter 5 and how we can help the body through vaccination and the use of monoclonal antibodies.

Some other diseases, such as coronary heart disease, are linked with lifestyle. You will learn about the structure of the heart, how it beats and how blood is transported around the body in Chapter 6. Then this chapter looks in more detail at heart disease and its causes.

What you already know

Whilst the material in this unit is intended to be self-explanatory, there is certain information from GCSE that will prove very helpful to the understanding of the content of this unit. A knowledge of the following elements of GCSE will be of assistance:

- Living organisms are made up of cells.

- Cell membranes control what enters and leaves a cell.

- Reactions in cells are controlled by enzymes.

- The human lungs carry out gas exchange.

- Nutrients and gases are transported around the body in the blood.

- Some microorganisms cause diseases.

- Human health is affected by a range of environmental and inherited factors.

1.1 Balanced diet

Learning objectives:

- What is a balanced diet?
- Why do we need energy even when we are not active?
- What types of sugars are best for you?

Specification reference: 3.1.1

Cystic fibrosis is an inherited condition affecting about one child in every 2500 born in the UK. There is no cure for the condition, although improvements in medicine mean that these children can now lead almost normal lives, and expect to live until middle age. Before we look at cystic fibrosis in detail, it is important to understand what makes a body healthy.

A balanced diet should be balanced in terms of energy and food groups. A balanced diet needs the right amounts of fibre, water, carbohydrates, fats, proteins, vitamins and minerals. These food groups will be looked at in the rest of this chapter.

Energy balance

Most of our energy is obtained from carbohydrates and fats. Protein can be used as an energy source too, when there is more than enough for growth and repair. In simple terms, if you take in more energy in your food than you use up in everyday activities, you will put on weight. If this continues over a long period of time, you may become obese. This is because the body stores the extra energy as body fat. Body fat is stored under the skin and around internal organs. On the other hand, if you take in less energy in your food than you need to carry out your everyday activities, then you will lose weight. Stores of body fat will be used up. If this happens over a long period of time, e.g. during starvation, the body will start to break down other parts of the body. This means that body proteins, for example muscle tissue, are used up. Therefore it is important that a diet is balanced in terms of energy.

All carbohydrates (except fibre) provide similar amounts of energy per gram. However, the type of carbohydrate that you eat can have an impact on your health. Nutritionists classify sugars into three groups:

- Intrinsic sugars: These are sugars contained within the cells of food, e.g. sugars within the cells of an apple or banana.
- Extrinsic sugars: These are not contained inside cells. Examples are those sugars found in processed foods like chocolate or soft drinks. These sugars are most likely to lead to tooth decay.
- Milk sugars: These are found in milk and milk products such as cheese. The most important milk sugar is lactose.

Nutritionists recommend that we should not obtain more than 10% of our daily energy requirements from extrinsic sugars. Starches, intrinsic sugars and milk sugars should make up about 40% of our daily energy intake. However, it is recommended that we obtain most of this energy from starches. As seen in Topic 1.2, this is because the energy from starches is released more slowly. It is sensible to eat more starch and to reduce sugar consumption, because it stops blood glucose levels rising too sharply, and stops you feeling hungry for much longer.

Figure 1 *Fruit is important in a balanced diet*

Applications and How science works

Basal metabolic rate

Even when your body is at rest, it needs energy for all the many processes going on in the body. For example, your brain is using energy to process information; your intestines are using energy to push food along and absorb nutrients into the blood; your heart is pumping blood around the body; you need heat energy to maintain your body temperature; and energy is needed for processes such as active transport and protein synthesis. The energy you need to keep yourself alive, when you are at rest but not asleep, is called your **basal metabolic rate (BMR)**. Your BMR varies according to your age, sex and body size.

- Women have a lower BMR than men, because they have a higher ratio of adipose (fat-storage) tissue to muscle. Muscle has a higher metabolic rate than adipose tissue.
- People with a higher body mass have a higher BMR because they have more respiring tissue.
- Tall, slim people have a higher BMR than a short, fat person with the same body mass. This is because the slimmer person has a higher surface area to volume ratio, and loses more body heat.
- Children have a higher BMR for their size than adults because they are growing and developing rapidly.
- Older people tend to have a lower BMR than younger people, because older people usually have a lower proportion of muscle tissue.
- Pregnant women have a higher BMR because the foetus is growing and respiring rapidly. It gets all its energy needs from its mother.

However, the amount of energy you need in food also depends on your level of activity.

Figure 2 *Exercise and outside play are important for a healthy up-bringing*

1. Explain why a man has a higher BMR than a woman of the same height and body mass.

2. Explain why a pregnant woman has a higher BMR than a non-pregnant woman of the same size.

Applications and How science works

Anorexia nervosa

Some people can be starving, even though they have plenty of food available to them. They can suffer from a psychological condition called anorexia nervosa. This affects far more girls than boys, and mainly affects teenagers. It usually starts when a person goes on a diet to try to lose weight, but the person becomes obsessed about food. Anorexics lack confidence and see the ability to control their food intake as a way of taking charge of their lives. To others, they may appear unnaturally thin, but they see themselves as unattractively fat. Unless the condition is successfully treated, an anorexic may starve herself to death.

1. When a person is in advanced starvation, they may still die despite being given enough food and water. Suggest why.

Summary questions

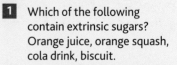

1. Which of the following contain extrinsic sugars? Orange juice, orange squash, cola drink, biscuit.

2. Suggest why the energy in starch is released more slowly than the energy in sugars.

1.2 Glycaemic index and glycaemic load

Learning objectives:

■ What are glycaemic index and glycaemic load?

■ Are low carbohydrate diets good for you?

Specification reference: 3.1.1

Glycaemic index

You will remember from GCSE that starch is a carbohydrate found in many foods. It is digested into glucose which is absorbed into the blood. The glycaemic index tells us how much glucose a food contains and how quickly the glucose is released. This information can be used by people who are trying to lose weight. Foods with a low glycaemic index release their glucose content more slowly, so the person is likely to feel full for longer. In turn, this means the person is less likely to overeat.

To find the **glycaemic index** (**GI**) of a food, scientists feed volunteers enough of one specific food to give 50 g of carbohydrates (excluding dietary fibre). They take blood samples afterwards, to see how much the food has raised the level of glucose in the blood. The concentration of glucose in the blood is measured several times over a period of two hours. Some kinds of starch are digested more slowly than others, while foods containing sugars release glucose more quickly. The more glucose that is released by the food, and the more quickly the glucose is released, the greater the area under the curve in Figure 1 will be. The test is carried out on 10 different human subjects and then the average value found. This is converted to a figure known as the glycaemic index. The GI is a figure out of 100; 50 g of glucose has the highest possible glycaemic index, so this is 100. Other foods are compared to glucose.

The effects of a high GI food and a low GI food on blood glucose concentration

You will remember from GCSE that when your blood glucose level increases, the pancreas is stimulated to release insulin. Insulin causes the liver and muscle cells to store the glucose as glycogen. However, if the blood glucose level stays too high for too long, the excess glucose will be stored as fat. Furthermore, the release of insulin causes the blood glucose level to fall. If a lot of insulin is released, it may cause the blood glucose level to fall more sharply. This can lead to a dip in blood glucose levels that can make you feel hungry again. Overeating can result and, eventually, obesity. For this reason, it is recommended that we should avoid too many sugary foods with a high GI.

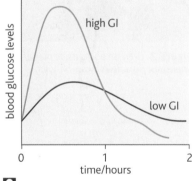

Figure 1 *Graph showing the effects of a high GI food and a low GI food*

■ A GI of 70 or over is high.

■ A GI of 56–69 is medium.

■ A GI of 55 or less is low.

The glycaemic index can only be calculated for foods with a reasonable carbohydrate content, as the test relies on human subjects eating enough of the food to contain 50 g of carbohydrate (excluding fibre). Many fruits and vegetables contain very little carbohydrate per serving, so they have very low GI values. For example, to eat enough carrots to contain 50 g of carbohydrate you would need to eat about 700 g – which is a very large portion!

Factors that affect the glycaemic index of foods

■ Starch molecules can be different in different plants – the exact shape of the starch molecule and the amount of branching it has can vary.

This will affect how quickly it is hydrolysed by enzymes and absorbed into the blood.

■ Whether the starch is combined with dietary fibre, as dietary fibre slows down the absorption of sugars into the blood.

■ The presence of other components in the food. For example, the presence of fat affects the rate of carbohydrate digestion, and adding vinegar to food, which lowers its pH, can also slow down the digestion and absorption of carbohydrates.

Sometimes, glycaemic index is calculated using white bread, instead of glucose, as a standard. This is because many people eat white bread so they can compare the other foods they eat with it.

💡 Glycaemic load

As we have already seen, glycaemic index does not always tell you the effect that a portion of food will have on your blood glucose level. For this reason, many people think that the **glycaemic load** is a better measurement. The glycaemic load (GL) for a portion of food is calculated as the quantity (in grams) of its carbohydrate content, multiplied by its GI and divided by 100.

$$\text{glycaemic load} = \text{carbohydrate content of food (g)} \times \frac{\text{GI of food}}{100}$$

For example, watermelon has a GI of 72, so it is classed as a high glycaemic index food. However, a normal portion of watermelon might be a slice weighing 100 g. Watermelons have a high water content, so this slice will only contain 5 g of carbohydrate. Its glycaemic load, therefore, will be $5 \times \frac{72}{100} = 3.6$, so its glycaemic load is 3.6.

■ A GL of 20 or more is high.
■ A GL of 11–19 is medium.
■ A GL of 10 or less is low.

■ Low carbohydrate diets

Diets based on glycaemic index and glycaemic load aim to reduce overeating by eating foods that do not increase blood glucose too suddenly or too much. Remember that fats and proteins in the diet do not increase blood glucose levels when they are absorbed. Some diets, such as the Atkins diet, aim to cut carbohydrates to a minimum. However, some people are concerned that these diets can be unhealthy in other ways. These diets are often high in fats, especially saturated fats, which can be a cause of heart disease. Current dietary advice is to reduce our consumption of fats. Also, by reducing carbohydrates, people may not eat enough fibre.

Table 1 *Table showing GI and GL of some foods*

Food	GI	GL
white rice	98	33
cornflakes	84	21
French fries/ chips	75	30
ice cream	61	10
all bran	42	9
strawberries, fresh	42	1
apple	38	6

Summary questions

1. What is: a glycaemic index, b glycaemic load?

2. Fifty grams of glucose has a glycaemic index of 100. What would be the glycaemic load of this portion?

3. Explain why strawberries have a glycaemic index of 42 but a glycaemic load of only 1.

4. Explain why a portion of brown rice has a lower glycaemic load than a portion of white rice.

5. If spaghetti is boiled for 15 minutes, it has a higher glycaemic load than if it is boiled for 7 minutes. Suggest why.

1.3 Vitamins and mineral salts

Learning objectives:

- What are vitamins and mineral salts?
- Why do we need them?
- Is it a good idea to take vitamin supplements?

Specification reference: 3.1.1

Vitamins

Vitamins are organic molecules that are needed by the body in very small amounts. Many of them interact with important enzymes involved in cell processes. Most of the vitamins we need are taken in from the food we eat. There are two vitamins that we can obtain from other sources, so we do not have to rely on our food for them. One of these is vitamin D. This is found in egg yolks, oily fish (such as mackerel), meat, margarine and low-fat spreads. However, it is also made in the body by the action of ultraviolet rays from sunlight on the skin. This means that light-skinned people who are exposed to enough sunlight do not have to rely on vitamin D from their diet. However, darker-skinned people have more of the pigment melanin in their skin. This means that they will make less vitamin D in their skin, especially in a temperate climate such as that of the UK.

Mineral salts

A number of mineral salts are important in the body, and these are shown in the table. Some mineral salts are needed in fairly high amounts, and these are called macronutrients. Others are needed in much smaller (or trace) amounts, so these are called micronutrients.

Table 1 *Minerals required by humans*

Mineral ion	Major food source	Function
Calcium (Ca^{2+})	Dairy foods, eggs	Constituent of bones and teeth, needed for blood clotting
Phosphate (PO_4^{3-})	Dairy foods, eggs, meat	Constituent of nucleic acids, ATP, phospholipids, bones and teeth
Iron (Fe^{2+}/Fe^{3+})	Liver, green vegetables	Constituent of haemoglobin and myoglobin
Sodium (Na^+)	Table salt, dairy foods, meat, eggs, vegetables	Needed for nerve and muscle action

AQA Examiner's tip

You don't need to learn the details of the vitamins and minerals mentioned here. You just need to know that they are important for processes in the body, often because they interact with enzymes.

Applications and How science works

Should we take vitamin and mineral supplements?

Vitamin D can be stored in our muscles and body fat. It is needed so that we can absorb calcium ions from the food in our guts, and also to assist in depositing calcium in bone cells. Lack of a vitamin can lead to a **deficiency disease**. Vitamin D deficiency can lead to the disease, rickets, in children. A child with rickets has soft bones that do not grow properly. The joints may become swollen and the limb and chest bones may bend. In adults, vitamin D deficiency causes a gradual softening of the bones. The bones may become painful, and more likely to fracture. Pregnant women should increase their intake of vitamin D because it is needed for the developing bones of the foetus.

Figure 1 *A child with rickets*

You will read on page 10 that bacteria in our guts can produce vitamin K. This is a vitamin that is important in blood clotting. However, we also obtain this vitamin in our diet, from dark green vegetables such as broccoli.

Another important vitamin is vitamin A. This is found in milk, egg yolks and carrots. Vitamin A is used to make the pigment rhodopsin, present in the rod cells in the eye. These cells are needed for vision in dim light. This vitamin can also be stored in the liver. A lack of vitamin A eventually leads to blindness, through inflammation and scarring of the cornea of the eye. It also causes 'night blindness', which is an inability to see in dim light.

1   Give two examples of a deficiency disease.

Many people believe that they should take vitamin and mineral supplements to make sure they are healthy. Some people even believe that high doses of some vitamins have health benefits. One useful vitamin is vitamin E, found in many fruits and vegetables. This acts as an antioxidant, and seems to be beneficial in preventing cancer. There do not appear to be any dangers of consuming too much vitamin E. On the other hand, high amounts of vitamin D can cause kidney damage and kidney stones, while high levels of vitamin A are toxic and can lead to serious side-effects including liver damage. Experts may recommend supplements for certain people, such as pregnant women or the elderly.

2   Suggest why a pregnant woman or an elderly person might need a vitamin supplement.

3   Should fit, young people take vitamin and mineral supplements? Explain your answer.

Summary question

1   Explain the difference between a macronutrient and a micronutrient.

1.4 Bacteria in the gut

Learning objectives:

- Do the bacteria in our guts do anything?

- Are probiotic drinks good for your health?

Specification reference: 3.1.1

Everybody has a wide range of bacteria in their guts. Most of these are not harmful bacteria, and indeed, there is evidence that some of the bacteria can be useful. Some of the bacteria are thought to release useful compounds into the gut, or they may compete with harmful bacteria that have been taken in with food, reducing their harmful effects. Biologists often talk about these bacteria as a 'healthy gut flora'.

Vitamin K is essential in humans and most animals. It is needed by the liver to synthesise thrombin. This is an enzyme needed for blood clotting. Humans cannot synthesise vitamin K themselves, so it has to come from another source. There are two forms of vitamin K, vitamin K1 and vitamin K2. Vitamin K1 is found in dark green vegetables such as broccoli and spinach, and also in some oils, such as soybean oil. This means that we can obtain vitamin K1 from our diet. Vitamin K2 is produced by some bacteria that live in the intestines. One of these bacteria is *E. coli*. This bacterium uses vitamin K2 in its respiration, and when the bacteria die, vitamin K2 is released from their cells. It is thought that this vitamin is absorbed by the body to be used in the liver.

Applications and How science works

Research on vitamin K and *E. coli*

Some scientists carried out an investigation to find out whether vitamin K made by *E. coli* in the gut is absorbed into the body and used by the liver. They used rats that had been born and raised in a completely sterile environment, without any bacteria present. They injected different groups of rats with different bacteria, including *E. coli*. They found that these *E. coli* bacteria made vitamin K in the rats' guts. They also showed that the rats that had been infected with vitamin K-producing bacteria also had a higher concentration of vitamin K in their livers than the rats infected with other bacteria.

A different study was carried out in humans who had just died. All of them, because they were adults, had a fully developed population of bacteria in their guts, including *E. coli*, but with many other kinds present as well. Some of these humans had been taking broad-spectrum antibiotics before they died. Broad-spectrum antibiotics kill many of the species of bacteria in the human gut. The other humans had not been taking antibiotics, so they had a normal range of bacteria in their guts. The scientists found that the group who had not taken antibiotics had a much higher level of vitamin K in their livers than the group who had taken antibiotics.

1. Does this study show that *E. coli* in the human gut is an important source of vitamin K?

2. Do studies like this show that bacteria like *E. coli* are important for human health?

Establishing a gut flora

All babies are born with sterile guts. In other words, there are no bacteria anywhere in their intestines. This is because the baby has developed inside its mother's uterus. However, as soon as it is born, a baby starts to take in bacteria from the environment around it. These bacteria may come from the mother's skin, or from people who handle the baby. Provided that the baby picks up the right kind of bacteria, this will help the baby to resist any harmful bacteria that come along. This is one of several arguments for promoting breastfeeding. Breastfed babies pick up 'healthy' bacteria from their mother's breast when they feed. These bacteria will then breed in the baby's gut.

Figure 1 *A newborn baby being given vitamin K*

In the first few days of life, babies can sometimes suffer from haemorrhagic disease of the newborn. This is a condition in which the blood does not clot properly. In the UK, it occurs in 8.6 babies in every 100 000. Among the symptoms are: bleeding in the intestines; bleeding from the skin and mucous membranes, e.g. nose and gums; prolonged bleeding after circumcision; and bleeding from the umbilical stump. Fortunately, this disease can be prevented by giving the baby vitamin K on the first day of life. This can be by mouth or by injection. This is more important for breastfed babies, as formula milk contains vitamin K.

Applications and How science works

Probiotic bacteria

Recently, **probiotic** drinks have become very popular. These contain a number of different microorganisms, mainly certain bacteria (lactobacilli and bifidobacteria). Some people believe that these bacteria are beneficial to health in a number of ways. It is believed that they compete with disease-causing organisms (pathogens) that may get into the gut; bind cancer-causing chemicals (mutagens) that may be present; they may produce vitamins, like the *E. coli* referred to above; and they may bind to the intestine wall, preventing harmful bacteria from attaching. Other people think that the type of bacteria present in the gut depends on the food you eat. They believe that if you eat a healthy, balanced diet you are likely to have 'healthy' bacteria in your gut, without the need to consume probiotic drinks regularly.

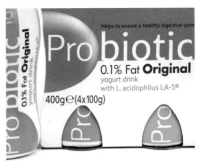

Figure 2 *Probiotic drinks*

1. How could you carry out a study to find out whether probiotic drinks taken every day can improve your health?
2. What are the difficulties involved in carrying out a study like this?

Summary questions

1. What do biologists mean by a 'healthy gut flora'?
2. What is vitamin K needed for?
3. Do you think that it is a good idea to consume probiotic drinks regularly? Give reasons for your answer.

1.5 Water

Learning objectives:

■ Why do we need to drink water?

■ How much water should we drink every day?

■ Is it healthier to drink bottled water?

■ Are sports drinks useful when you are exercising hard?

Specification reference: 3.1.1

Water in our bodies

Water is essential in our bodies. About 60% of our body mass is water. Our cells are mainly water, there is water in the blood and there is water in the intercellular fluid between the cells. If the water level in the body falls too low, reactions inside the cells will slow down or stop. If there is too little water in our blood plasma, blood cannot be pumped around the body so easily.

We lose water from our bodies all the time. We lose water vapour when we breathe out, we lose water in sweat and we also lose water in faeces and urine. As a result, it is estimated that we must drink approximately 1.1–1.5 litres of liquid (8 to 10 cups) every day. This is on top of the water we obtain from our food. In hot weather, or when we exercise, we need to drink even more. Dehydration can have serious health consequences. Recently, it has been suggested that mild dehydration in school children can lead to minor health problems such as a lack of concentration.

Replacing water

We can replace the water we lose by drinking water-based drinks, as well as pure water. However, some drinks can have diuretic effects. This means that they cause you to lose even more water because they increase the amount of water lost in urine. Alcohol can have a diuretic effect as well, depending on the strength of the drink. Spirits, such as whisky or vodka, have a greater diuretic effect than beer or lager. Caffeine is also diuretic. This is found in drinks such as tea, coffee and cola drinks. A small amount of caffeine will not cause significant dehydration, but several caffeine-containing drinks a day may cause some dehydration.

How science works

Tap water or bottled?

Tap water is safe to drink all over the UK, although its taste will vary depending on how hard or soft it is. Tap water is carefully treated, and it is monitored to check that it meets safety standards. Water is treated with chlorine or ultraviolet light to make sure no harmful bacteria are present. The safety limit for bacteria in tap water is 100 per cm^3, but in practice it is normally 2 per cm^3. Soft water contains fewer mineral salts than hard water, but this does not mean that a person living in a soft water area will be short of mineral salts in their diet. We get most of the mineral salts we need from our food.

Recently, there has been a trend towards buying bottled water. Bottled water is often mineral or spring water. The content of this water will depend on the place it is taken from. There are no legal limits for bacteria in bottled water, although no bacteria must be added during the bottling process. Some bottled water contains many more bacteria than tap water, although these bacteria are unlikely to cause any harm.

In the western world, tap water is about as safe as it can be and it is relatively cheap. Yet many people are prepared to pay up to 1500 times as much when the water comes in a bottle. Many people drink bottled mineral water because they believe it is healthier and safer and tastes better. What do you think?

Isotonic sports drinks

A person exercising for a long time may lose a lot of water in sweat. If this water is not replaced quickly, the person's performance may be impaired. However, sweat also contains inorganic ions. These are needed for the body to work properly, for example, for muscles to contract. These also need to be replaced. In addition, a person who has been exercising hard will have used up a lot of glucose in respiration. The body does store carbohydrate as glycogen in liver and muscle tissue, but this can be used up during a long period of exercise.

Many people find it useful to drink an isotonic sports drink when they are exercising hard. You will find out on page 52 that isotonic means a solution that has the same water potential as blood plasma. So, a sports drink will have roughly the same water potential as the person's body fluids. It should replace the lost water and ions, as well as providing glucose for respiration.

Figure 1 *An isotonic sports drink*

> **Hint**
>
> Remember that isotonic means a solution that has the same water potential as your blood plasma. Water potential measures the energy of water molecules in a solution, and their ability to move freely. The more water there is, the higher the water potential and the more freely the molecules can move.

> **How science works**
>
> Make your own isotonic sports drink!
>
> Mix together:
>
> 50–70 g sugar
>
> a pinch of salt
>
> 200 cm³ sugar-free fruit squash
>
> 1 litre of warm water

> **Summary questions**
>
> 1. Give **three** ways in which the body loses water.
> 2. Why should you avoid drinking too much cola or coffee in a day?
> 3. What is an isotonic sports drink?
> 4. If you made an isotonic sports drink using the recipe on this page, but added only half a litre of water, would this have a higher or lower water potential than your blood plasma?

1.6 Diet and disease

Learning objectives:

- What is a healthy diet and why?

- What information should go on food labels?

- Why are additives added to our food?

- Why is food processed and are processed foods harmful for our health?

- What are the problems associated with obesity?

- What is Type 2 diabetes?

Specification reference: 3.1.1

The Food Standards Agency in the UK recommends that, for a healthy diet, you should:

- base your meals on starchy foods such as wholegrain bread, pasta and rice,

- eat at least five portions of fruit and vegetables every day (both these foods have a low GI, contain vitamins, minerals and plenty of fibre),

- include some protein-based foods, such as meat, pulses, fish, milk and dairy foods,

- keep the amount of fat you eat, especially saturated fat, to a minimum. Fat contains far more energy per gram (high calorific value) than carbohydrate-based foods, therefore if someone eats a lot of fat they are more likely to become obese,

- keep the amount of sugars and salt that you eat to a minimum. High salt levels in the diet can cause hypertension or high blood pressure. This then leads to damage to the walls of the arteries, increasing the amount of fatty plaque that is built up and the risk of suffering from coronary heart disease (CHD). Foods with high sugar content have a high GI.

Fibre

Dietary fibre, as you will see on page 19, consists of polysaccharides that cannot be broken down by the enzymes in the gut. As a result, they make the absorption of carbohydrates slower, reducing insulin release and making the development of diabetes less likely. Fibre also increases the feeling of 'fullness', reducing the overeating that leads to obesity. It also reduces the chances of developing other diseases, such as colon cancer.

Processed food

Much of the food we buy and consume is processed. Food processing means altering the raw food product in some way to make it taste better, last longer, or to make it more appealing. Processing food is very important for preserving foods and making food more palatable. It is also very popular because of our lifestyles. People are often busy and find that buying processed food saves time. However, this means that people may be unaware of exactly what is in the food they are eating. For example, tomato ketchup and pasta sauces may contain more sugar and salt than you realise.

It is therefore very important that the content of the food is clearly labelled, so that consumers can check their diet is within the guidelines above. If we have too much of a food type or too little it can cause disease. Type 2 diabetes and obesity are conditions that have been linked to the increased consumption of processed food, because they may contain more ingredients, like fat or sugar, than the consumer is aware of.

Figure 1 *High fibre foods include pasta, cereals, fruit and vegetables*

Applications and How science works

Food labelling

The Food Standards Agency has introduced a 'traffic light' labelling system. The aim of this scheme is to let consumers see, at a glance, whether there are high, medium or low amounts of saturated fat, sugars and salt in 100 g of the food. This information has been on food labels previously, but it has taken time to evaluate the information. In addition to the traffic light colours, you can see the amount of these nutrients that are present in a portion of the food.

- red = high
- amber = medium
- green = low

Consumers will realise that if there is a red light on the front of the pack, the food is high in something they should be trying to cut down on. This does not mean that you should avoid the food completely, but you should only eat this kind of food occasionally. You should try to eat foods with green lights on the front most of the time.

This new food labelling system is being used by some of the major supermarkets, but not all of them. One of the supermarkets that has chosen not to use the traffic light system says that they give the nutritional information in a different way. They claim that customers are confused about what the amber light means. Instead, this supermarket gives the following information on their labels:

- how much sugar, fat, saturated fat and salt there is in one serving,
- the percentage of the guideline daily amount for each nutrient.

Guideline daily amounts (GDAs) are a guide to the amount of calories (energy), sugar, fat, saturated fat and salt a typical adult should be eating in a day. However, adults with a more or less active lifestyle would need a different amount, and the GDAs do not apply to children.

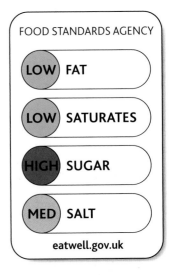

FOOD STANDARDS AGENCY

LOW **FAT**

LOW **SATURATES**

HIGH **SUGAR**

MED **SALT**

eatwell.gov.uk

Figure 2 *Traffic light labelling*

Table 1 *Guideline daily amounts used by a major supermarket*

calories	2000 kcal
sugar	90 g
fat	70 g
saturated fat	20 g
salt	6 g

Each serving (half of the can) contains

Calories	Sugar	Fat	Saturates	Salt
125	7.9g	1.1g	0.2g	1.3g
6%	9%	2%	1%	21%

of your guideline daily amount

Figure 3 *Alternative food labelling system*

1 Compare the food labelling systems shown in Figure 2 and Figure 3. Which system do you think is best? Give reasons for your answer.

Food additives

Processed food from supermarkets often contains food additives. Some food additives have an E number. This means it has passed safety tests and has been approved for use throughout the European Union. Most food additives are identified, either by their name or E number, on the ingredients list. Table 2 tells you the main reasons why additives are added to processed food.

Some people say that additives are not harmful, and many additives are natural products. They also say that they make food safer, for example, by preventing bacterial growth. However, other people say that these additives would not be needed if we ate more fresh food, and that some of these additives are used to make poor quality ingredients taste better. They claim that some of the additives can be harmful if you eat a lot of processed food. For example, some people are concerned that some of the colourings added to processed food can affect children's behaviour.

1 When an additive has an E number, what does this mean?

2 Give **three** reasons why additives are added to foods.

3 Do you think that we should reduce the number of additives used in processed foods? Give reasons for your answer.

Table 2 *Some additives added to processed food*

Type of additive	Why added	Examples
antioxidants	make food last longer by stopping the fats, oils and some vitamins from combining with oxygen; this can make the food taste 'off', become rancid and lose colour	vitamin C (ascorbic acid or E300)
colours	replace the natural colour lost during processing or storage	caramel (E150a)
emulsifiers	help mix ingredients that would normally separate, e.g. oil and water, to give food a consistent texture	lecithins (E322)
stabilisers	give food a consistent texture, e.g. in low-fat spreads	locust bean gum (E410)
gelling agents	change the consistency of food, making it thicker	pectin (E440)
flavour enhancers	bring out the flavour of savoury and sweet foods, e.g. soups, savoury snacks, ready meals	monosodium glutamate (E621)
flavourings	added in small amounts to give a particular taste or smell	do not have E numbers and do not have to be named, but food label must say if flavourings have been used
preservatives	give foods a longer shelf-life, e.g. by stopping bacteria and mould growing	sulfur dioxide (E220)
intense sweeteners	used instead of sugar in low-calorie products; only added in small amounts	aspartame (E951)
		saccharin (E954)
bulk sweeteners	used in similar amounts to sugar	sorbitol (E420)

Obesity

On page 4, you saw that we need to consider the energy content of our food. If we eat more energy in our food than we use up in our daily activities, then we will store the excess energy as fat. Over time, this will lead to obesity. People who are **obese** have a **body mass index** (BMI) over 30.

Obesity is now very common in developed countries, especially North America, Europe and Australasia. At the time of writing, 23% of adults in the UK are obese, which is the highest of any European country. The government predicts that, by 2010, about a third of people in the UK will be obese. The obesity rate in children has also risen dramatically. As many as 22% of girls and 19% of boys aged 2–15 years old are obese.

There are many reasons for this increase in obesity, including:

- People spend more leisure time on computers and watching TV than playing sport.
- People tend to drive to school or work rather than cycling or walking.
- Incomes have increased so people can afford plenty of food.
- More people have sedentary jobs, involving sitting down or working on a computer, rather than traditional manual jobs.
- Fast-food outlets selling cheap processed food are common.

Problems with obesity

Obese people are more likely to develop certain medical conditions, which can lead to premature death:

- Hypertension, or high blood pressure, is linked to obesity.
- Some cancers are more likely to develop in people who are overweight. One example of this is breast cancer. Colon, rectal and kidney cancer are also more likely to occur in people who are obese.
- Osteoarthritis and rheumatoid arthritis are both more likely to occur in obese people. This is because the extra body weight puts additional strain on the bones and joints.
- Obese people are at higher risk of coronary heart disease (CHD) than others. This is partly because obesity increases blood pressure and increases blood cholesterol levels. Although, other factors to do with the diet can increase the risk of CHD. You will learn more about CHD in Topic 6.5.
- A major risk for obese people is Type 2 diabetes.

Type 2 diabetes

Type 2 diabetes occurs when a person cannot control their blood glucose levels. However, this kind of diabetes is not controlled by insulin injections. Many people with Type 2 diabetes produce enough insulin, but their body has stopped responding to it. About 90% of people with Type 2 diabetes are overweight. Until recently, this kind of diabetes was rare until late in life. The government is now worried because a significant number of children are developing Type 2 diabetes. A diet high in dietary fibre can reduce the chance of Type 2 diabetes.

The reason that they are worried is that people with Type 2 diabetes tend to have a higher blood pressure. This means that they are more likely to develop heart disease or angina, or suffer from strokes. People with diabetes are more likely to develop blindness, poor nerve function and poor circulation in the limbs, leading to amputation.

Hint

Remember that body mass index (BMI) =

$$\frac{\text{body mass in kilograms}}{(\text{height in metres})^2}$$

Figure 4 *The obesity rate has increased dramatically in the UK, especially among children*

Summary questions

1. Suggest **two** more reasons, other than those given earlier, to account for the increase in obesity in the UK in recent years.

2. Suggest **three** things that the government could do to reduce the amount of disease in the UK that is caused by obesity.

3. Should the government take action to reduce obesity in the UK, or is a person's body mass their own responsibility? Give reasons to support your answer.

1.7 Carbohydrates

Learning objectives:

■ What is a carbohydrate?

■ What are they needed for?

Specification reference 3.1.1

Carbohydrates are composed of the elements carbon, hydrogen and oxygen. There are many forms of carbohydrate ranging from very simple molecules to very complex molecules.

🔺 💡 Monosaccharides and disaccharides

Monosaccharides are the simplest kind of carbohydrate. These are single sugar units, such as glucose. Monosaccharides join together to form **disaccharides**, such as maltose. These contain two glucose units. Another disaccharide is sucrose, the sugar you add to your tea or coffee. This is made of two different monosaccharides, glucose and fructose.

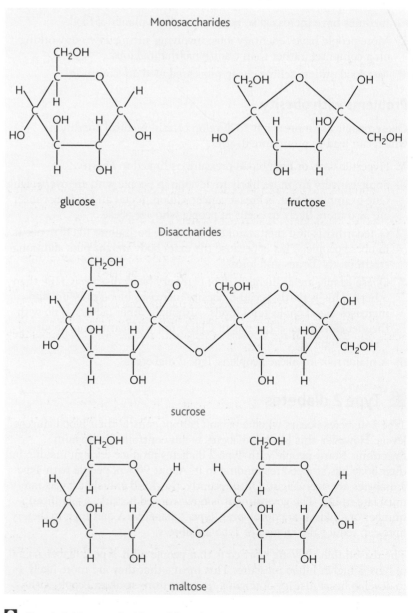

💡 **Figure 1** *Monosaccharides and disaccharides*

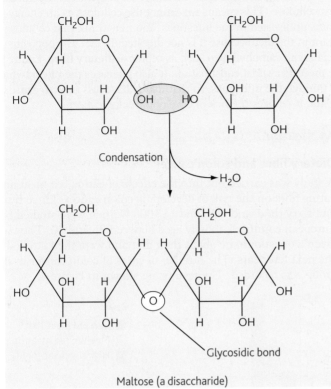

Two glucose molecules (monosaccharides)

Condensation

H_2O

Glycosidic bond

Maltose (a disaccharide)

Figure 2 *Formation of a disaccharide*

Two monosaccharides join together by a **condensation** reaction to form a disaccharide. A condensation reaction is when two molecules are joined together by removing a molecule of water. This is shown in Figure 2.

Both monosaccharides and disaccharides are classed as sugars. They have names ending in –ose. Sugars such as glucose are absorbed from the intestines very quickly. This means they can be used as an energy boost. For example, an athlete may have a drink containing glucose while running a marathon. However, sugar in the diet can lead to tooth decay. Sugary foods like soft drinks, sweets and biscuits provide a great deal of energy while containing very few other useful nutrients. This means they are more likely to lead to obesity.

Polysaccharides

Polysaccharides are made of many sugar units joined together. These are **polymers** of monosaccharides. You may remember from GCSE that a polymer is a large molecule made from many similar smaller units joined together. Polysaccharides are made by many monosaccharides joining together by condensation.

Starch is a polymer of glucose that is found in plant tissues (Figure 3). Foods like potatoes, rice, pasta and bread are rich in starch because these are all plant-based foods. Plants store starch because it is a compact molecule. It is insoluble so it does not interefere with osmosis. It also has a branched structure, so it has lots of 'ends'. This means that glucose can be released easily when it is needed.

Glycogen is very similar to starch. Like starch, it is a polymer of glucose, but it is found in animal cells. In humans, glycogen is stored in muscle and liver cells. Like starch, it is compact, insoluble and branched.

glucose monomer

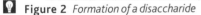

Figure 3 *Starch*

Cellulose is also a polymer of glucose, but the bonds are a different shape from those in starch or glycogen. There are no enzymes in the human body to digest cellulose. This means we cannot use cellulose as an energy source. It remains undigested in the intestines. You may think that cellulose is not important in the diet because it is not digested. In fact, the opposite is true – dieticians call carbohydrates such as cellulose **dietary fibre**. Eating plenty of fibre protects against constipation. It also increases the rate at which food moves through the intestines, so that toxins have less time to cause damage. As a result, it reduces the risk of developing colon cancer.

■ Application

Dietary fibre and colon cancer

A study was carried out into the effects of eating red meat and eating fibre on the risk of developing colon cancer. Three hundred and sixty thousand men and 153 000 women were studied from 10 European countries, mostly aged between 35 and 70. They were given a questionnaire about their diet and were then studied over the next few years. The number of cases of colon cancer in the group was recorded. The results are shown in Figure 4.

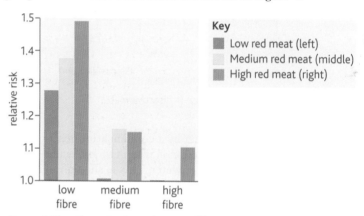

Figure 4 *The effects of eating red meat and fibre on the risk of developing colon cancer*

1 The relative risk is calculated as the

$$\frac{\text{number of people per 10 000 in the group developing colon cancer}}{\text{number of people per 10 000 in the high fibre low red meat group developing cancer}}$$

Explain why this is a better way to present the data than by counting the total number of cases of colon cancer in each group.

2 What do these data suggest about the effects of red meat and fibre on the risk of developing colon cancer?

3 Describe three ways in which these data may not be completely reliable.

Summary questions

1 What is a condensation reaction?

2 What is: a a disaccharide, b a polysaccharide?

3 Explain why cellulose and starch are both polysaccharides, but cellulose is classed as dietary fibre.

1.8 Proteins

Learning objectives:

- Why are proteins needed in the diet?
- What are proteins made of?
- How is their structure related to their function?

Specification reference: 3.1.1

Proteins are very important in our diet, because protein makes up more than half the dry mass of our bodies. Children need to eat more protein as a proportion of their diet than adults do, because they are still growing. They need proteins for growth as well as repair. Adults only need proteins to repair the body. An average adult needs only 60 g of protein a day. In practice, most adults eat rather more protein than this. Excess protein is used as an energy source. It is recommended that about 15% of our daily energy should come from proteins.

Proteins contain the elements carbon, hydrogen, oxygen, nitrogen and sometimes sulfur. They are composed of small units called amino acids. We digest the proteins in our food into their constituent amino acids. These amino acids are then reassembled in a different order to make the proteins we need.

Amino acids

Figure 1 shows the structure of an amino acid. All amino acids have a carboxylic acid group (COOH) and an amino group (NH_2). However, each kind of amino acid has a different side chain, or R-group. There are 20 different amino acids that make up proteins in our body. Some of these are essential amino acids. This means that we have to eat them in our diet. Some others are non-essential, because we can make them from other amino acids that we have eaten. You will remember that food is made of animal and/or plant cells. Because we are more closely related to animals than to plants, animal proteins contain more of the essential amino acids. However, this does not mean that a vegetarian cannot eat a healthy diet. Vegetarians simply need to eat a wide variety of plant proteins if they are to make sure they eat all the essential amino acids.

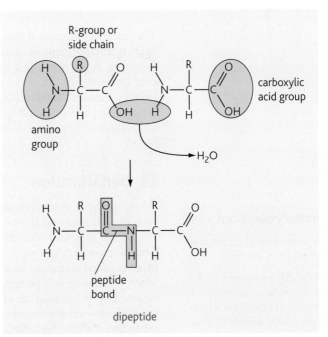

Figure 1 *Amino acids join together by a condensation reaction*

■ Polypeptides

Amino acids join together by condensation reactions to form a polypeptide chain. The bonds between the amino acids are called peptide bonds. Proteins usually contain tens or hundreds of amino acids. In other words, a protein is a **polymer** made of amino acids.

■ Tertiary structure

The polypeptide chain coils and bends, then it coils up again into an overall three-dimensional shape called its **tertiary structure**. You can see this in Figure 2. The specific shape of a protein is very important in its function.

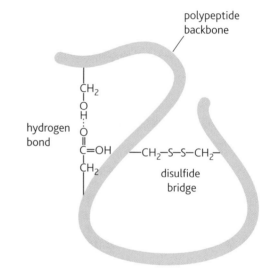

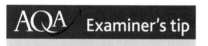 Examiner's tip

You do not need to learn the molecular structure of these molecules.

💡 **Figure 2** *The tertiary structure of a protein*

The tertiary structure is held together by bonds between the amino acids in the polypeptide chain. These bonds form between the different R-groups. A few amino acids have sulfur in their R-groups. These sulfur-containing amino acids can form fairly strong bonds called **disulfide bridges**. Another kind of bond that can form between the amino acids is a **hydrogen bond**. Hydrogen bonds are formed because of weak attractions between atoms, so they are quite weak. However, proteins usually contain several of these hydrogen bonds, so they are important.

■ Denaturation

When the hydrogen bonds in a protein break, the tertiary structure of the protein is altered and the protein can no longer carry out its function. We say the protein is **denatured**. Denaturation is usually non-reversible. This is what happens when we cook food. For example, egg white is a protein called albumen. In a raw egg, it is clear and runny. However, when you boil or fry the egg, the egg white very quickly becomes solid and white. This is because the albumen protein is denatured. The polypeptide chains lose their tertiary structure and the chains tangle up with each other. Even when the food cools down, the egg white stays denatured. You cannot make it go back to its clear, runny form again.

Summary questions

1   How is one kind of amino acid different from another?

2   Explain why a pregnant woman needs to eat more protein in her diet than a non-pregnant woman of the same age and body mass.

1.9 Lipids

Lipids are a varied group of molecles. They all contain carbon and hydrogen, with some oxygen. The group includes fats and oils as well as some other compounds, like sterols and waxes. The most important lipids in our diet are fats and oils. The scientific name for these is **triglycerides**. They are so called because they are made up of a glycerol molecule with three fatty acids attached. Unlike proteins and carbohydrates such as starch and glycogen, they are not polymers.

🔺 💡 Fatty acids

In Figure 1 you will see that glycerol has three –OH groups. Each fatty acid has COOH at the end. The fatty acids line up alongside the glycerol so that they join together. Three condensation reactions result in a triglyceride being formed.

There are two different kinds of fatty acids. All fatty acids have a –COOH group at the end. The rest of the molecule is made of a hydrocarbon chain (a chain of carbon atoms with hydrogens attached). However, in **saturated** fatty acids all the bonds between the carbon atoms are single bonds. This means the maximum possible number of hydrogen atoms is attached. This is why they are called saturated fatty acids.

AQA Examiner's tip

You do not need to learn the molecular structure of these molecules.

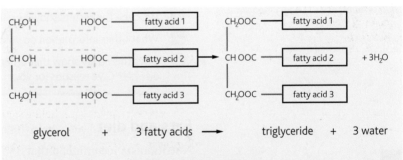

The three fatty acids may all be the same, thereby forming a simple triglyceride, or they may be different, in which case a mixed triglyceride is produced. In either case it is a condensation reaction.

💡 **Figure 1** *The formation of a triglyceride*

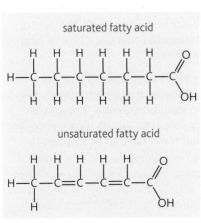

Figure 2 *Saturated and unsaturated fatty acids*

In **unsaturated** fatty acids, some of the carbon atoms join together by double bonds. This means that, for the same number of carbon atoms, they contain less hydrogen. If there is only one double carbon–carbon bond, the fatty acid is said to be **monounsaturated**. If there is more than one double bond present, the fatty acid is said to be **polyunsaturated**. If a triglyceride contains an unsaturated fatty acid, we say it is an unsaturated fat. The more unsaturated a fatty acid, the more liquid it is. Unsaturated fats tend to be classed as oils.

Food from animal sources tends to be high in saturated fats, while food from plant sources tends to be high in unsaturated fats.

Lipids and cell membranes

We need lipids in the diet to make phospholipids for our cell membranes. You will learn more about this on p 44. We also need lipids so that we can synthesise certain hormones, and we need cholesterol for our cell membranes. We can make many of the fatty acids that we need from other foods that we eat, but some fatty acids cannot be made in the body. These are called **essential fatty acids**. Recently, there has been a lot of publicity about omega-3 fatty acids. These are essential fatty acids found in fish oils. A membrane with lots of these fatty acids in it is more flexible.

Applications and How science works

Fish oil supplements

Studies suggest that children who take fish oil supplements behave better and have longer concentration spans. In older people, it is thought that they may reduce the risk of coronary heart disease, by reducing blood pressure and cholesterol levels. Some people suggest they are effective in reducing the symptoms of depression, rheumatoid arthritis and even some kinds of cancer.

A study was carried out to investigate whether a diet high in omega-3 fatty acids protected against sudden cardiac death. All the people who took part were men, and all had no symptoms of heart disease at the start of the study. The level of omega-3 fatty acids was measured in their blood. The number of men in the study who died of sudden cardiac death was recorded over the next 17 years. The results are shown in the graph.

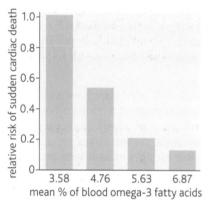

Figure 3 *Blood levels of long-chain n-3 fatty acids and the risk of sudden death Source: Albert et al. N Engl J Med 2002*

1 Describe the results shown in the graph.

2 What other information do you need to know to evaluate this study?

3 Does this study show that omega-3 fatty acids protect against heart disease? Give reasons for your answer.

Fats and diet

Nutritionists recommend that 35% of total energy requirements should come from fats. One gram of carbohydrate produces about 17 kJ of energy in the body, but 1 g of fat produces about 39 kJ. You can see from this that a high-fat diet can lead to obesity. There is a great deal of evidence that saturated fats lead to heart disease, mainly by raising blood cholesterol levels. For this reason, nutritionists recommend that only 11% of total energy intake should come from saturated fats.

Recently, there has been concern about trans-fatty acids. These are unsaturated fats, but most unsaturated fats occurring naturally are not trans-fatty acids. Trans-fatty acids have straighter chains. They have been developed by the food industry because they have a longer shelf life. However, recent reports have shown that trans-fatty acids increase the risk of CHD.

Summary questions

1 What is a triglyceride?

2 How does a saturated fatty acid differ from an unsaturated fatty acid?

3 Why should we avoid too much fat in the diet?

4 Give **three** reasons why it is difficult to carry out studies to find out whether a particular component in food gives health benefits.

1.10 Polymers and digestion

Learning objectives:

- What is a polymer?
- Why do we need to digest polymers?
- How are polymers digested?

Specification reference: 3.1.1

A polymer is a large molecule made of many similar smaller molecules (**monomers**) joined together in a **condensation** reaction. We have already looked at polysaccharides in Topic 1.7, which are polymers of simple sugars (monosaccharides). Proteins, which we looked at in Topic 1.8, are polymers of amino acids.

🔬 Digesting food

We eat proteins and polysaccharides in our food. However, these molecules are very large, and often insoluble, so they cannot be absorbed from the gut into the blood. Before they can be absorbed, they need to be digested – broken up into the monomers they are made from. These monomers are soluble, and are transported in the blood to the parts of the body where they are needed.

▪ Enzymes and digestion

Enzymes in the gut digest these food substances. You will remember from GCSE that different enzymes are needed to digest different food molecules. Also, the pH varies in different parts of the digestive system. The stomach has an acid pH whereas the small intestine is slightly alkaline. The enzymes in the digestive system therefore have to function at a specific pH depending on the part of the digestive system in which they are working.

Breaking the bonds between amino acids, and breaking the bonds in polysaccharides, involves a reaction called **hydrolysis**. Hydrolysis is the opposite of condensation. It is the splitting of a molecule by adding a molecule of water. You can see this reaction in Figure 1.

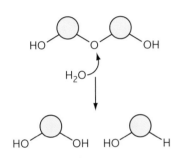

Figure 1 *Hydrolysis reaction*

Triglycerides (fats and oils) are not polymers, but you will remember from Topic 1.9 that they are also made from smaller molecules joined together in condensation reactions. Like proteins and polysaccharides, triglycerides also need to be digested: they are also hydrolysed into smaller molecules which can be absorbed.

Enzymes are used to hydrolyse food molecules in the digestive system. Digestive enzymes allow these reactions to occur quickly at body temperature (37 °C). Different enzymes digest different polymers, and physiological conditions found in the digestive system vary in pH, so each of these enzymes works best at different pHs. You will learn more about how enzymes do this in the next chapter.

Summary questions

 Explain why proteins and polysaccharides are polymers, but lipids are not.

2 Copy and complete the table:

Food molecule	Composed of
proteins	
polysaccharides	
lipids	

3 What is a hydrolysis reaction?

4 Explain why food substances have to be digested in the gut.

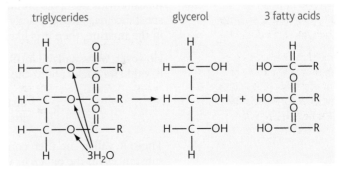

Figure 2 *Digestion of triglycerides*

1.11 Chromatography

Learning objectives:

- What is chromatography used for?

- How is it carried out?

Specification reference: 3.1.1

Chromatography

Chromatography is a technique used to separate a mixture of substances. It is very useful in biology, because biological samples often contain a mixture of many different substances. There are several different kinds of chromatography used in research laboratories, but the easiest kind to carry out is paper chromatography. The method is shown in Figure 1.

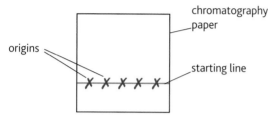

1   A starting line is marked on a piece of chromatography paper (which is very absorbent) using a pencil. Some crosses or **origins** are marked along this line.

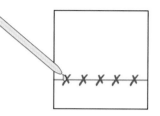

2   A micropipette is used to make a small, concentrated spot of the fruit juice on the first origin. A spot is applied, allowed to dry, then another spot is applied on top of the first. This is done several times. Solutions of known sugars are then spotted individually on to the other origins.

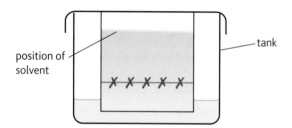

3   The paper is then suspended in a tank of a solvent and left until the solvent is nearly at the top of the paper. The final position of the solvent is marked in pencil. This is called the **solvent front**.

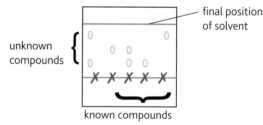

4   The chromatogram is removed from the tank and dried. Sometimes the compounds cannot be seen without adding another chemical called a **locating agent**.

Figure 1 *Paper chromatography – finding out which amino acids are present in fruit juice*

Identifying the mixture

One way to decide what is in the mixture is to compare the spots from the mixture with the spots produced by the known substances. If the known substance has moved exactly the same distance as an unknown substance in the mixture, then it is likely that they are both the same substance.

However, we usually identifty the spots by calculating the R_f value. The R_f value for each spot in the mixture can be calculated using the equation:

$$R_f = \frac{\text{distance travelled by the spot}}{\text{distance travelled by the solvent}}$$

These R_f values are then compared with the R_f values for the known substances on the paper, or with R_f values for the same solvent in reference tables.

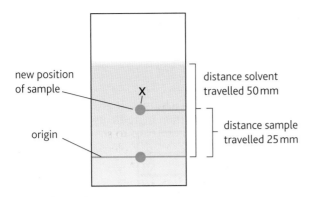

Figure 2 *Measuring the R$_f$ value*

How science works

A key technique

Paper chromatography has been a very important technique in biology and biochemistry. For example, it was one of the key techniques that Frederick Sanger used to determine the amino acid sequence of insulin. This was the first protein sequence to be discovered. Frederick Sanger won the Nobel Prize for this work in 1958.

Figure 3 *A chromatogram*

Summary questions

1. Why is it important that the origin line and the solvent front are drawn in pencil?

2. How do you calculate an R$_f$ value?

3. Calculate the R$_f$ value of the spot marked X in Figure 2.

1   **Figure 1** shows some information from the packaging of a burger. It gives the percentage of the guideline daily amounts (GDA) of certain ingredients for a woman.

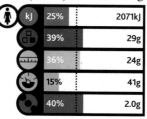

Figure 1 Key: purple, calories; red, protein; amber, fat; green, carbohydrates; blue, salt.

   (a) (i)   Give **one** advantage and **one** disadvantage of labelling food products in this way.

   (ii)   The burger contains 2 g of salt, which is 40% of the guideline daily amount of salt for a woman. Calculate the guideline daily amount of salt that is recommended for a woman, in grams. Show your working.   *(4 marks)*

   (b) Some nutritionists would say that this burger is *not* a healthy food item. Give **two** reasons for this, and explain your answers.   *(4 marks)*

2   **Table 1** shows some statements about four carbohydrates. Copy and complete the table with a tick (✓) if the statement is true or a cross (✗) if it is not true.   *(3 marks)*

   Table 1

	Sucrose	Maltose	Glycogen	Cellulose
Made only from glucose molecules joined together				
Branched molecule				
Soluble in water				

AQA, 2007

3   (a) Chromatography can be used to separate amino acids from a mixture. Describe how you would apply a solution containing a mixture of amino acids to a piece of chromatography paper.   *(3 marks)*

   (b) **Figure 2** shows a chromatogram produced by a mixture of amino acids.

   Table 2 shows Rf values for some amino acids.

   Identify amino acid X. Explain how you got your answer.   *(2 marks)*

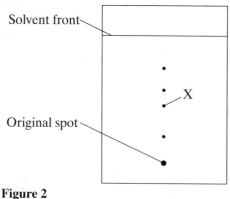

Figure 2

Table 2

Amino acid	Rf value
Alanine	0.38
Arginine	0.20
Phenylalanine	0.68
Threonine	0.35
Tyrosine	0.45

AQA, 2003

4   Read the following passage.

Scientists carried out a study to compare different kinds of weight-loss diet. They compared diets reducing fat intake with the GI diet. The GI diet is based on eating carbohydrates that have a low glycaemic index.

The benefits of a low-GI diet for people with diabetes are clear. However, the scientists wanted to find out whether the low-GI diet is also good for reducing obesity. Some   5
studies with small numbers of humans suggest that the low-GI diet leads to weight loss, but some people think that the GI value of the foods is not the crucial factor. Other explanations are that low-GI foods are less tempting, or contain more fibre, meaning that people eat less.

In the new study, scientists fed two groups of rats on diets that were identical apart   10
from their starch content. At first the rats were allowed to eat as much as they liked. But after eight weeks the high-GI group began to gain weight, so to rule out the possibility that they were eating more because the high-GI food is more palatable, their portions were reduced.

At the end of four-month study, both groups had similar body weights. However there   15
was a striking difference: the high-GI group had 71 per cent more body fat than the low-GI group, and 8 per cent less muscle. The high-GI group also had higher blood levels of substances linked to heart disease, such as triglycerides.

(Source: Pawlak et al., *The Lancet*, vol. 364, 2004)

(a)   What is *glycaemic index* (line 3)?   *(2 marks)*

(b)   Explain why a low-GI diet may benefit people with diabetes (line 4).   *(2 marks)*

(c)   Use information in the passage to evaluate whether a low-GI diet is beneficial to health.   *(4 marks)*

5   (a)   **Table 3** contains some statements about different molecules. Copy and complete the box with a tick (✔) if the statement is true, or a cross (✗) if the statement is not true.

Table 3

	Protein	Triglyceride	Maltose	Starch
Molecule is a polymer				
Molecule is formed by condensation reaction(s)				
Contains hydrogen bonds				

(4 marks)

(b)   **Tables 4** and **5** show nutritional information from the packages of two different foods.

(i)   Which of these foods would have the highest glycaemic index? Explain your answer.

Table 4 Food A

Typical composition	100g contains
Energy	1484 kJ
Protein	12.0 g
Carbohydrates	72.0 g
Of which sugars	2.5 g
Fat	1.5 g
Of which saturates	0.5 g
Fibre	0.8 g
Sodium	trace

Table 5 Food B

Typical composition	100g contains
Energy	1080 kJ
Protein	14.8 g
Carbohydrates	4.1 g
Of which sugars	1.1 g
Fat	20.5 g
Of which saturates	9.3 g
Fibre	0.3 g
Sodium	0.8 g

(ii)   Explain why it is important to know how much sodium is present in food.   *(4 marks)*

2.1 Enzymes and how they work

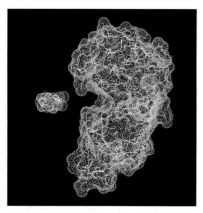

Figure 1 *A computer-generated model showing an enzyme and its substrate*

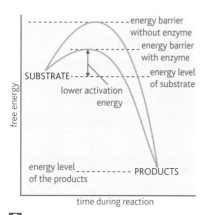

Figure 2 *How enzymes lower activation energy*

Enzymes are complex globular proteins. This means that they have a roughly spherical tertiary structure with a very specific shape. Most of the metabolic reactions in the body depend on them. This is because enzymes act as catalysts, speeding up reactions in the body. They also control the rate at which reactions take place.

How enzymes work

Enzymes have a specific three-dimensional shape, as a result of their tertiary structure. You learned about the tertiary structure of proteins in Topic 1.8. You can see this in Figure 1. Each enzyme has a specific part of their structure called the **active site**. This is exactly the right shape for the substrate to fit into. In other words, the active site is **complementary** to the substrate. The substrate fits into the active site, making the reaction occur more quickly. Enzymes are **highly specific**, because only one substrate can fit into the enzyme's active site.

Enzymes and activation energy

For a reaction to occur, molecules need enough energy to get the reaction 'kick-started'. We call this input of energy **activation energy**. There is an energy barrier that needs to be overcome. One way for molecules to gain enough activation energy to overcome the energy barrier is to add heat. This gives the molecules more kinetic energy. When they collide there is enough energy to overcome the energy barrier. However, reactions in the human body take place at 37 °C. At this temperature, most molecules do not have enough kinetic energy to overcome the energy barrier. This is why enzymes are needed in the body. Enzymes work by lowering the activation energy needed for a reaction to occur, making it possible for the reaction to occur at 37 °C.

In Figure 2 the energy barrier is much higher without the enzyme. The molecules need far more activation energy to overcome the energy barrier. However, when the enzyme is present, the energy barrier is much lower. Therefore the activation energy needed for the reaction to occur is much lower.

How enzymes work

Enzymes work in a similar way to a lock and key. Each key has a specific shape that will only fit into one particular lock. Similarly, each substrate will only fit into the active site of one specific enzyme. You can see this in Figure 3. The way that an enzyme works is called the **lock and key theory**.

This is how enzymes lower the activation energy needed for a reaction to occur. They bring the substrates very close together in the active site. This means that the reaction can happen much more easily.

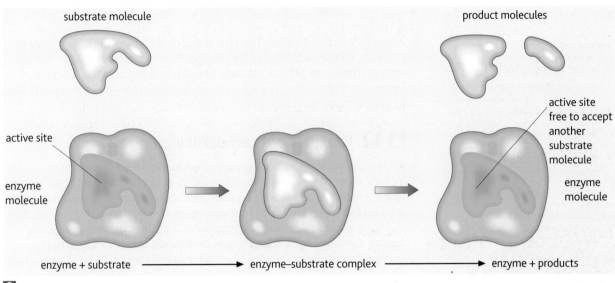

Figure 3 *The lock and key theory of enzyme action*

Induced fit

This theory suggests that the enzyme has a basic shape that is flexible. When the substrate collides with the enzyme, the enzyme's shape changes, so that the active site becomes a close fit for the substrate. This lowers the activation energy needed for the reaction. Because the enzyme's active site changes once the substrate is present, it is called the **induced fit theory**. You can see this in Figure 4.

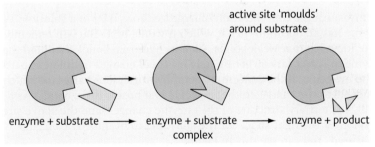

Figure 4 *The induced fit theory of enzyme action*

AQA Examiner's tip

Remember that it is the enzyme which has the active site, and that the substrate fits into it. Many candidates say that the active site is the same shape as the substrate, but it isn't! Remember that it is complementary to the substrate.

Summary questions

1 Use the lock and key theory of enzyme action to explain why:

   a an enzyme is highly specific to one substrate,

   b enzymes lower the activation energy needed for a reaction to occur.

2 Name **two** of the bonds that are important in holding the enzyme in its tertiary structure.

3 Give **one** difference between the induced fit theory and the lock and key theory.

4 Starch and cellulose are both polysaccharides made from glucose. However, the bonds in cellulose are a different shape from those in starch. Enzymes in the human gut can digest starch into sugars which are absorbed into the body but they cannot hydrolyse cellulose. It is therefore known as 'dietary fibre'. Use your knowledge of enzymes to explain why the enzyme that digests starch cannot digest cellulose.

2.2 Factors affecting enzyme activity

A number of factors affect the rate at which enzymes work. Enzymes are proteins, so they are affected by changes in temperature and pH. Certain temperatures and pHs can change the shape of the enzyme, so it no longer works properly. The rate at which an enzyme works is also affected by the concentration of substrate available.

The effect of temperature on enzymes

An increase in temperature increases the kinetic energy of molecules, making them move faster. This means they collide more often. If the rate at which substrates collide with an enzyme's active site is increased, the rate of reaction increases. However, increasing temperature also makes the enzyme molecule vibrate more. You will remember that the enzyme has a specific tertiary structure. Some of the bonds holding the enzyme in its tertiary structure are hydrogen bonds. These are relatively weak. If the enzyme vibrates too much, the hydrogen bonds break. This changes the shape of the enzyme's active site. At first, the substrate still fits in, but not as easily, so the rate of reaction is slowed down. However, as more bonds break, the active site changes so much that the substrate cannot fit in at all. At this point, we say that the enzyme is **denatured**. You can see this in Figure 1.

The enzyme's optimum temperature is the temperature at which the rate of reaction is fastest. Human enzymes have an optimum temperature of 37 °C. However, other organisms may have enzymes with optimum temperatures much higher or lower than this.

The effect of pH on enzymes

pH measures the concentration of hydrogen ions (H^+) in a solution. Each enzyme has an optimum pH at which it works best. You will remember from Topic 1.8 that weak bonds, such as hydrogen bonds that hold the enzyme in its tertiary structure, rely on small charges in different parts of the molecule. If the concentration of hydrogen ions varies too much, this changes the charge on the molecule and breaks these bonds. As a result, the tertiary structure of the enzyme changes, and the active site is no longer the right shape for the substrate to fit into. The enzyme is **denatured**. You can see this in Figure 2.

The effect of substrate concentration on the rate of enzyme activity

If a fixed amount of enzyme is present, and the amount of substrate present is slowly increased, the rate of reaction increases. This is because a low substrate concentration means that some of the enzymes will have empty active sites. There are not enough substrate molecules present for the enzymes to work at their fastest rate. You can see this in Figure 3.

As substrate is added, more active sites are being used so the rate of reaction increases. However, when the substrate concentration reaches a certain point, adding more substrate makes no difference at all to the rate of reaction. This is because all the active sites are being used. Substrate molecules are 'waiting' for an active site.

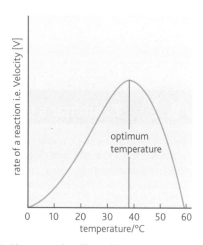

Figure 1 *The effect of temperature on the rate of an enzyme-controlled reaction*

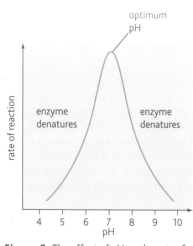

Figure 2 *The effect of pH on the rate of an enzyme-controlled reaction*

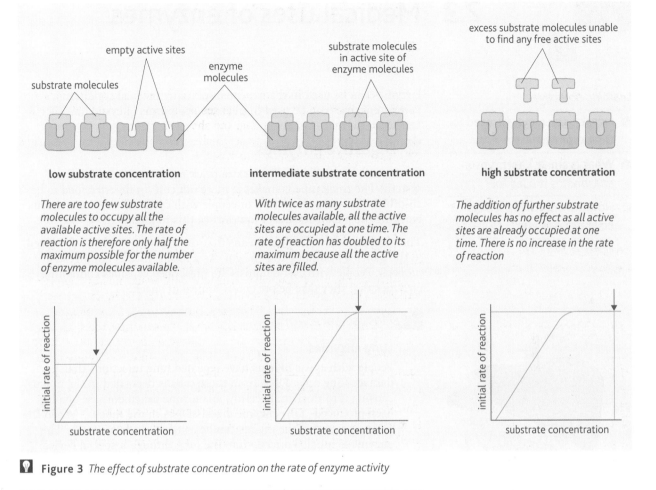

Figure 3 *The effect of substrate concentration on the rate of enzyme activity*

Within the figure:

low substrate concentration

There are too few substrate molecules to occupy all the available active sites. The rate of reaction is therefore only half the maximum possible for the number of enzyme molecules available.

intermediate substrate concentration

With twice as many substrate molecules available, all the active sites are occupied at one time. The rate of reaction has doubled to its maximum because all the active sites are filled.

high substrate concentration

The addition of further substrate molecules has no effect as all active sites are already occupied at one time. There is no increase in the rate of reaction

Summary questions

1 Enzymes can cause the spoilage of stored food. Use your knowledge of enzymes to explain why:

   a food can be stored for longer if you keep it in a refrigerator,

   b food is heated before sealing it in tins or bottles,

   c some foods are preserved by putting them into vinegar.

2 Solutions called **buffer solutions** prevent changes in pH. A student carried out a laboratory investigation to find the optimum temperature of an enzyme. She measured the rate of reaction of an enzyme at several different temperatures. At each temperature, the same amounts of enzyme and substrate were used, together with a buffer solution. Why was it important to include a buffer solution?

2.3 Medical uses of enzymes

Learning objectives:

- How can enzymes be used to treat disease?

- What is alpha 1 antitrypsin and what is it used for?

- How are enzymes used to diagnose disease?

Specification reference: 3.1.2

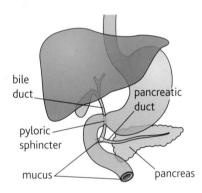

bile duct

pancreatic duct

pyloric sphincter

mucus

pancreas

 Figure 1 *Many people with cystic fibrosis have thick mucus blocking the pancreatic duct*

Link

Cystic fibrosis is covered in more detail in Chapter 3.

Enzymes can be used in the treatment of many medical conditions. Several enzymes can be used to treat the symptoms of cystic fibrosis.

Digestive enzymes

People with cystic fibrosis have extra thick mucus in their digestive system. The thick mucus makes it more difficult for digested food to be absorbed. However, about 85% of people with cystic fibrosis have mucus blocking the pancreatic duct. You can see this in Figure 1.

The blocked pancreatic duct means that the digestive enzymes produced in the pancreas cannot enter the gut. As a result, food is not digested properly. People with cystic fibrosis are prescribed capsules containing enzymes that they take before eating a meal or snack.

How science works

Lung enzymes

People with cystic fibrosis have repeated lung infections that damage lung cells. DNA from these cells is deposited in the mucus, causing it to thicken. Recently, an enzyme called dornase alfa has been produced. This enzyme digests DNA in the mucus. When the DNA is digested, the mucus can be coughed up more easily. The enzyme is inhaled directly into the lung through a special device called a jet nebuliser.

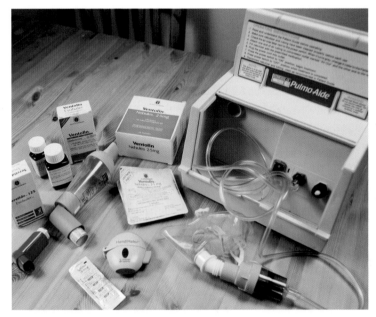

The enzyme dornase alfa and a jet nebuliser

Enzymes in the lungs: alpha-1-antitrypsin

In cystic fibrosis sufferers, the repeated lung infections cause certain white blood cells, called **phagocytes**, to come to the lungs. Here, they engulf bacteria. At the same time, they release an enzyme called **elastase**. This is a protein-digesting enzyme. It digests many different kinds of protein, including the elastic fibres in the lungs and airways. Recently, a protein called **alpha-1-antitrypsin** (**A1AT**), an inhibitor of elastase, has been used to reduce the damage caused by elastase. Some studies have shown that treatment with A1AT can reduce the amount of lung damage experienced by people with cystic fibrosis.

Another kind of lung disease, emphysema, results in the walls of the alveoli breaking down (Figure 2). The disease usually results from damage caused by cigarette smoking. Instead of having many tiny alveoli supplied by thin-walled capillaries, the lungs contain fewer alveoli which are much bigger. This greatly reduces the surface area available for gas exchange. In addition, many of the capillaries disappear. People with emphysema have great difficulty getting enough oxygen into their blood. A1AT is used in the treatment of emphysema. It slows down the breakdown of the walls of the alveoli.

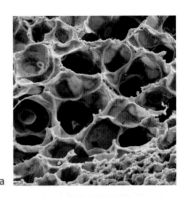

a

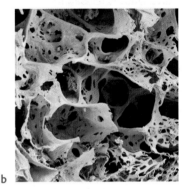

b

Figure 2 *Photomicrographs of (a) healthy alveoli and (b) the lungs of a person with emphysema*

🧪 Diagnostic enzymes

Because enzymes are highly specific, they can also be used to diagnose disease. One example of this is in detecting glucose. Normally, the urine of a healthy person does not contain glucose. However, the urine of a person with diabetes may contain glucose. Test strips have been developed to test whether glucose contains urine. You can see this in Figure 3. The test strip has two enzymes, glucose oxidase and peroxidase, immobilised on a cellulose fibre pad at the end of the strip.

The test strip is dipped into a sample of urine. If glucose is present, this combines with the glucose oxidase enzyme to form gluconic acid:

glucose + oxygen $\xrightarrow{\text{glucose oxidase enzyme}}$ gluconic acid + hydrogen peroxide

Chromagen is also present in the test strip. It is normally colourless. Peroxidase on the test strip breaks down the hydrogen peroxide. When this happens, the chromagen dye is oxidised and becomes coloured.

colourless chromagen + hydrogen peroxide $\xrightarrow{\text{peroxidase enzyme}}$ coloured chromagen + water

The colour of the test strip is compared with a colour chart on the bottle. The colour tells you how much glucose is present in the urine.

Figure 3 *Glucose test strip and colour chart*

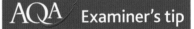

Summary questions

1. When a person with cystic fibrosis is prescribed dornase alfa, they are told to store it in a refrigerator at 2–8 °C. Use your knowledge of enzymes to explain the reason for this advice.

2. Explain why a glucose test strip detects glucose, but not any other substance present in the urine.

3. Explain why a glucose test strip containing glucose oxidase, but not peroxidase or chromagen, would not be very useful.

AQA Examiner's tip

You need to understand why enzymes are so useful in detecting and treating disease. The examiner may give you a different example that you haven't heard of to check that you understand the sensitivity and specificity of enzymes.

2.4 Problems with enzymes

Learning objectives:

■ What is the cause of lactose intolerance?

■ What are the symptoms of lactose intolerance?

■ What is pancreatitis?

■ What affects does pancreatitis have on digestive enzymes?

Specification reference: 3.1.2

Sometimes, problems are caused when the body does not produce enough of an enzyme, or the enzyme ends up in the wrong place. People who do not produce enough lactase enzyme in their guts are **lactose intolerant**. **Pancreatitis** occurs when pancreatic enzymes cannot enter the gut, so they are present in the blood instead.

🚹 Lactose intolerance

Lactose is a sugar found in milk, and in products made using milk, such as cheese, butter, yogurt and ice cream. Lactose may also be added to some processed foods such as bread and some breakfast cereals. However, some people are unable to digest the lactose in the food they eat, because they do not produce enough lactase enzyme. They are said to be lactose intolerant. The undigested lactose causes the growth of bacteria in the gut that feed on the lactose. The bacteria produce gas, causing nausea, bloating and stomach cramps. The undigested sugar lowers the water potential of the gut contents, leading to diarrhoea.

There are many causes of lactose intolerance. A few people are born with the condition but it usually develops after the age of two. Some diseases and injuries to the small intestine can reduce the amount of lactase produced.

Lactose intolerance is not life-threatening and can be treated by a change in diet. People who are lactose intolerant should stop eating foods containing lactose. People who cannot tolerate even tiny amounts of lactose can use lactase enzyme. This can be added to milk, or a tablet can be chewed when eating food containing lactose.

Reducing the lactose content in milk

People who are lactose intolerant can buy milk that has had its lactose content reduced by using enzymes. Most cats are also lactose intolerant, so lactose-reduced milk is also available for cats, produced in the same way. The milk is treated using the enzyme lactase.

Figure 1 *Reduced-lactose milk*

Pancreatitis

The pancreas is an organ found just below the stomach (see Figure 2). It produces hormones that regulate blood glucose concentration, but it also secretes digestive enzymes. These enzymes include trypsin, which digests proteins, lipase which digests fats and amylase which digests starch into maltose.

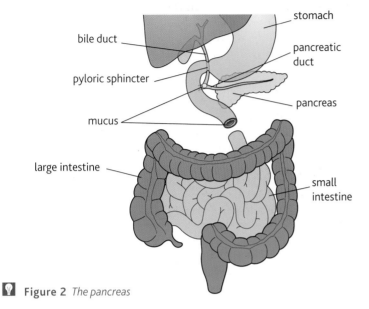

Figure 2 *The pancreas*

Pancreatitis is a severe inflammation of the pancreas. Trypsin is an enzyme that digests protein. It is usually produced in an inactive form, so that it does not start to digest protein until it is in the intestine. Pancreatitis is caused when the enzymes are active in the pancreas and start to break down the tissue of the pancreas. Acute pancreatitis is when the disease occurs suddenly, and chronic pancreatitis is when the disease is long term. People with cystic fibrosis may develop chronic pancreatitis as a result of the thick mucus blocking the pancreatic duct.

Pancreatitis is diagnosed by a blood test. In acute pancreatitis, the enzymes from the damaged pancreas cells are released into the blood. If the levels of amylase and lipase are high in a blood sample, then the person almost certainly has acute pancreatitis. In chronic pancreatitis the pancreas tissue is destroyed more slowly. This is diagnosed by measuring the amounts of enzymes in the person's faeces. Normally, fairly high levels of digestive enzymes should be present in the faeces. In a person with chronic pancreatitis the amount of digestive enzymes in the faeces will be much lower.

Summary questions

1. Suggest how thick mucus blocking the pancreatic duct in a person with cystic fibrosis can lead to pancreatitis.

2. Explain why the amount of digestive enzymes in a person's faeces would normally be fairly high.

3. How can manufacturers of lactose-free milk be sure that the lactase enzyme has completely hydrolysed the lactose by using chromatography?

1   **Figure 1** shows how a test strip is used to detect glucose in urine.

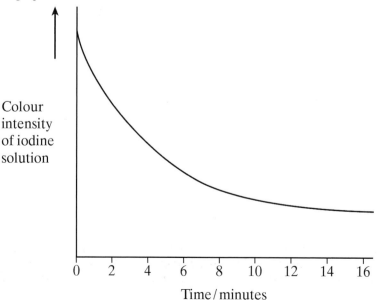

1
Plastic strip has blue band at the end, containing enzymes and dye

2
The strip is dipped into a urine sample

3
The blue band changes colour if glucose is present in the urine

Figure 1

Two enzymes are present on the strip: glucose oxidase and peroxidase. They catalyse the following reactions:

Glucose + oxygen + water $\xrightarrow{\text{glucose oxidase}}$ gluconic acid + hydrogen peroxide

Blue dye + hydrogen peroxide $\xrightarrow{\text{peroxidase}}$ brown dye + water

(a) (i)   Explain why this strip will detect glucose, but not other sugars.
     (ii) Explain why peroxidase is needed on the strip in addition to glucose oxidase.   *(4 marks)*

(b) Suggest **two** advantages of having these enzymes attached to a plastic strip rather than adding them to a urine sample in a test tube.   *(2 marks)*

AQA, 2003

2   In an investigation into carbohydrase activity, the contents from part of the gut were collected. The contents were added to starch solution at pH 7 and kept in a water bath at 25 °C. At one minute intervals, samples were removed and added to different test tubes containing dilute iodine solution. Dilute iodine turns blue-black in the presence of starch. The graph shows the results.

Colour intensity of iodine solution

0   2   4   6   8   10   12   14   16
Time / minutes

(a) Explain the change in colour intensity. *(2 marks)*

(b) Copy the graph and add clearly labelled curves to show the expected results if the experiment was repeated at:

    (i) 35 °C,

    (ii) pH 2. *(2 marks)*

(c) (i) Explain how raising the temperature to 35 °C affects carbohydrase ativity.

    (ii) Explain how decreasing the pH affects carbohydrase activity. *(7 marks)*

AQA, 2005

3 (a) Describe the induced fit theory of enzyme action. *(4 marks)*

(b) A student investigated the effect of pH on the action of amylase. They cut six holes in an agar plate containing starch. They added enzyme and different pH buffers to each hole. The plates were incubated for 4 hours and then iodine added. Iodine turns blue-black in the presence of starch. Clear areas around the hole could be measured.

The widths of the clear areas are shown in the table.

pH	Width of clear ring/mm
4	1
5	2
6	6
7	12
8	9
9	3

    (i) Give **two** factors that should be controlled in this investigation.

    (ii) What conclusion would you draw from these results?

    (iii) Use an appropriate method to estimate the maximum rate of reaction that was observed in this investigation. Show your working. *(5 marks)*

AQA, 2002

4 Lactose is a disaccharide found in milk. In the human small intestine, the enzyme lactase catalyses the hydrolysis of lactose to the monosaccharides galactose and glucose. The monosaccharides are then absorbed into the blood.

(a) Copy and complete **Figure 2** to show the hydrolysis of lactose to galactose and glucose. *(2 marks)*

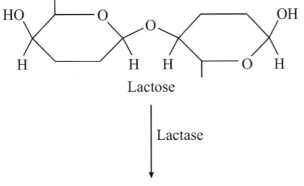

Figure 2

(b) Some people are lactose intolerant because they do not produce enough lactase enzyme in the small intestine. Lactose accumulates in the small intestine and remains unhydrolysed. Explain how this could lead to diarrhoea in these individuals. *(2 marks)*

AQA, 2006

3.1 The lungs and ventilation

Learning objectives:

- How does air get into our lungs?

- How do we breathe in and out?

- How do our lungs stay clean?

Specification reference: 3.1.3

People with cystic fibrosis suffer from frequent lung infections and experience a number of symptoms, including breathing difficulties. Before we look at cystic fibrosis, it is important to understand how healthy lungs work.

The structure of the lungs

Humans need to take in oxygen for respiration from the air, and to get rid of carbon dioxide produced in respiration. These gases are exchanged inside the lungs. You will remember from GCSE that we have a breathing (or **ventilation**) mechanism to force air into and out of the lungs.

Figure 1 shows how air enters and leaves the lungs through a tube called the **trachea**. This is supported by rings of cartilage. The lungs are situated inside the chest cavity, called the **thorax**. The ribs surround the thorax, forming a **rib cage**. The **diaphragm** lies across the bottom of the thorax. The lungs are attached to the inside of the rib cage and diaphragm by the pleural membranes. The ribs can be moved by the **intercostal muscles** which lie between them. The trachea divides into two tubes called **bronchi**, one leading to each lung. The bronchi subdivide into smaller tubes called **bronchioles**. The bronchioles are highly branched, giving many pathways for air to enter and leave the lung. The bronchioles end in clusters of tiny air sacs called **alveoli**. This is where gas exchange takes place.

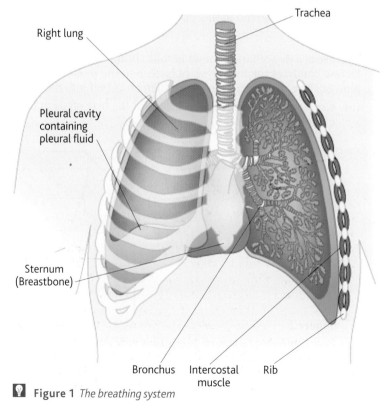

Right lung

Trachea

Pleural cavity containing pleural fluid

Sternum (Breastbone)

Bronchus   Intercostal muscle   Rib

Figure 1 *The breathing system*

◼ Ventilating the lungs

When you breathe in, the intercostal muscles contract, pulling the rib cage up and out. At the same time, the diaphragm muscles contract, pulling the diaphragm flatter. This increases the volume of the thorax and reduces the pressure inside it. As a result, air is pulled into the lungs.

When you breathe out, the intercostal muscles relax, so the rib cage returns to its starting position. The diaphragm muscles relax, moving the diaphragm back to its original domed shape. This reduces the volume of the thorax, and increases the pressure within it. As a result, air is forced out of the lungs.

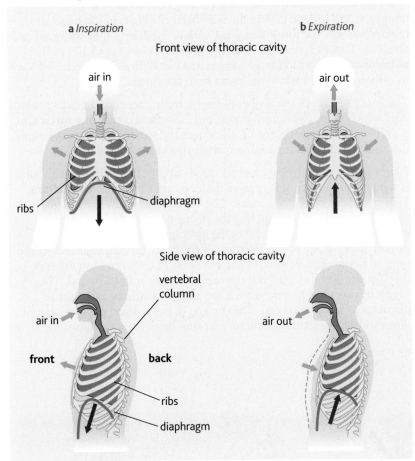

a *Inspiration*   **b** *Expiration*

Front view of thoracic cavity

air in   air out

ribs   diaphragm

Side view of thoracic cavity

vertebral column

air in   air out

front   **back**

ribs

diaphragm

Figure 2 *Ventilating the lungs*

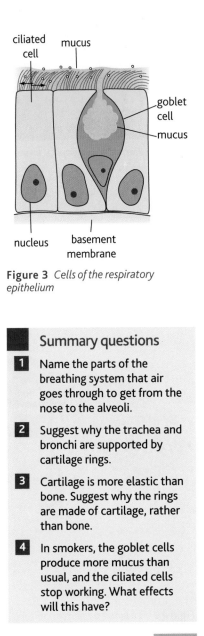

Figure 3 *Cells of the respiratory epithelium*

◼ Keeping the lungs clean

The trachea and bronchi are lined by a layer of cells called an epithelium. There are two main types of cells in this epithelium. Most of the cells are ciliated cells. Cilia are tiny extensions of the cytoplasm that form many tiny hair-like structures on the surface of the cells (see Figure 3). These can bend and beat in time with each other. In between the ciliated cells there are also goblet cells. These cells make and secrete mucus. Mucus is a slimy, sticky substance. Particles of dust and dirt, or bacteria, in the air that is breathed in, get trapped in the mucus. The cilia sweep the mucus back up the bronchi and trachea towards the throat, where it is swallowed. This stops these particles and bacteria entering the lungs, keeping them clean and free from infection. The main reason why people with cystic fibrosis have frequent lung infections is because these cilia cannot move the mucus away from the lungs.

Summary questions

1. Name the parts of the breathing system that air goes through to get from the nose to the alveoli.

2. Suggest why the trachea and bronchi are supported by cartilage rings.

3. Cartilage is more elastic than bone. Suggest why the rings are made of cartilage, rather than bone.

4. In smokers, the goblet cells produce more mucus than usual, and the ciliated cells stop working. What effects will this have?

3.2 Gas exchange

Learning objectives:

- What are the features of an efficient gas exchange surface?

- How are the alveoli adapted for efficient gas exchange?

Specification reference: 3.1.3

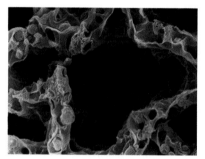

Figure 1 *Electronmicrograph of alveoli*

The alveoli are where gas exchange takes place. Alveoli are tiny hollow sacs. There are many of them in each lung, providing a very large surface area for gas exchange (Figure 1). Alongside the alveoli and the bronchioles that bring air to them, there are many blood vessels (see Figure 2). The **pulmonary artery** brings deoxygenated blood (low in oxygen and high in carbon dioxide) from the heart to the lungs. It branches inside the lungs into a network of capillaries that surround each alveolus. These capillaries eventually join up to form branches of the **pulmonary vein**, which takes oxygenated blood (high in oxygen and low in carbon dioxide) back to the heart from the lungs.

The inner surface of the alveoli is always moist, because the cells produce fluid which stops them from drying out. The fluid contains a **surfactant**. A surfactant is like a detergent. It reduces the surface tension, and stops the alveoli from sticking together when you breathe in and out.

Figure 3 shows an alveolus and its blood supply. The wall of the alveolus is made up of a layer of very thin, flattened cells called an **epithelium**. This is the gas exchange surface. The capillary also has a thin wall made of thin, flat cells. When you breathe in, air which is high in oxygen and low in carbon dioxide enters the alveolus. The capillary brings deoxygenated blood to the alveolus all the time. Oxygen dissolves in the layer of liquid on the inside of the alveolus. The oxygen then diffuses through the alveolus wall and the capillary wall, into the blood. The capillaries surrounding the alveoli are narrow, with about the same diameter as a red blood cell. This means that red blood cells are slowed down as they flow through them, allowing more time for diffusion.

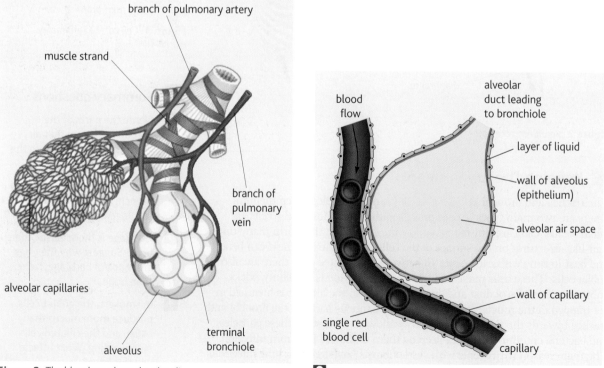

Figure 2 *The blood supply to the alveoli*

Figure 3 *An alveolus and blood capillary*

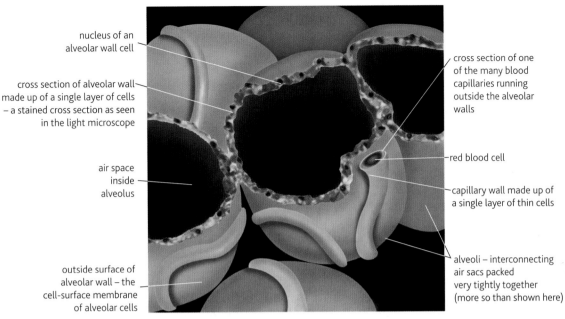

nucleus of an alveolar wall cell

cross section of alveolar wall made up of a single layer of cells – a stained cross section as seen in the light microscope

air space inside alveolus

outside surface of alveolar wall – the cell-surface membrane of alveolar cells

cross section of one of the many blood capillaries running outside the alveolar walls

red blood cell

capillary wall made up of a single layer of thin cells

alveoli – interconnecting air sacs packed very tightly together (more so than shown here)

Figure 4 *External appearance of a group of alveoli*

💡 Features of an efficient gas exchange surface

Alveoli are a good exchange surface because they have these features:

A large surface area

- There are millions of tiny alveoli in each lung.
- Each alveolus is folded, so that there is an even greater surface area in the space available.

A thin permeable surface

- The epithelium of the alveolus is made of very thin, flattened cells.
- The wall of the capillary is also made of very thin, flat cells.
- The capillary walls are in close contact with the alveolus walls.

A large diffusion gradient

- Ventilation brings air high in oxygen and low in carbon dioxide into the alveoli, and takes away air high in carbon dioxide and low in oxygen.
- The capillaries constantly bring deoxygenated blood to the alveoli, and remove oxygenated blood.

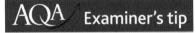 **Examiner's tip**

The inside of the alveoli are moist to maintain their structure and to stop the alveoli sticking together. Oxygen has to dissolve in this layer so that it can diffuse through the capillary wall. However, dissolving in this layer does not speed up gas exchange.

Summary questions

1. Name:

   a the blood vessel that brings deoxygenated blood to the lungs,

   b the blood vessel that takes oxygenated blood away from the lungs.

2. What is the role of surfactant in the alveoli?

3. What features should an efficient gas exchange surface have?

4. Give **three** ways in which the alveoli are adapted for efficient gas exchange.

AQA **Examiner's tip**

The walls of the alveoli are made of thin, flattened cells. Don't write about thin cell walls.

3.3 Plasma membranes

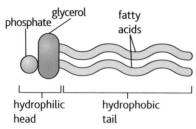

Figure 1 *The structure of a phospholipid*

Plasma membranes are found on the outside of every cell. You will remember from GCSE that plasma membranes control the molecules that enter and leave the cell. The basic structure of the membrane is made up of molecules called **phospholipids**.

⚠ 💡 Phospholipid bilayer

A phospholipid is made up of a glycerol molecule (see page 23) with a phosphate group and two fatty acid chains attached to it. The fatty acid chains are made of carbon and hydrogen only, so they do not have a charge. They are insoluble in water. The fatty acid chains form the 'tail' of the molecule. Because they are insoluble in water, the 'tail' is said to be **hydrophobic**. The phosphate group, however, is charged and it is soluble in water. You will see that the glycerol and phosphate form the 'head' of the molecule. Because the 'head' is water soluble, it is said to be **hydrophilic** (meaning water loving).

In a membrane, phospholipids pack together to form a double layer, or a **bilayer**. The 'heads' face the outside of the membrane so that they are in contact with water. Remember that there is water surrounding all cells, as well as water in the cytoplasm. The 'tails' are found in the middle of the membrane, away from the water. Lipid-soluble molecules can pass through the phospholipid bilayer. Oxygen, carbon dioxide and water molecules pass between the phospholipids because they are very small, but most other molecules and ions cannot pass through the phospholipid bilayer. For this reason, a membrane is said to be **partially permeable**.

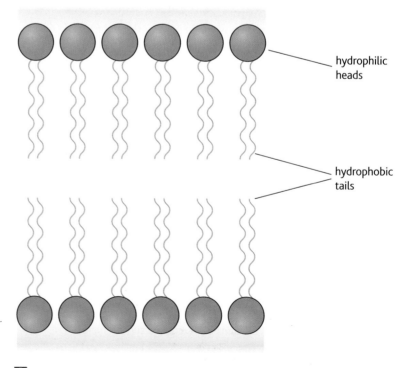

hydrophilic heads

hydrophobic tails

💡 **Figure 2** *A phospholipid bilayer*

Fluid-mosaic model of a membrane

Phospholipids are not the only molecules found in a membrane. Scattered among the phospholipids are many different proteins. Some of the proteins pass all the way through the phospholipid, so they are called **intrinsic** proteins. Some of these act as carriers to transport water-soluble substances across the membrane. People with cystic fibrosis have a faulty protein in the membrane that does not transport chloride ions properly. Other intrinsic proteins are enzymes.

Some proteins are found in only one of the phospholipid layers, so these are called **extrinsic** proteins. These give mechanical support to the membrane, or act as cell receptors. Some of the proteins have carbohydrate chains attached to them. These proteins are called glycoproteins. Glycoproteins act as antigens, allowing cells to recognise each other. You will find out later how these help the body's immune system to distinguish the body's own cells from pathogens. They also act as recognition sites for hormones. You will remember from GCSE that hormones travel all around the body in the blood, but only affect certain organs. This is because hormones can only affect cells that have specific receptors for that hormone.

Carbohydrates may also attach to the phospholipids, forming glycolipids. Scattered among the phospholipids are **cholesterol** molecules. Cholesterol keeps the membrane stable.

The way the molecules are arranged in a membrane is called the **fluid-mosaic** structure. The membrane is fluid because the phospholipid heads move around within their layer. Floating among them are the protein molecules, giving a mosaic appearance.

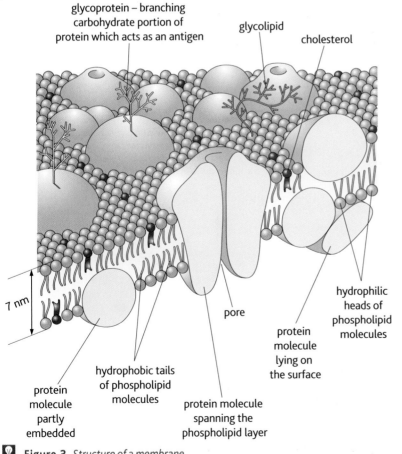

glycoprotein – branching carbohydrate portion of protein which acts as an antigen

glycolipid

cholesterol

7 nm

hydrophilic heads of phospholipid molecules

pore

protein molecule lying on the surface

protein molecule partly embedded

hydrophobic tails of phospholipid molecules

protein molecule spanning the phospholipid layer

Figure 3 *Structure of a membrane*

Summary questions

1. Describe the structure of a phospholipid.

2. Explain how the phospholipids form a double layer in the membrane.

3. Give **three** functions of proteins in a plasma membrane.

4. Explain why the membrane is described as a 'fluid-mosaic'.

3.4 Diffusion

Learning objectives:

■ How does oxygen from the air get into our blood?

■ What is diffusion?

■ What is facilitated diffusion?

Specification reference: 3.1.3

All molecules are constantly in motion because of the kinetic energy they possess. They move around at random. Molecules continually collide with each other, and when they do, they change direction. The closer together they are, the more likely they are to collide with each other.

Diffusion is the net movement of molecules from a region of high concentration to a region of lower concentration. We say that this occurs **down** a concentration gradient. No additional energy is needed for this to happen, so it is described as a **passive** process. This process means that a group of molecules concentrated together in an area will move about at random. As a result, they will eventually end up evenly distributed within the area. This process is shown in Figure 1.

1 *If 10 particles occupying the left-hand side of a closed vessel are in random motion, they will collide with each other and the sides of the vessel. Some particles from the left-hand side move to the right, but initially there are no available particles to move in the opposite direction, so the movement is in one direction only. There is a large concentration gradient and diffusion is rapid.*

2 *After a short time the particles (still in random motion) have spread themselves more evenly. Particles can now move from right to left as well as from left to right. However, with a higher concentration of particles (7) on the left than on the right (3), there is a greater probability of a particle moving to the right than in the reverse direction. There is a smaller concentration gradient and diffusion is slower.*

3 *Some time later, the particles will be evenly distributed throughout the vessel and the concentrations will be equal on each side. The system is in equilibrium. However, the particles are not static but remain in random motion. With equal concentrations on each side, the probability of a particle moving from left to right is equal to the probability of one moving in the opposite direction. There is no concentration gradient and no net diffusion.*

4 *At a later stage, the particles remain evenly distributed and will continue to do so. Although the number of particles on each side remains the same, individual particles are continuously changing position. This situation is called **dynamic equilibrium**.*

Figure 1 *Diffusion*

You will remember from Topic 3.2 that this is how oxygen from the air enters the blood in the alveoli, and how carbon dioxide leaves the blood and enters the air in the alveoli. You will also remember that diffusion is fastest when there is:

■ a large surface area,

■ a short distance,

■ a large concentration gradient.

Cell membranes are very thin because they are only two phospholipid molecules thick. However, many molecules find it difficult to pass through the cell membranes. Small, lipid-soluble molecules pass through the membrane most easily, because they can pass through the phospholipid bilayer (Figure 2). Larger molecules, and molecules that are soluble in water, do not pass through the phospholipid bilayer.

■ Facilitated diffusion

Facilitate means 'to help', so facilitated diffusion is another kind of diffusion in which the proteins in the membrane help molecules to diffuse. Some proteins form water-filled pores that span the membrane, see Figure 3. These allow small water-soluble molecules and ions, such as glucose or amino acids, to pass through. These channels are **specific**. In other words, they only let one kind of molecule or ion through.

Another kind of facilitated diffusion uses **carrier** proteins. These are also intrinsic proteins which span the membrane. This process is shown in Figure 4. Carrier proteins, like channel proteins, are specific. When the molecule binds with the protein, the protein changes shape. This causes the molecule to be released on the other side of the membrane. However, both these kinds of facilitated diffusion require no additional energy. Both use only the kinetic energy of the molecules themselves, so they are passive. Both move molecules from a region where they are in a higher concentration to a region where they are in a lower concentration.

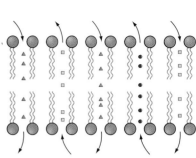

Figure 2 *Small lipid-soluble molecules can pass through the phospholipid bilayer*

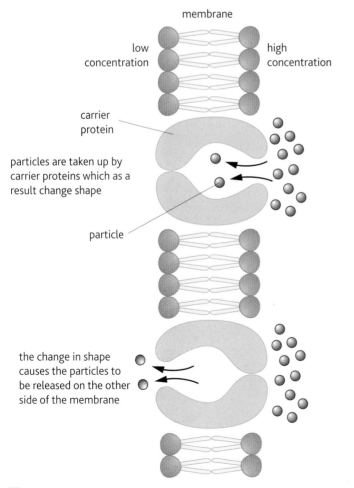

membrane

low concentration

high concentration

carrier protein

particles are taken up by carrier proteins which as a result change shape

particle

the change in shape causes the particles to be released on the other side of the membrane

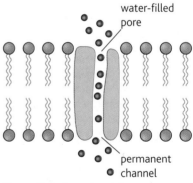

water-filled pore

permanent channel

Figure 3 *A channel protein*

💡 **Figure 4** *Facilitated diffusion*

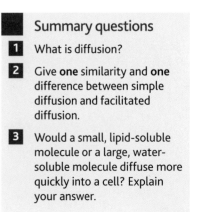

Summary questions

1 What is diffusion?

2 Give **one** similarity and **one** difference between simple diffusion and facilitated diffusion.

3 Would a small, lipid-soluble molecule or a large, water-soluble molecule diffuse more quickly into a cell? Explain your answer.

3.5 Active transport

Learning objectives:

- How are molecules and ions transported into or out of a cell against their concentration gradient?

Specification reference: 3.1.3

Sometimes molecules need to be transported into a cell or out of a cell against their concentration gradient. Additional energy is needed for this process, so it is called **active transport**. The energy needed comes from **ATP**. You will learn in Topic 10.4 that ATP is an energy-storage molecule made in cellular respiration. ATP is short for adenosine triphosphate. It can be broken down to adenosine diphosphate and phosphate. When this happens, a small amount of energy is released. We usually write this as:

$$ATP \xrightarrow{\text{ATPase}} ADP + P_i + energy$$

P_i is shorthand for 'inorganic phosphate ion'.

Carrier proteins which span the whole membrane are needed for active transport. Each carrier protein is specific for one or a few molecules.

The molecule binds to the carrier protein. ATP also binds to the carrier protein. The carrier protein changes shape and energy from the breakdown of ATP is used to transport the molecule across the membrane, against its concentration gradient. As the molecule is released, the carrier protein goes back to its original shape. It is now ready to take up more molecules. This is shown in Figure 1.

AQA Examiner's tip

Be careful not to confuse active transport with facilitated diffusion. Both processes use protein carriers, but active transport carries substances against a concentration gradient and uses ATP as an energy source.

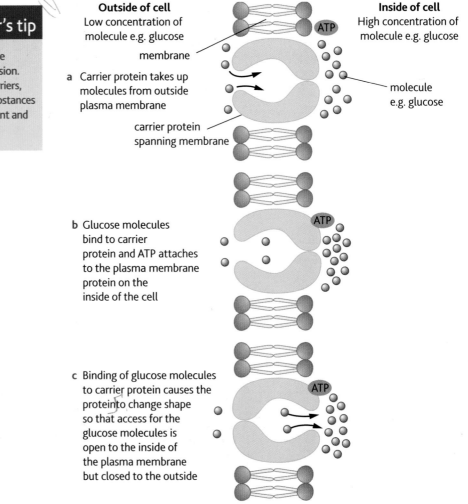

Outside of cell
Low concentration of molecule e.g. glucose

membrane

a Carrier protein takes up molecules from outside plasma membrane

carrier protein spanning membrane

Inside of cell
High concentration of molecule e.g. glucose

ATP

molecule e.g. glucose

b Glucose molecules bind to carrier protein and ATP attaches to the plasma membrane protein on the inside of the cell

ATP

c Binding of glucose molecules to carrier protein causes the protein to change shape so that access for the glucose molecules is open to the inside of the plasma membrane but closed to the outside

ATP

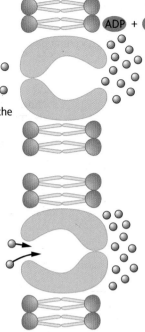

d This new shape of the protein no longer binds the glucose molecules and so they are released to the inside of the plasma membrane with the aid of energy released from the breakdown of ATP to ADP + P_i

e The release of the glucose molecules causes the protein to go back to its original shape and so it is available to take up more glucose molecules from the outside

Figure 1 *Active transport*

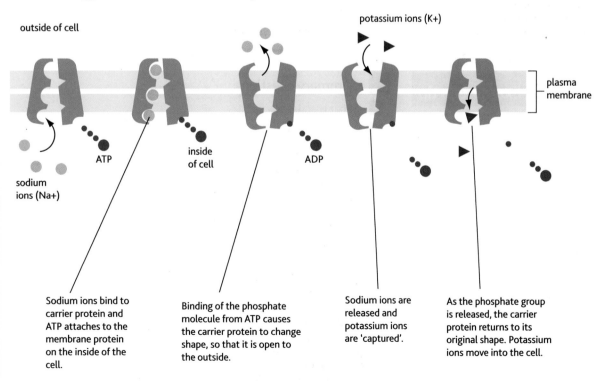

Applications and How science works

Interpreting data about active transport

Some carrier proteins actively transport one ion into a cell at the same time as another ion is moved out. An example of this is the **sodium–potassium pump**. This uses ATP to remove sodium ions from the cell at the same time as bringing potassium ions into the cell. This happens all the time in most body cells.

Sodium ions bind to carrier protein and ATP attaches to the membrane protein on the inside of the cell.

Binding of the phosphate molecule from ATP causes the carrier protein to change shape, so that it is open to the outside.

Sodium ions are released and potassium ions are 'captured'.

As the phosphate group is released, the carrier protein returns to its original shape. Potassium ions move into the cell.

Figure 2 *Sodium–potassium pump*

49

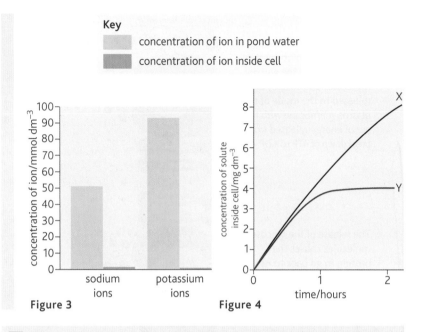

Key

concentration of ion in pond water

concentration of ion inside cell

Figure 3

Figure 4

1. Plant cells move ions in and out of cells in a similar way to animal cells. Figure 3 shows the concentrations of sodium and potassium ions inside the cells of a water plant and in the pond water they were growing in.

   What evidence from the bar graph suggests that:

   a sodium and potassium ions enter the plant cells by active transport?

   b ion uptake is selective?

2. Some animal cells were placed in a solution containing two different solutes, X and Y. The solution contained $4\,mg\,dm^{-3}$ of each solute. The cells did not contain any X or Y at the start of the investigation. The concentration of X and Y inside the cells was measured regularly over a period of 2 hours. Figure 4 shows the results. How were X and Y entering the cells? Explain your answer.

Summary questions

1. What is active transport?

2. Copy the table below and complete it, using a tick if the statement does apply or a cross if the statement does not.

Process	Moves molecules against a concentration gradient	Uses ATP energy	Uses protein carrier molecules
diffusion	✗	✗	✗
facilitated diffusion	✗	✗	✓
active transport	✓	✓	✓

3.6 Osmosis

- How is water potential measured and what does it mean?

- What is osmosis?

- How are animal and plant cells adapted to osmosis?

Specification reference: 3.1.3

Hint

It may help you to think about temperatures. For example –5 °C is a higher temperature than –8 °C. Similarly, –5 kPa is a higher water potential than –8 kPa.

Hint

Remember that partially permeable means that the membrane allows water and some other molecules through, but it is not permeable to many molecules.

Osmosis is a special kind of diffusion involving only water molecules. It is a passive process because it relies only on the kinetic energy of the water molecules. To understand osmosis, you need to understand the term **water potential**. Water potential measures the pressure water molecules exert in a solution, and their ability to move freely. The more water there is, the higher the water potential and the more freely the molecules can move.

Water potential

Water potential is measured in pressure units, usually kilopascals (kPa). It is represented by the Greek letter ψ (psi, pronounced 'sigh'). The water potential of pure water at standard temperature and pressure is said to be zero. When dissolved molecules (solutes) are present, this makes the water potential lower, so the value becomes negative. Water molecules move by osmosis from a region of higher (less negative) water potential to a region of lower (more negative) water potential.

Osmosis

The definition of osmosis is the movement of water molecules from a region of higher water potential to a region of lower water potential across a partially permeable membrane.

Figure 1 shows osmosis. There is a much higher concentration of water molecules on one side of the membrane than on the other side. This difference in concentration is called a **water potential gradient**. The water and solute molecules are moving randomly because they have kinetic energy. However, the membrane is partially permeable, so only the water molecules can pass through it. Water molecules diffuse through the membrane from the left-hand side, where there is a higher water potential, to the right-hand side, where there is a lower water potential. In other words, the water molecules diffuse down a water potential gradient. Eventually, the water potential on both sides of the membrane will be the same. At this point equilibrium is reached, and there is no net movement of water.

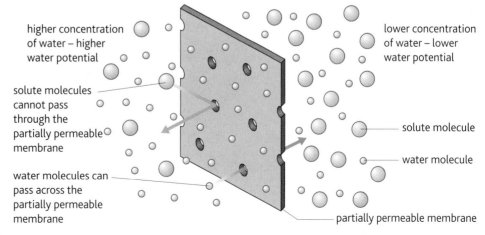

higher concentration of water – higher water potential

lower concentration of water – lower water potential

solute molecules cannot pass through the partially permeable membrane

solute molecule

water molecule

water molecules can pass across the partially permeable membrane

partially permeable membrane

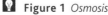 **Figure 1** *Osmosis*

Osmosis in animal cells

We can study osmosis in animal cells by placing them in different solutions.

- If the solution has a **higher** water potential than the solution inside the cell, we say it is a **hypotonic** solution.
- If the solution has a **lower** water potential than the solution inside the cell, we say it is a **hypertonic** solution.
- If the solution has the **same** water potential as the solution inside the cell, we say it is an **isotonic** solution.

If an animal cell, such as a red blood cell, is placed in pure water, it will take in water by osmosis. This is because the water has a higher water potential than the solution inside the red blood cell. As the cell takes in water, it swells up. However, you will remember that cell-surface membranes are very thin, and they are not able to stretch very much. If the cell takes in more than a small amount of water it will burst, releasing its cell contents.

If a red blood cell is placed in a hypertonic solution, such as a concentrated salt solution, it will lose water. This is because the salt solution has a lower water potential than the red blood cell. The red blood cell will shrink and shrivel up.

Normally, cells inside the body do not swell up or shrink as a result of osmosis. This is because the water potential of the fluids surrounding body cells, such as blood plasma, is carefully controlled. Blood plasma is **isotonic** with body cells.

Figure 2 *Summary of osmosis in an animal cell, e.g. a red blood cell*

Type of external solution	Hypotonic	Isotonic	Hypertonic
water potential (ψ) of external solution compared to cell solution	higher (less negative)	equal	lower (more negative)
net movement of water	enters cell	neither enters nor leaves	leaves cell
state of cell	swells and bursts	no change	shrinks

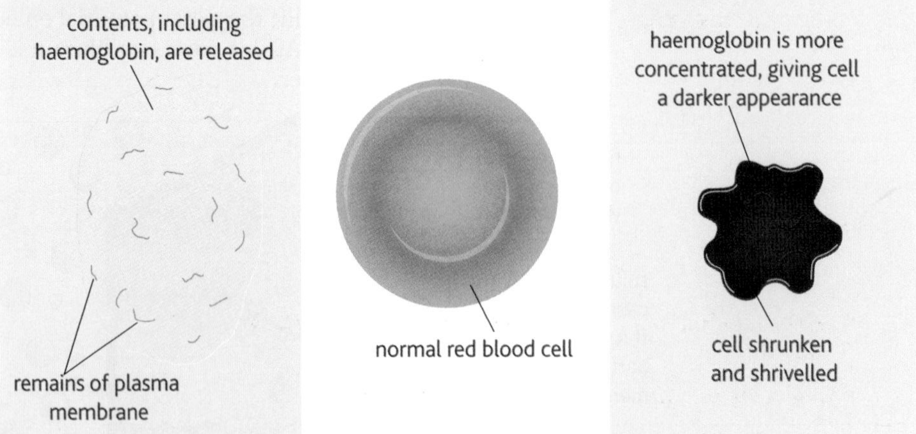

contents, including haemoglobin, are released

remains of plasma membrane

normal red blood cell

haemoglobin is more concentrated, giving cell a darker appearance

cell shrunken and shrivelled

Osmosis in plant cells

You will remember from GCSE that plant cells also have a cell-surface membrane, like animal cells. However, they also have a strong cellulose cell wall surrounding the membrane. This means that when a plant cell is placed in pure water, it swells up but it cannot burst because the cell wall acts like a 'cage'. The cell pushes against the cell wall, like an inflated bladder inside a football pushing against the leather outer. When a plant cell is in this condition, we say it is **turgid**.

When a plant cell is placed in a solution with a much lower water potential than the cell solution, it loses water by osmosis. The plasma membrane shrinks away from the cell wall, and external solution is pulled into the space between the plasma membrane and the cell wall. A cell in this condition is said to be **plasmolysed**.

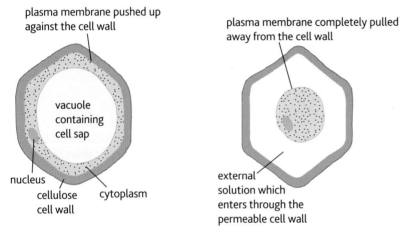

Figure 3 *A turgid plant cell and a plasmolysed plant cell*

Summary questions

1. Define: a osmosis, b water potential.

2. Explain why osmosis is said to be a passive process.

3. Copy the cells shown below. Add arrows to show the direction in which water will move between them.

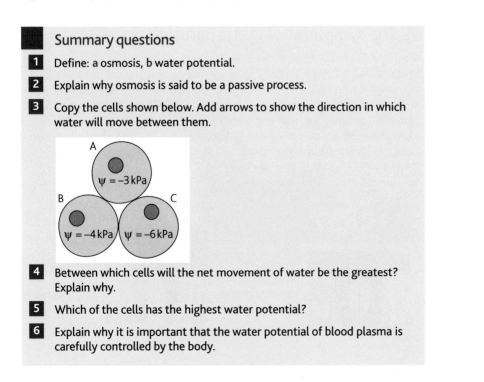

4. Between which cells will the net movement of water be the greatest? Explain why.

5. Which of the cells has the highest water potential?

6. Explain why it is important that the water potential of blood plasma is carefully controlled by the body.

3.7 Cystic fibrosis

Learning objectives:

- What causes cystic fibrosis?
- How does cystic fibrosis affect gas exchange?
- What are the symptoms of cystic fibrosis?

Specification reference: 3.1.3

Link

Remember from GCSE that an allele is a form of a gene.

Link

Revisit Topics 3.3 and 3.4 to revise the structure of membranes and transport of substances across membranes.

Cystic fibrosis is a disorder that affects plasma membranes. It is a genetic disorder, which means that it is caused by a faulty gene. One child in every 2500 is born with cystic fibrosis. The disease is the most common genetic disorder amongst Europeans and Ashkenazi Jews. One person in every 22 people of European descent carries the allele for cystic fibrosis. Cystic fibrosis is a lifelong condition and there is currently no cure. However, the treatment available has improved dramatically over the past 20 years. Fifty years ago, a baby born with cystic fibrosis had a life expectancy of only 5 years. By contrast, a baby born today with cystic fibrosis has an excellent chance of living into their mid-forties. The treatment available also means that sufferers can live reasonably normal lives.

You will remember from Topic 3.3 that membranes contain proteins. These proteins can actively transport ions across the membrane. One of these proteins is called **CFTR**. This stands for *cystic fibrosis transmembrane conductance regulator*. It is made by the CFTR gene. CFTR transports chloride ions (Cl^-) across the membrane. You saw in Topic 3.1 that the cells lining the respiratory tract produce mucus, which is moved by tiny cilia up towards the throat. When chloride ions are actively transported out of the epithelium cells into the mucus, this lowers the water potential of the mucus. Water moves by osmosis out of the epithelium cells into the mucus. This means that the mucus is sticky enough to trap dirt and bacteria that enter the airways, but is also thin enough for the cilia to move the mucus upwards, preventing bacteria from settling in the lungs.

The symptoms of cystic fibrosis

People with cystic fibrosis have a faulty version of the CFTR protein. The protein has a different tertiary structure. Tertiary structure is explained in Topic 1.8. This means that the protein cannot transport chloride ions out of the cells. Instead, the water potential of the mucus increases and water leaves the mucus. You will remember from Topic 3.1 that the epithelium is covered with mucus produced by goblet cells. The lack of water in the mucus means that it is very thick and sticky.

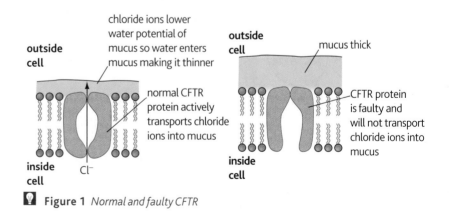

Figure 1 *Normal and faulty CFTR*

Lung infections

You will remember that the ciliated epithelium cells in the respiratory tract move mucus upwards, to prevent bacteria entering the lungs. It is very difficult for the cilia to move the sticky mucus, so it builds up in the air passages. This means that people with cystic fibrosis develop a persistent cough and wheezing. They may experience shortness of breath and breathing difficulties, as the mucus blocks some of the bronchioles. People with cystic fibrosis are prone to repeated lung infections, which can be very severe. Eventually, these infections cause lung damage. Bacteria grow in a layer in the lungs, called a biofilm. When bacteria grow in this way it is very difficult for antibiotics and the immune system to destroy them. White blood cells, especially phagocytes, migrate to the lungs to destroy the bacteria. However, they end up damaging the alveoli instead. This reduces the surface area available for gas exchange.

Other symptoms

CFTR affects other parts of the body too.

- In the digestive system the thick mucus blocks the pancreatic duct. As a result, the enzymes that the pancreas produces cannot get into the gut, so food is not digested properly. People with cystic fibrosis may develop pancreatitis, which you have learned about in Topic 2.4. The thick mucus also means that digested food is not absorbed properly.

- In the reproductive tract, mucus blocks the ducts carrying the gametes. This can lead to infertility, especially in males.

How science works

Screening for cystic fibrosis

Since April 2002 all newborn babies in Scotland have been screened for cystic fibrosis. The test has only recently become routine over the whole of the UK. A small 'heel prick' blood test is taken about the sixth day after birth. This can detect an enzyme called trypsin, which is high in the blood of babies with cystic fibrosis. If it is high, then further tests can be done to confirm the diagnosis.

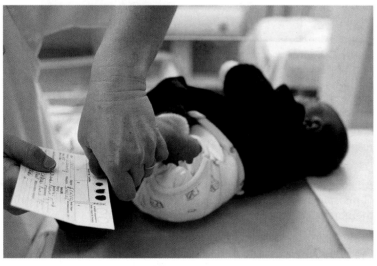

Figure 2 *Screening for cystic fibrosis*

AQA Examiner's tip

Be sure to use the correct terminology to explain the symptoms of cystic fibrosis: diffusion, diffusion gradient, surface area to volume ratio.

Be sure to use the correct terminology to explain the development of thick mucus in a person with cystic fibrosis: osmosis, water potential, water potential gradient.

Summary questions

1 Use water potential terminology to explain why people with normal CFTR have thinner mucus than people with cystic fibrosis.

2 Explain why people with cystic fibrosis:

   a have a persistent cough,

   b have frequent lung infections,

   c may be short of breath.

3 Give **one** advantage and **one** disadvantage of routinely screening all newborn babies in the UK for cystic fibrosis.

3.8 Cell structure

Learning objectives:

■ What are the roles of endoplasmic reticulum, ribosomes, the Golgi body and vesicles in producing CFTR protein and mucus?

■ What is the role of mitochondria?

■ What is the cell structure of a ciliated cell?

■ What are cilia and what is their function?

Specification reference: 3.1.3

The gene that codes for making the CFTR protein, and the genes that code for all the other proteins needed in a cell, are found in the nucleus. However, these proteins are actually made in the cytoplasm.

To understand the structure of cells, you need a microscope. A light microscope can be used to see the overall structure of a cell. However, cells contain many smaller structures, and to see these an electron microscope is needed. This is much more powerful and it allows us to see the cell's **ultrastructure**.

An electron microscope uses a beam of electrons. This has a much shorter wavelength than light, so it gives much better **resolution**. Resolution is the ability to see two objects close together as separate objects. In a transmission electron microscope, a beam of electrons is passed through a very thin section of a specimen. Different parts of the specimen absorb more or less of the electrons, producing a black and white image on a computer screen. However, the electron beam will only operate in a vacuum. This means that you cannot view living material in an electron microscope. Light microscopes are useful because you can see the specimen in colour, and you can view living specimens.

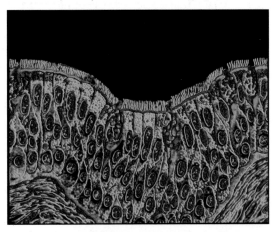

Figure 1 *Light micrograph of cells from the respiratory epithelium*

⚠ 💡 Ultrastructure of a goblet cell

You will remember from Topic 3.1 that there are goblet cells in the respiratory epithelium. These are so called because of their shape. Their function is to secrete mucus.

All cells are surrounded by a plasma membrane. This is made up of phospholipids and protein molecules (see Topic 1.8). The plasma membrane controls what enters or leaves the cell.

In the cell cytoplasm there is an extensive membrane system called the **rough endoplasmic reticulum** (RER). It links up with the nuclear membrane. Inside the membranes are cavities called cisternae. On the outside of the RER are darkly-staining structures called **ribosomes**. Proteins are synthesised (made) by the ribosomes. The RER transports proteins around the cell. Ribosomes attached to the RER make proteins

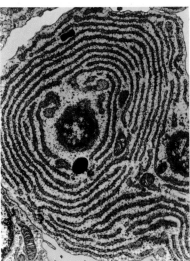

Figure 2 *Electronmicrograph showing rough endoplasmic reticulum*

that will be secreted by the cell to be used elsewhere in the body. There are also ribosomes free in the cytoplasm. These synthesise enzymes to be used in the cell itself.

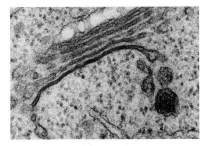

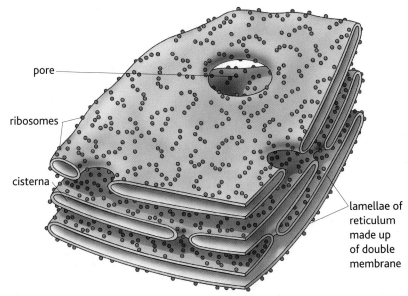

pore

ribosomes

cisterna

lamellae of reticulum made up of double membrane

Figure 3 *A three-dimensional diagram of rough endoplasmic reticulum*

Figure 4 *The Golgi body – electronmicrograph and three-dimensional diagram*

Another kind of endoplasmic reticulum in the cell does not have ribosomes attached. This is called **smooth endoplasmic reticulum** (SER). It is more tubular in appearance. SER has different functions depending on the kind of cell it is found in. Enzymes in the SER are important in synthesising fats, phospholipids and steroids. For example, in the ovaries and testes it makes hormones such as oestrogen and testosterone.

The **Golgi body** is a stack of flattened, curved cisternae surrounded by membranes. Vesicles are pinched off at the edges of the cisternae. Proteins and lipids produced by the endoplasmic reticulum pass through the Golgi body. Here, they are modified and packaged into vesicles.

Mucus is made of glycoprotein. In other words, it is a protein with carbohydrate attached to it. In goblet cells, prtoteins made by the ribosomes on the RER travel through the RER to the Golgi body. Here, carbohydrates are added to the proteins to make mucus. The mucus is packaged into vesicles, which pinch off the Golgi body and move towards the plasma membrane. The membrane surrounding the vesicles fuses with the plasma membrane, so that the mucus is released outside the cell.

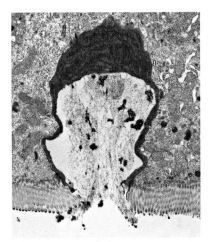

Figure 5 *Electronmicrograph of mucus being secreted from the goblet cells*

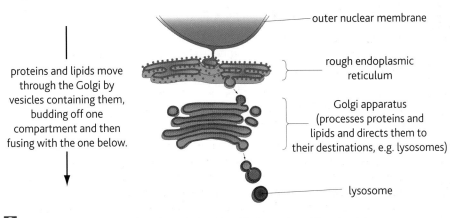

outer nuclear membrane

rough endoplasmic reticulum

Golgi apparatus (processes proteins and lipids and directs them to their destinations, e.g. lysosomes)

proteins and lipids move through the Golgi by vesicles containing them, budding off one compartment and then fusing with the one below.

lysosome

Figure 6 *The Golgi body and its relationship with the nucleus, ER and vesicles*

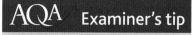
In the cytoplasm of the cell are many rod-shaped organelles called **mitochondria**. These organelles are surrounded by two membranes. The inner membrane is folded to form **cristae**. Filling the space in the middle is a fluid called the **matrix**. The mitochondria contain enzymes involved in the production of ATP during aerobic respiration. ATP is an energy storage molecule.

ATP produced in the mitochondria is used for many energy-requiring processes in the cell, including protein synthesis and active transport.

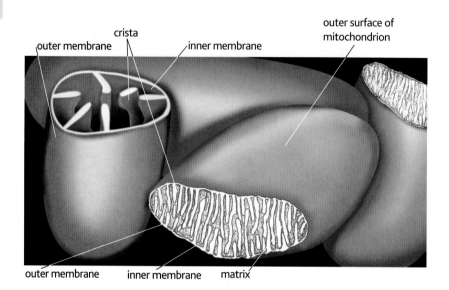

💡 **Figure 7** *Cross-section of mitochondria showing the arrangement of the cristae (magnification × 25 000 approx.)*

🔢 Ultrastructure of a ciliated epithelium cell

On page 56 you saw a light micrograph of the respiratory epithelium, which contains two main kinds of cell. You looked at the detailed structure of one of these kinds of cell – the goblet cell, which secretes mucus. Here we are going to look at the structure of the other kind of cell – the ciliated epithelium cell.

You will see from Figures 8 and 9 that a ciliated cell from the respiratory epithelium has many of the same features as a goblet cell. For example, it has a plasma membrane, endoplasmic reticulum, ribosomes, Golgi body and mitochondria.

CFTR protein is one of the proteins that is synthesised by the ribosomes on the RER. It travels to the Golgi body. Here it is packaged into vesicles. After this, it is carried to the plasma membrane where it becomes a membrane protein.

You will also see that the ciliated epithelium cell has many tiny threads extending from its plasma membrane. These are called **cilia**. One ciliated epithelium cell in the respiratory tract has about 200 cilia. These all beat together in a regular rhythm, producing a wave-like motion, rather like a Mexican wave. This enables the cells to move mucus up the respiratory tract, back towards the throat.

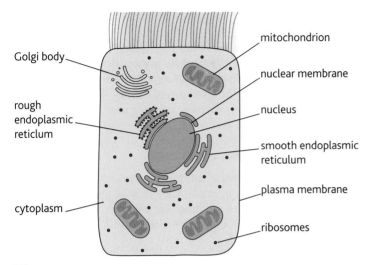

Golgi body

mitochondrion

nuclear membrane

rough endoplasmic reticlum

nucleus

smooth endoplasmic reticulum

plasma membrane

cytoplasm

ribosomes

Figure 8 *Drawing of the structure of a ciliated cell from the respiratory epithelium*

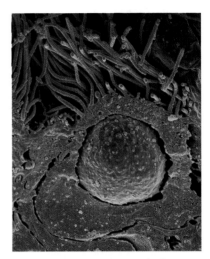

Figure 9 *Electronmicrograph of a ciliated cell from the respiratory epithelium*

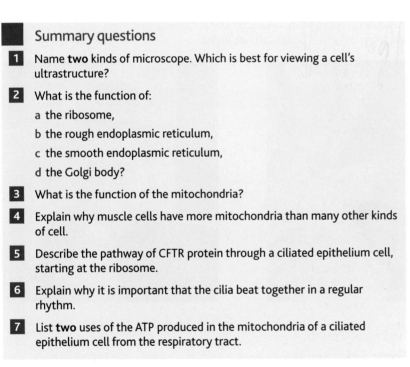

Summary questions

1 Name **two** kinds of microscope. Which is best for viewing a cell's ultrastructure?

2 What is the function of:

a the ribosome,

b the rough endoplasmic reticulum,

c the smooth endoplasmic reticulum,

d the Golgi body?

3 What is the function of the mitochondria?

4 Explain why muscle cells have more mitochondria than many other kinds of cell.

5 Describe the pathway of CFTR protein through a ciliated epithelium cell, starting at the ribosome.

6 Explain why it is important that the cilia beat together in a regular rhythm.

7 List **two** uses of the ATP produced in the mitochondria of a ciliated epithelium cell from the respiratory tract.

3.9   Living with cystic fibrosis

Learning objectives:

■ How can people with cystic fibrosis be treated?

■ How do people with cystic fibrosis usually die?

■ What is gene therapy and what could be its benefits to cystic fibrosis sufferers?

■ How can cystic fibrosis symptoms and treatments be applied to other conditions that can impair gas exchange?

Specification reference: 3.1.3

Regular chest physiotherapy is very important for children with cystic fibrosis. A physiotherapist will usually show parents how to carry this out on their children. It helps to remove the thick mucus from the airways. The child lies head-down, so they can cough out the sputum and mucus, while the parent pats the chest firmly in a special way. Usually, this treatment is carried out twice a day. If the child has a chest infection, physiotherapy may be needed more often. Children with cystic fibrosis are encouraged to exercise and play sport, as keeping active and fit improves their health.

Most children with cystic fibrosis take antibiotics regularly to prevent lung infections. If they get a lung infection they may be given other antibiotics in addition. Sometimes the lungs become infected with a fungus, so an antifungal medicine may be needed as well.

People with cystic fibrosis often take a drug to dilate the airways so that they can breathe more easily. This is similar to the inhaler used by people with asthma. They may also take a drug that thins down the mucus. This makes it easier for them to cough up the mucus and clear the airways. It may reduce the number of lung infections and improve lung function. People with advanced cystic fibrosis who have lung damage may be given oxygen, particularly at night.

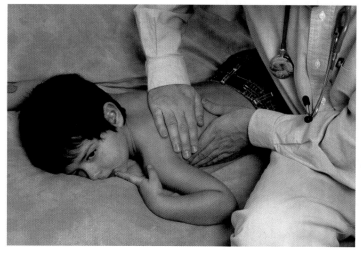

Figure 1 *A child with cystic fibrosis being given physiotherapy*

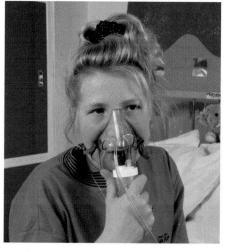

Figure 2 *A person with cystic fibrosis receiving drugs using a nebuliser*

People with cystic fibrosis need a high fat, protein and carbohydrate diet, and probably high-energy food and drink supplements because they do not digest and absorb food properly. They will also need vitamin supplements because they do not absorb vitamins from their food very well either. Most people with cystic fibrosis swallow enzyme capsules before eating food, to help them to digest their food more easily.

Lung infections, and the resulting damage to the lungs, are the main cause of death for people with cystic fibrosis. Although there is no cure for cystic fibrosis at present, there is a great deal of hope. People with advanced cystic fibrosis, which has caused severe lung damage, may have a heart-lung transplant. There is also research taking place into gene therapy. This involves inserting a normal copy of the CFTR gene into the cells lining the respiratory tract. If this treatment can be made to work, someone with cystic fibrosis would need to repeat the therapy every few weeks for life.

Applications and How science works

Smoking and emphysema

Smoking has a number of harmful effects on the body. However, one effect is that, over time, the walls of the alveoli break down. This means that the number of alveoli in the lungs gets much lower, while the size of the alveoli is much larger. Many of the capillaries that normally surround the alveoli also disappear. This condition is called **emphysema**. People with emphysema have great difficulty getting enough oxygen into their blood. They become breathless, even when carrying out gentle activities. Eventually they need to breathe pure oxygen. The lung tissue gradually loses its elasticity, making breathing out more difficult.

Another effect of smoking is that the tissues lining the trachea and bronchi are damaged. As the tissue repairs itself, fibrous tissue is laid down. This is thicker than the original tissue, so the airways become narrower. This also makes it much harder for the smoker to get air into and out of the lungs.

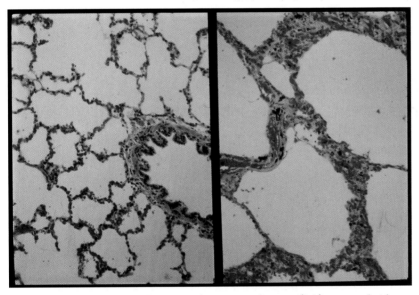

Figure 3 *Light micrograph of lung tissue from a normal person (left) compared with lung tissue from a person with emphysema (right). Same magnification shown.*

1. Explain why the alveoli in a person with emphysema are not efficient at gas exchange.

Summary questions

1. Explain why it is important to remove as much mucus as possible from the lungs of a person with cystic fibrosis.

2. Explain how a drug that dilates the airways can help a person with cystic fibrosis.

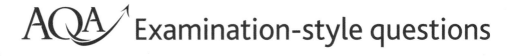

AQA Examination-style questions

1   **Figure 1** shows some of the structures involved in ventilating human lungs.

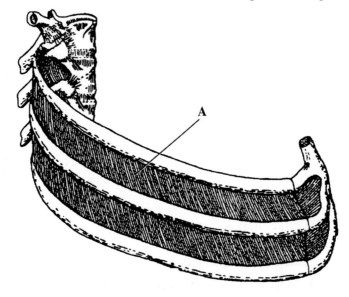

   Figure 1
   (a) Name structure **A**.   *(1 mark)*
   (b) (i)   Describe the role of structure **A** in inspiration.
        (ii) Explain how ventilation increases the rate of gas exchange in the alveoli.   *(5 marks)*

AQA, 2003

2   **Figure 2** shows part of a plasma membrane.

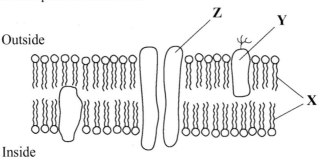

   Figure 2
   (a) Describe **two** functions of the structure made from the parts labelled **X**.   *(2 marks)*
   (b) Give **one** function of the part labelled **Y**.   *(1 mark)*
   (c) The part labelled **Z** is involved in facilitated diffusion of substances across the membrane.
        (i)   Give **one** similarity in the way in which active transport and facilitated
              diffusion transport substances across the membrane.
        (ii) Give **one** way in which active transport differs from facilitated diffusion.
        Figure 3 shows the relationship between the concentration of a substance outside
        a cell and the rate of entry of this substance into the cell.

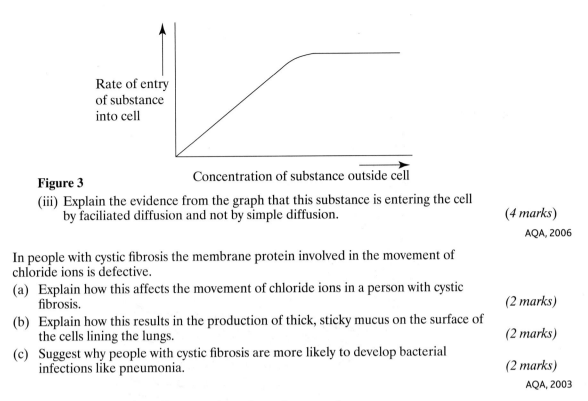

Figure 3

(iii) Explain the evidence from the graph that this substance is entering the cell by faciliated diffusion and not by simple diffusion.

(4 marks)

AQA, 2006

3   In people with cystic fibrosis the membrane protein involved in the movement of chloride ions is defective.

(a) Explain how this affects the movement of chloride ions in a person with cystic fibrosis.

(2 marks)

(b) Explain how this results in the production of thick, sticky mucus on the surface of the cells lining the lungs.

(2 marks)

(c) Suggest why people with cystic fibrosis are more likely to develop bacterial infections like pneumonia.

(2 marks)

AQA, 2003

4   **Figure 4** shows part of a cell as seen through an electron microscope.

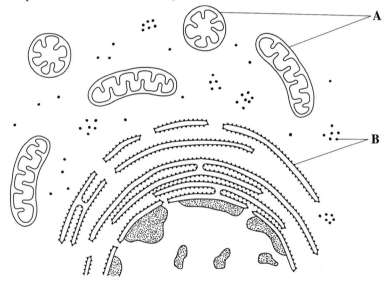

Figure 4

(a) Name the organelles labelled **A** and **B**.

(2 marks)

(b) Explain why the shapes of the two organelles labelled A appear different.

(2 marks)

(c) Give the function of organelle **B**.

(1 mark)

AQA, 2005

5   (a) (i)   Give **two** functions of the proteins found in a plasma membrane.

(ii) Explain why the structure of the plasma membrane is described as a 'fluid-mosaic'.

(4 marks)

(b) Describe the role of the rough endoplasmic reticulum and the Golgi body in producing mucus in cells lining the respiratory tract.

(3 marks)

AQA, 2007

4 Microorganisms

4.1 Bacteria

Learning objectives:

■ What are bacterial cells like?

■ How is a bacterial cell different from a human cell?

Specification reference: 3.1.4

Bacteria are very small organisms. A typical bacterial cell is about $2\,\mu m$ long. This means that 500 bacteria placed end-to-end would stretch across 1 mm on your ruler! Most people associate bacteria with disease, and some bacteria do cause disease. However, you will remember from page 10 that some bacteria are very useful.

⚠ 💡 The structure of a bacterial cell

Figure 1 shows the structure of a typical bacterial cell. Bacteria have a different kind of cell structure from those of humans. You will notice that a bacterial cell does not have a nucleus with a nuclear membrane around it. Biologists believe that bacteria were among the first organisms to evolve on Earth. They are called **prokaryotic** cells (pro = before, karyon = nucleus). Human cells are **eukaryotic** (eu = true).

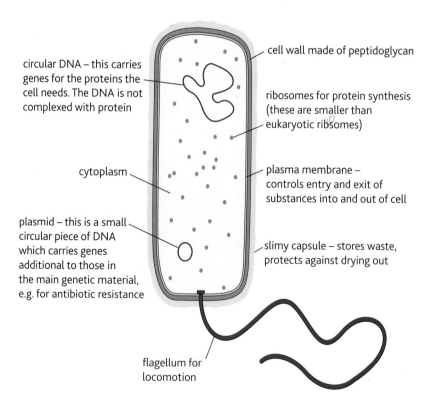

circular DNA – this carries genes for the proteins the cell needs. The DNA is not complexed with protein

cell wall made of peptidoglycan

ribosomes for protein synthesis (these are smaller than eukaryotic ribosomes)

cytoplasm

plasma membrane – controls entry and exit of substances into and out of cell

plasmid – this is a small circular piece of DNA which carries genes additional to those in the main genetic material, e.g. for antibiotic resistance

slimy capsule – stores waste, protects against drying out

flagellum for locomotion

💡 **Figure 1** *The structure of a typical bacterial cell*

The functions of the structures found in a typical bacterial cell are summarised in Table 1 on the next page.

Table 1 *Structures found in a bacterial cell*

Cell structure	Structure	Function
cell wall	made of a substance called peptidoglycan; peptidoglycan contains carbohydrates and amino acids	keeps some substances out of the cell; stops the cell bursting if it takes in water by osmosis, and holds the cell in shape
plasma membrane	made of phospholipids and proteins just like in eukaryotic cell membranes	partially permeable; controls what molecules may enter or leave the cell
nuclear material	made of a long circular DNA molecule, with no proteins attached to it	contains the genes needed for the bacterial cell to grow and reproduce
plasmid	a small circular piece of DNA, found in some bacterial cells only	carries genes in addition to those in the main nuclear material, e.g. carries genes that code for enzymes to destroy antibiotics
capsule	a slimy layer found outside the cell wall of some bacteria only	protects the cell from drying out and makes the cells slippery so it is harder for white blood cells to engulf them
ribosome	made of RNA and protein, like eukaryotic ribosomes, but bacterial ribosomes are smaller	protein synthesis
flagellum	found only in some bacterial cells; rigid and a corkscrew shape, so it has a different structure from the flagella found in eukaryotic cells (e.g. sperm cells)	rotates from the base and helps the bacterium move through fluids

Summary questions

1. Name **three** organelles that are found in a human cell but are not found in a bacterial cell.

2. Copy and complete the table to show differences between a prokaryotic cell and a human cell.

Prokaryotic cell	Human cell
no true nucleus with a nuclear envelope	
	DNA in the form of chromosomes inside the nucleus; these chromosomes are linear
	flagella (if present) can beat and move from side to side
no membrane-bound organelles	
	ribosomes are larger
	does not have a capsule

4.2 Salmonella food poisoning

Learning objectives:

■ What causes salmonella food poisoning?

■ How can we prevent the spread of the disease?

Specification reference: 3.1.4

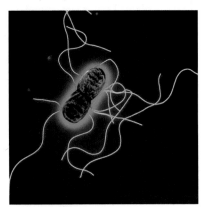

Figure 1 *Electronmicrograph of Salmonella*

Some bacteria can grow in the human body, where they obtain food and shelter. Some beneficial bacteria live in the human gut. For example, you learned about bacteria that produce vitamins on page 10. However, some of the bacteria that get into the human body can cause disease by damaging the cells of the human body and producing toxins.

💡 The cause of salmonella food poisoning

Salmonella food poisoning is caused by a bacterium called *Salmonella*. About 10 different species of *Salmonella* cause food poisoning. The bacteria are naturally present in the intestines of many animals, so they may be present in animal faeces. People who have had salmonella food poisoning may still have the bacteria in their intestines for some time after they have recovered.

Salmonella is spread when a person consumes food or drink that is contaminated, directly or indirectly, with faeces. Chickens that are not vaccinated against *Salmonella* may also have the bacteria in their oviducts. Eggs laid by infected chickens may contain the bacteria. The bacteria are killed by thorough cooking, but can be spread if the egg is eaten raw or only partially cooked. Large numbers of bacteria must be consumed to cause an infection, so the disease is usually caught after eating contaminated food that has been left to stand for a few hours, especially if the conditions are warm and damp.

How the bacteria cause disease

Salmonella bacteria invade the cells lining the small intestine where they divide rapidly. When the bacteria die they release an **endotoxin**. Endotoxins are found inside the bacterial cells, so they are only released when the cells burst open after the bacteria have died. It is this endotoxin that causes the symptoms of salmonella food poisoning, which are:

■ vomiting,

■ diarrhoea,

■ abdominal pain,

■ fever.

The symptoms start about 12–24 hours after the contaminated food was eaten, and may last for 2–5 days. The faeces produced are very watery, containing mucus and sometimes blood. The infection can cause severe dehydration, especially in the very young or elderly.

Treatment

Most cases of salmonella are left to run their course. The patient is advised to drink plenty of fluids and to rest while they recover from their symptoms. In the very young and elderly, or in severe cases, **oral rehydration therapy** is given. This is a drink of water containing sugars and salts which replaces mineral ions lost by the body, as well as fluids. Antibiotics are only given in very severe cases.

Preventing food poisoning

The best way to deal with salmonella food poisoning is to avoid getting it in the first place. This can be done by following good food-hygiene rules. For example, frozen chicken might be contaminated with *Salmonella* bacteria from the abattoir. If the chicken is completely thawed and then cooked all the way through, any bacteria present will be killed. However, if the chicken is put into the oven before it is fully thawed, some of the meat may not reach a sufficiently high temperature to kill the bacteria. Good personal hygiene, such as washing your hands after going to the lavatory and before handling food, also helps to prevent the spread of the disease.

Figure 2 *Food hygiene – using a meat thermometer to check that meat is cooked thoroughly all the way through*

Summary questions

1. Explain why the symptoms of salmonella food poisoning do not usually appear until at least 12 hours after the contaminated food has been eaten.

2. Suggest why antibiotics are not normally used to treat salmonella food poisoning.

3. The table shows some food hygiene rules that should be applied to prevent the spread of salmonella food poisoning. Copy and complete the table to explain the reason for each rule.

Food hygiene rule	Reason for the rule
Do not refreeze frozen food that has thawed out.	
Store raw meat at the bottom of the refrigerator, and cooked food, or food that is to be eaten raw, at the top.	
Boil dishcloths regularly, or use disposable ones.	
Do not use a board or knife that has been used to prepare raw meat for any other food preparation, until it has been thoroughly washed.	
Keep food you have prepared, such as ham sandwiches, in a refrigerator until it is ready to be eaten.	

4. A woman bought a frozen chicken and left it in the refrigerator to thaw out. She also bought some cooked ham, which she placed on the shelf below the chicken in the refrigerator. Later, she used the ham to make some sandwiches for a child's birthday party. She put the sandwiches on a plate and wrapped them with cling film. She left the sandwiches on the worktop in the kitchen for 3 hours before they were eaten. Two days later, several children who had been at the party were diagnosed with salmonella food poisoning. Explain how the infection was probably caused.

4.3 Tuberculosis

Learning objectives:

- What causes tuberculosis?
- What are the symptoms?
- How can the disease be treated?

Specification reference: 3.1.4

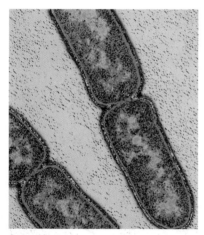

Figure 1 *Mycobacterium tuberculosis*

The cause of tuberculosis

Tuberculosis (TB) is caused by the bacterium *Mycobacterium tuberculosis*. It is an infectious disease that can affect any part of the body, although it usually affects the lungs as this is the part of the body that is most easily infected. Every year, about 8 million people in the world become infected with TB, and 2.6 million die from it.

TB is spread by **droplet infection**. This means that it is spread through the air. When an infected person coughs or sneezes, they release tiny droplets of mucus that contain the bacteria. When another person breathes in these droplets, the bacteria enter their lungs. However, people usually have to be in close contact with another infected person for a prolonged period of time before they become infected. The disease is more likely to be spread when people live in overcrowded, poorly ventilated homes.

Some forms of TB are caused by the bacterium *Mycobacterium bovis* which infects cattle. Meat from infected animals can spread TB, but it is much more likely to be spread by drinking milk from infected animals.

How the bacterium causes disease

In many people, the bacterium does not cause disease. Instead the infection lies dormant, although it can become active many years later, especially if the person later becomes infected with HIV.

Most cases of TB affect the lungs. The droplets containing the bacterium are inhaled, and enter the lungs. Phagocytic white blood cells called **macrophages** engulf the *Mycobacterium* cells. The macrophage cells act like a 'shell' that surrounds the bacteria and keeps them under control. Most people who become infected with TB do not go on to develop the full symptoms of the disease.

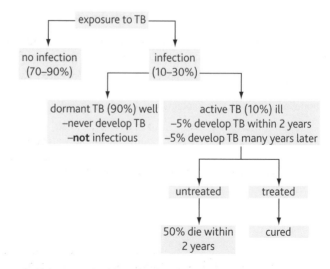

Figure 2 *The stages of pulmonary tuberculosis*

The next stage of the disease is when **tubercles** develop. These consist of a mass of dead lung tissue surrounding the *Mycobacterium* bacteria. The bacteria cannot multiply inside the tubercles due to a low pH and lack of oxygen. However, they can remain alive inside the tubercles for a long time.

The tubercles are surrounded by many macrophages. *Mycobacterium* is able to multiply inside some of the macrophages which causes the tubercles to grow. The tubercles may invade the bronchioles and spread to other parts of the lung. Alternatively, the bacteria may enter a blood vessel and cause an infection in another part of the body. The secondary infection can occur anywhere in the body, but usually occurs in the reproductive system, urinary system, bones, joints, lymph nodes or peritoneum (the membrane surrounding the body cavity).

In the final stages of TB, the centres of the tubercles begin to liquefy. This causes the *Mycobacterium* to multiply very quickly. The tissues of the bronchioles die and break open, leaving cavities in the lungs. This causes *Mycobacterium* to spread quickly to other parts of the lungs.

TB from milk

Mycobacterium bovis is a bacterium that causes TB in cattle. The bacterium can also infect humans. Humans can develop TB by consuming unpasteurised milk from TB-infected cattle. In these cases, the bacteria usually infect the bones rather than the lungs.

Symptoms of TB

People with a TB infection in their lungs are likely to develop a mild cough and they may feel slightly sick. At this stage, the symptoms of TB are similar to many other infections of the respiratory system. As the disease progresses, they may cough up small amounts of greenish or yellow sputum, and the sputum may contain blood. Later, they may develop a slight fever and loss of appetite. They may experience mild chest pain, difficulty in breathing and night sweats. If the TB bacteria spread to other parts of the body, other symptoms such as skin infections may develop. They may also suffer severe weight loss. However, modern antibiotic treatment can be used to treat the disease before these severe symptoms develop.

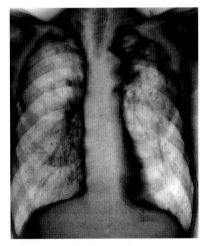

Figure 3 *In this chest X-ray, you can see areas where the bacteria that cause TB have damaged the lung tissue*

Diagnosing TB

A chest X-ray can show whether there is any infection in the lungs. Tubercles show up as shadowy areas. You can see this in Figure 3. However, to show that the lung infection is caused by *Mycobacterium*, a skin test must be carried out.

TB can be detected by administering the **Mantoux** or **tuberculin** test (see Figure 2 on page 87). A protein from *Mycobacterium* (an antigen) is injected into the skin. The tissue surrounding the injection site becomes red and swollen. If the swollen red area is greater than 15 mm in diameter, the person is infected with *Mycobacterium*, or has previously been infected.

Treating TB

TB can be treated successfully with antibiotics. If just one drug is given, the bacterium is likely to develop resistance, so a mixture of four different

Figure 4 *TB killed many people in the days before antibiotics, including the novelist Emily Bronte (above) and the composer Frederic Chopin*

antibiotics is usually given. However, it is very difficult for the antibiotics to penetrate the tubercles and kill the bacteria. This means that the drugs need to be taken regularly for a period of 6 months. Many people feel better during this time and stop taking the drugs, so medical staff have difficulties in making sure that patients complete their course of treatment. One way to do this is to make the patient come to a clinic, where they are observed taking their medication.

TB can be prevented by a vaccination called the BCG vaccination. You will learn more about this in Topic 5.4.

■ Risk factors for TB

Tuberculosis seemed to be under control in developed countries by the 1980s. However, there has recently been a large increase in the number of cases. Two million people die of TB every year worldwide, and 30% of the world's population is infected with TB. There are several reasons for this increase in TB, including the following:

■ People who are infected with HIV are more likely to develop TB.

■ More people travel internationally, and this has spread the disease worldwide.

■ Drug-resistant forms of TB have developed, which are difficult to treat.

■ More people are homeless and living on the streets or in overcrowded accommodation.

How science works

Koch's Postulates

In 1885 the German microbiologist Robert Koch discovered the tubercle bacillus and showed that this microorganism was responsible for tuberculosis. At the time, TB was responsible for one out of every seven deaths that occurred in Europe. He showed that *Mycobacterium* caused TB by using the following set of rules. These are now known as Koch's Postulates.

1 The microorganism must be found in all organisms suffering from the disease, but not in healthy organisms.

2 The microorganism must be isolated from a diseased organism, and grown in pure culture.

3 When the cultured microorganism is introduced into a healthy organism, it should cause the disease.

4 The microorganism must be reisolated from the inoculated, diseased organism from stage 3 and be identical to the original microorganism from stage 2.

Summary questions

1 Explain why TB is more likely to spread when people live in overcrowded conditions.

2 Explain why people with developing TB have chest pains and cough up sputum containing blood.

3 Suggest why homeless people who are living on the streets are more likely to develop TB.

4.4 Antibiotics

Learning objectives:

- What diseases can be treated with antibiotics?

- How do antibiotics work?

Specification reference: 3.1.4

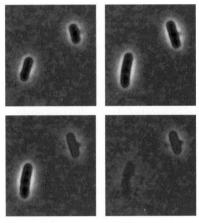

Figure 1 *How penicillin kills bacteria*

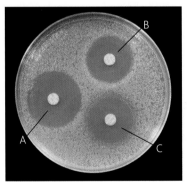

Figure 2 *Action of antibiotics on bacterial cells. The clear regions around the paper discs containing antibiotic show that the antibiotic has killed the bacteria. These clear zones are called inhibition zones*

Examiner's tip

Do not confuse antibiotics with antibodies! Antibodies are proteins made by the body's immune system to destroy pathogens. They are completely different from antibiotics, which are chemicals that kill bacteria.

Antibiotics are substances produced by microorganisms that kill or inhibit bacteria. They were first developed in the 1930s and 1940s. More recently, antibiotics have been found in other organisms. There are also synthetic antibiotics.

Antibiotics kill bacteria by interfering with their metabolism. The antibiotic penicillin works by stopping bacteria synthesising new cell walls when the cells divide. You can see this in Figure 1. The cells swell up because they take in water by osmosis. The weakened cell wall is not strong enough to withstand the pressure, so they burst.

Several antibiotics stop bacteria making proteins. You will remember from Topic 4.1 that proteins are made at the ribosomes. Chloramphenicol stops amino acids being brought to the ribosomes. Tetracycline binds to bacterial ribosomes and stops proteins being made.

How science works

The discovery of antibiotics

The story of Alexander Fleming's accidental discovery of penicillin in 1928 is well known. He was studying bacteria, and left a Petri dish of bacteria in his laboratory while he went away on holiday. When he returned, he found that *Penicillium* fungus had started growing in the dish. He also noticed that the bacteria growing near the fungus had died. You can see this in Figure 3.

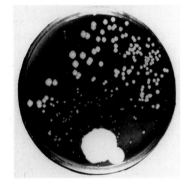

Figure 3 *Alexander Fleming's Petri dish of bacteria, showing the growth of* Penicillium *mould (bottom)*

Fleming thought that the fungus was producing a chemical that killed bacteria, and he made an extract that he called penicillin. However, he could not obtain enough to test it properly.

It was in 1939 that Ernst Chain and Howard Florey managed to obtain enough penicillin to test. They found that it was effective in treating bacterial infections in mice. In 1941 they carried out the first trial of penicillin on a human. They used penicillin to treat a policeman who had osteomyelitis, an infection of the bone and bone marrow. The man did show some improvement, but he died when the supply of penicillin ran out. They were so short of penicillin that they purified penicillin from the man's urine to use again. However, this trial was enough to create interest in penicillin.

Hint

Mould is a general term often used for fungus, especially *Penicillium*.

Summary questions

1 Use your knowledge of bacterial cells and eukaryotic cells to explain why penicillin and tetracycline do not harm human cells.

2 Use water potential terminology to explain how penicillin kills bacteria.

3 Lichens produce a number of chemicals that seem to inhibit bacterial growth. Some people think that lichens might be a source of useful antibiotics.

   a Describe an investigation you could carry out to find out whether lichens produce an antibiotic.

   b Suppose that you do find that lichens produce an antibiotic. Suggest what other tests would need to be done before you could use the antibiotic to treat human diseases.

   c Suggest why lichens might produce antibiotics.

4 Look at the photograph in Figure 2 on the previous page.

   a Which antibiotic is most effective in killing the bacteria? Explain your answer.

   b A doctor may decide *not* to use this antibiotic to treat an infection caused by this bacterium in a patient. Suggest why.

The Second World War was very important in the development of penicillin. The British and US governments wanted to be able to use the drugs to reduce the number of soldiers dying from their wounds. Florey and Chain developed a method for growing penicillin that led to tens of thousands of soldiers' lives being saved. In 1945, Fleming, Florey and Chain were jointly awarded the Nobel Prize for medicine for their work on penicillin.

Penicillin was very limited during the Second World War. Imagine that you are a doctor at this time, working in a field hospital. You have three patients and only enough penicillin to treat one of them.

Patient A is a soldier with very severe wounds that have become infected. He will die of his injuries unless the infection is cured. However, his injuries mean that he cannot return to army work even if he recovers.

Patient B is a child from a nearby village. She has a bacterial infection that will kill her unless she receives penicillin. Her mother has brought her to the field hospital, hoping that you will save her life.

Patient C is a soldier with gonorrhoea, a sexually transmitted disease he has picked up in a visit to a brothel. Penicillin can cure this condition quickly. If the soldier can be treated, he will soon be able to return to front-line duties.

Which patient would you treat, and why?

How science works

Ernest Duchesne

Ernest Duchesne was a French doctor. He noticed that the Arab stable boys at the army hospital kept the saddles in a dark, damp room so that mould would grow on them. The stable boys told Duchesne that the mould helped to treat the saddle sores on the horses. Duchesne tested the mould in an investigation. He took a suspension of the mould and injected it into guinea pigs that had a bacterial infection. They all recovered.

Duchesne also grew the fungus *Penicillium glaucum* with the bacterium *Escherichia coli*. He showed that the fungus completely killed the bacteria. He went on to inject an animal with enough typhoid bacteria to cause a lethal infection. However, by injecting *Penicillium glaucum* at the same time, he showed that the animal did not become ill.

He wrote a dissertation about the antibiotic effects of *Penicillium glaucum* in 1897 and sent it to the Pasteur Institute. However, because he was only 23 they ignored the dissertation.

4.5 Antibiotic resistance

Learning objectives:

■ How does antibiotic resistance develop?

■ What are the links between antibiotics and the development of MRSA and other antibiotic resistant bacteria?

Specification reference: 3.1.4

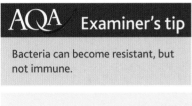

Examiner's tip

Bacteria can become resistant, but not immune.

When antibiotics were first used in the 1940s, they were seen as a major medical advance. Thousands of lives were saved. However, almost immediately, doctors started to notice that some bacteria were developing resistance. This problem has increased. Now, we have several strains of bacteria that are resistant to most antibiotics. These can cause infections that are very difficult to cure.

How does antibiotic resistance develop?

You will remember from Topic 4.1 that bacterial cells often contain circles of DNA called **plasmids**. A chance mutation can occur in this DNA, changing just one gene. As a result, the bacterium may be able to produce an enzyme that breaks down a particular antibiotic. This means that the bacterium would be resistant, and would not be killed by that antibiotic. Instead it would survive, and reproduce. All of its offspring would also contain the allele for antibiotic resistance. You can see this in Figure 1. Bacteria can also pass on copies of a plasmid to other bacteria. This means that antibiotic resistance can spread very quickly.

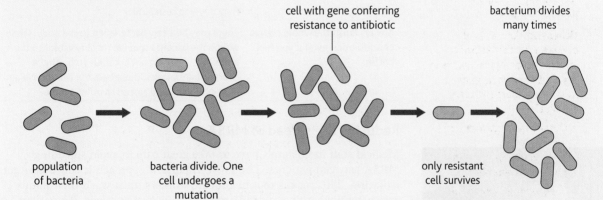

Figure 1 *How resistance to penicillin can spread in a population of bacteria*

cell with gene conferring resistance to antibiotic

bacterium divides many times

population of bacteria

bacteria divide. One cell undergoes a mutation

only resistant cell survives

Bacteria may contain several different alleles, each giving resistance to a different antibiotic. Bacteria with several different antibiotic resistance alleles are said to be **multi-drug resistant**. They can cause infections that are very difficult to treat.

MRSA

MRSA stands for methicillin-resistant *Staphylococcus aureus*. It is a type of bacterium, sometimes called the 'superbug' by journalists. About 30% of people have this bacterium growing on their skin or in their noses without developing an infection. However, if *Staphylococcus aureus* enters the body through a break in the skin they can cause infections such as boils and **abscesses**. If they get into the bloodstream they can cause more serious infections.

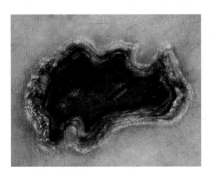

Figure 2 *MRSA infection*

Most *Staphylococcus aureus* infections can be treated with the antibiotic, methicillin. However, some strains of bacteria have developed resistance to methicillin. These strains are known as MRSA. They are often resistant to several other kinds of antibiotic, too.

MRSA is no more infectious than normal *Staphylococcus aureus*. However, it can be a serious problem because it is more difficult to treat. Sometimes it causes serious infections in people who are already very sick. The only way to treat MRSA may be to use very high doses of antibiotic, or to use an alternative antibiotic which may have unpleasant side-effects. MRSA contributes to thousands of deaths every year.

■ How we can reduce the spread of antibiotic resistance

Antibiotic resistance is more likely to develop when antibiotics are widely used. Everybody can help to reduce the spread of antibiotic resistance by following a few simple rules. These are summarised in Table 1.

Table 1 *Rules for reducing the spread of antibiotic resistance*

Rule	Reason
Doctors should avoid prescribing antibiotics for minor infections that present no danger.	If bacteria are not exposed to antibiotics, resistance is unlikely to develop.
Doctors should not prescribe antibiotics for infections caused by viruses.	Antibiotics do not destroy viruses, but any bacteria present will be exposed to antibiotics and may develop resistance.
Always finish the whole course of antibiotics, even if you feel better.	There may be a few bacteria left in the body. These will be the bacteria that are most resistant to the antibiotic. If you do not continue to finish the course of antibiotics, these bacteria will survive and multiply, and could spread to other people.

Reducing the spread of MRSA

Medical staff in hospitals have to take great care to avoid spreading MRSA between patients. The most important approach is called **contact isolation**. This means that healthcare workers must wash their hands very carefully both before and after touching every patient. If a patient has MRSA present in their nose, they may need to put the patient in a separate room. This means they cannot spread the bacteria to other patients by droplet infection. MRSA may be present in dust and on surfaces, so the surfaces need to be cleaned very thoroughly when a patient leaves the hospital. If several patients have MRSA they may be put in a room together, to keep them away from other patients.

Figure 3 *Precautions against MRSA – use of an alcohol-based hand rub*

Medical staff should wear clean, disposable gloves and a clean, disposable plastic apron if they are likely to become exposed to body fluids. Visitors to the hospital may also introduce MRSA. For this reason, visitors are asked to use alcohol-based hand rubs before visiting hospital patients.

MRSA infections

The graph shows the quarterly number of MRSA infections per 1000 acute occupied bed days (AOBD) for a group of hospitals in Scotland. One patient in one bed for one night is 1 AOBD.

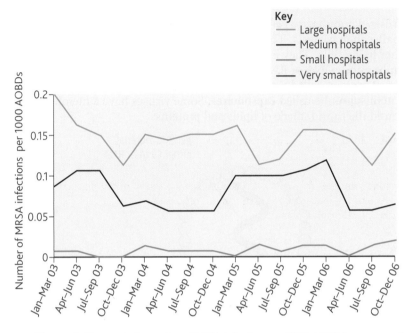

Key
— Large hospitals
— Medium hospitals
— Small hospitals
— Very small hospitals

Figure 4 *The quarterly number of MRSA infections per 1000 AOBD for a group of hospitals in Scotland*

1 Explain why the figures are given per 1000 AOBDs.

2 Describe the trend shown by the graph. Suggest an explanation for this trend.

Summary questions

1 Explain how a patient in a hospital who has MRSA present in their nose could spread the infection to other people 'by droplets'. (Hint: look again at Topic 4.3.)

2 Hospital patients who have had surgery are more likely to develop MRSA infections than some other types of patient. Explain why.

3 A bacterium carries an allele coding for an enzyme that destroys penicillin. Where in the bacterial cell will this enzyme be made?

4.6 Viruses

Learning objectives:

■ How do viruses cause disease?

■ What is the structure of the immunodeficiency virus (HIV) and how does it replicate?

■ How do the symptoms of AIDS develop?

■ How is HIV spread, and how can it be controlled?

■ Why are antibiotics ineffective against viruses?

Specification reference: 3.1.4

AQA Examiner's tip

Don't confuse bacteria and viruses. Make sure you are clear about the differences between them.

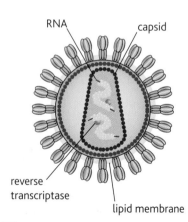

Figure 2 *The human immunodeficiency virus*

Structure

Viruses do not have a cell-like structure and they are about 50 times smaller than bacteria. They can only reproduce when they are inside other living cells. They have a core containing genetic material, which can be either DNA or RNA, but not both. Surrounding this is a protective coat of protein, called a **capsid** (Figure 1). The capsid is made up of protein sub-units called **capsomeres**. Some viruses have a membrane around the capsid, made of lipids and proteins.

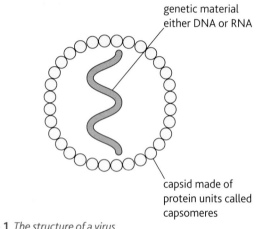

Figure 1 *The structure of a virus*

HIV

The human immunodeficiency virus (HIV) is shown in Figure 2. You can see that it is quite a complex virus. It is spherical in shape, with an envelope made of lipids and glycoproteins. There are protein knobs on the surface of the envelope. The capsid is cone-shaped. It contains RNA. It also contains an enzyme called **reverse transcriptase**. This enzyme allows the virus to make a DNA copy of its RNA when it infects a host cell. The DNA then inserts itself into the host cell's chromosomes. The DNA may remain inactive for a long time, sometimes many years. When the viral DNA becomes active, it instructs the cell to make new virus particles. This kind of virus is known as a **retrovirus.**

How HIV causes disease

■ HIV enters the bloodstream. Here, it infects a particular kind of white blood cell called a helper T-cell. You will learn more about these in Topic 5.2.

■ A DNA copy is made of the virus RNA. The DNA copy is inserted into the chromosome of the helper T-cell. Every time the helper T-cell divides it copies the virus DNA. However, the cell itself remains normal. During this time, the infected person has no symptoms. However, a blood test will show that the person has antibodies against HIV. During this stage, the person is said to be **HIV positive**.

■ Some years later, the virus DNA becomes active. It takes over the cell and causes more HIV to be made. As a result, the cell dies and releases thousands of HIV particles. These enter new helper T-cells. Gradually the helper T-cells are destroyed. These cells are very important in defending the body from disease.

▨ Now that the immune system is not working properly, the infected person suffers from diseases that might not have caused problems in a healthy person. These diseases are called **opportunistic diseases**. This stage is called full-blown AIDS. Examples of these diseases are Kaposi's sarcoma (a form of skin cancer that is otherwise very rare) and pneumocystis pneumonia (Figure 4). Other infectious diseases take hold, including tuberculosis. As a result of these diseases the person dies. At the moment there is no cure for AIDS, although there are drugs which can slow down the spread of the virus inside the body.

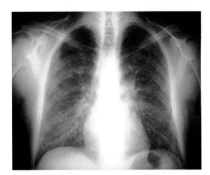

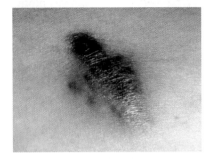

Figure 4 *Opportunistic infections: pneumocystis pneumonia (top) and Kaposi's sarcoma (bottom)*

How HIV is spread

HIV can pass from an infected person to another person when body fluids mix. The virus cannot survive outside the human body, so the body fluids must come into direct contact. The main ways in which HIV is passed on are:

▨ during sexual intercourse,

▨ when an intravenous drug abuser shares a needle already used by a person with HIV,

▨ when a transfusion of blood from a person infected with HIV is given to another person,

▨ from a mother to her unborn baby across the placenta.

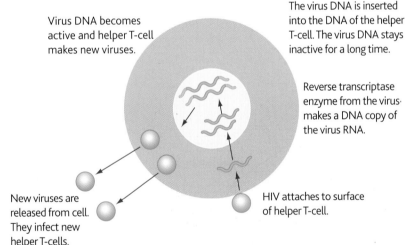

Virus DNA becomes active and helper T-cell makes new viruses.

The virus DNA is inserted into the DNA of the helper T-cell. The virus DNA stays inactive for a long time.

Reverse transcriptase enzyme from the virus makes a DNA copy of the virus RNA.

New viruses are released from cell. They infect new helper T-cells.

HIV attaches to surface of helper T-cell.

💡 **Figure 3** *How HIV infects body cells*

▨ Treating viral diseases

There are very few drugs available to treat viral diseases. Viruses do not show any activity until they are inside a living cell which means antiviral drugs have to get inside a host cell, where they may cause harm to the host cells. Most antiviral drugs interfere with the process by which the host cell makes new viruses.

Antibiotics are very effective against bacteria, as you saw in Topic 4.5. They kill bacteria by interfering with their metabolism. However, viruses do not have any metabolism of their own. For example, they do not have cell walls and they do not make their own proteins. This means that we cannot use antibiotics to destroy viruses.

■ Summary questions

1 Suggest why many biologists do not consider viruses to be living organisms.

2 Explain the difference between being HIV positive and having full-blown AIDS.

3 Use the information on this page, about the ways in which HIV can be spread, to suggest ways of controlling HIV infection.

4 Use your knowledge of how antibiotics work to explain why antibiotics cannot be used to treat a viral infection.

AQA Examination-style questions

1 (a) Give the function of each of the following organelles in a bacterial cell:

(i) cell wall,

(ii) capsule,

(iii) flagellum. *(3 marks)*

(b) Common symptoms of tuberculosis (TB) are coughing up blood and chest pains. Tuberculosis is spread by droplet infection. Explain how the common symptoms of tuberculosis are related to this method of spread. *(2 marks)*

(c) Give **two** ways in which HIV infection can spread. *(2 marks)*

(d) Suggest why people infected with HIV have an increased likelihood of dying from TB. *(1 mark)*

AQA, 2006

2 (a) Tuberculosis is caused by the bacterium, *Mycobacterium tuberculosis*. Describe how *Mycobacterium tuberculosis* enters the human body. *(2 marks)*

(b) Figure 1 shows the death rate from tuberculosis in England and Wales.

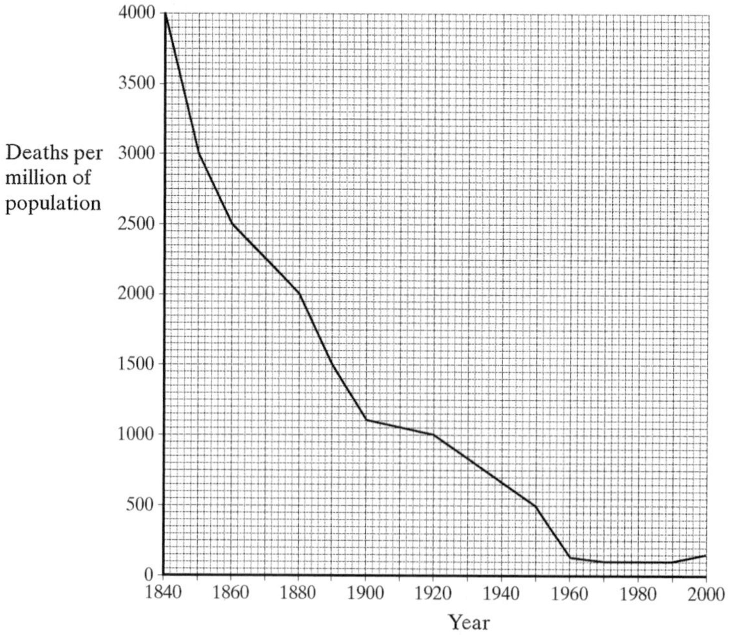

Figure 1

The population of England and Wales in 1860 was 20 066 000. Calculate the number of people who died of tuberculosis that year. Show your working. *(2 marks)*

(c) There was an increase in the number of cases of tuberculosis between 1990 and 2000. Suggest how each of the following might have contributed to this increase:

(i) an increase in antibiotic-resistant strains of *Mycobacterium tuberculosis*,

(ii) an increase in the number of people with AIDS. *(2 marks)*

AQA, 2004

3 Figure 2 shows a bacterium.

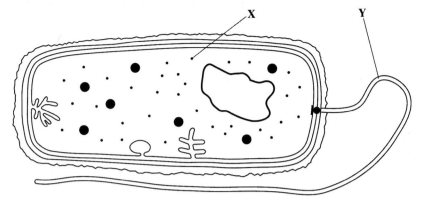

Figure 2

(a) Give the function of:
   (i) organelle **X**,
   (ii) organelle **Y**. *(2 marks)*

(b) Give **two** ways in which the structure of a bacterium is similar to the structure of a cell from a human. *(2 marks)*

(c) Give **two** ways in which the structure of a bacterium differs from the structure of a cell from a human. *(2 marks)*

AQA, 2005

4 (a) Give **two** ways in which antibiotics interfere with bacterial metabolism. *(2 marks)*

(b) Explain how the use of antibiotics has led to the development of antibiotic resistant bacteria such as MRSA. *(3 marks)*

(c) Explain why antibiotics are ineffective against viral diseases. *(2 marks)*

AQA, 2006

5 **Figure 3** shows some components of a human immunodeficiency virus (HIV)

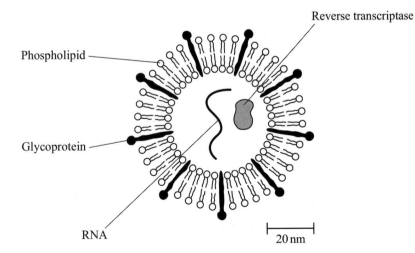

Figure 3

(a) A cell that HIV infects is 15 µm in diameter. Calculate how many times larger in diameter this cell is than HIV. Show your working. *(2 marks)*

(b) Give **two** ways in which HIV is spread. *(2 marks)*

(c) Describe how HIV leads to the development of the symptoms of AIDS. *(3 marks)*

AQA, 2006

How the body fights infectious disease

5.1 Antigens and phagocytosis

Antigens and antibodies

Most people associate bacteria with disease. Some bacteria do cause disease and are known as **pathogens**. Our body recognises invading bacteria or viruses as being 'foreign'. This is because they contain molecules that are different from those in our own body. These molecules are called **antigens**. Antigens are large molecules, usually proteins or polysaccharides. They may be 'free' molecules, or they may be on the surface of the microorganism.

In response to antigens, our immune system makes **antibodies**. Antibodies are proteins that have a specific shape to fit on to the foreign antigen. They are made by a kind of white blood cell called a B-lymphocyte. You will learn more about this in Topic 5.2. They are Y-shaped proteins made up of four polypeptide chains. You can see this in Figure 1. All antibodies have this same basic shape, but there is a 'variable region' at one end of the molecule. This variable region is different in each kind of antibody. The variable region is a specific shape so that it can bind to one specific kind of antigen, just as a key fits into a lock. Each antibody will bind to just one antigen.

When a microorganism enters the body, antibodies attach to the antigens on its surface. These act like a 'marker' and lead to the bacterium being destroyed. One way in which the bacterium is destroyed is by **phagocytosis**.

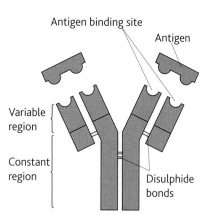

Antigen binding site

Antigen

Variable region

Constant region

Disulphide bonds

Figure 1 *Structure of an antibody*

Phagocytosis

When body cells and tissues have been damaged, they release certain chemicals. These chemicals cause a reaction called inflammation – when the area becomes red and swollen. The redness and swelling is because the capillaries have become more 'leaky' so that more antibodies and white blood cells can reach the site of infection.

Some white blood cells, called phagocytes, can engulf bacteria. Phagocytes are attracted to areas of inflammation. These phagocytes are able to recognise invading microorganisms. They engulf them by a process called phagocytosis. You can see this in Figure 2.

The lysosomes fuse with the phagosome, releasing their digestive enzymes. The enzymes break down the bacterium.

- The soluble products from the breakdown of the bacterium are absorbed into the cytoplasm of the phagocyte.
- The dead bacteria and phagocytes form **pus.**

Macrophages

Macrophages are a kind of phagocytic white blood cell. They engulf pathogens by phagocytosis. After the macrophages have engulfed the pathogen and digested it, they display the antigens from the pathogen on their plasma membranes.

1 The phagocyte is attracted to the bacterium by chemicals. It moves towards the bacterium along a concentration gradient.

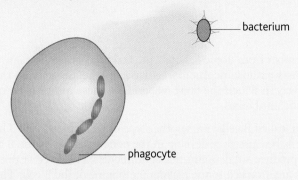

bacterium

phagocyte

2 Phagocytes bind themselves to the bacterium.

lysosome

nucleus

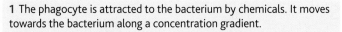

3 The cytoplasm of the phagocyte flows around the bacterium, engulfing it. A membrane-bound 'pocket', called a phagosome, forms around the bacterium. Inside the phagocyte are membrane-bound structures called lysosomes which contain powerful digestive enzymes. The lysosomes move towards the phagosome.

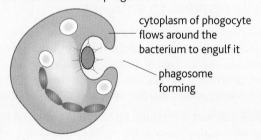

cytoplasm of phogocyte flows around the bacterium to engulf it

phagosome forming

4 The lysosomes fuse with the phagosome, releasing their digestive enzymes. The enzymes break down the bacterium.

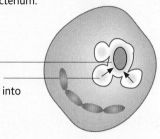

phagosome

lysosomes release digestive enzymes into phagosome

5 The soluble products from the breakdown of the bacterium are absorbed into the cytoplasm of the phagocyte. The dead bacteria and phagocytes form pus.

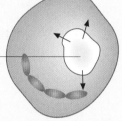

breakdown debris of bacterium

Figure 2 *Summary of phagocytosis of a bacterium by a phagocyte*

Summary questions

1 Antibodies are proteins. They are made up of many smaller molecules. Name these smaller molecules.

2 The enzymes inside lysosomes digest bacteria in the same way that enzymes in the human gut digest food molecules. Name the type of reaction involved in lysosome enzymes digesting bacteria.

3 The enzymes in the lysosomes are proteins. Where in the cell would they be made?

5.2 B cells

Learning objectives:

- How do B cells respond to antigens?

- There are two types of B cell, plasma cells and memory B cells. What are their functions?

Specification reference: 3.1.5

You will remember from Topic 5.1 that the body recognises foreign material, such as pathogenic microorganisms, by the antigens on their surface. One way in which the body responds to these antigens is to produce specific antibodies.

B lymphocytes (called B cells) are another type of white blood cell. They are called B cells because they develop in the bone marrow. As the B cells develop, they produce small quantities of antibodies. However, at this stage the antibodies are attached to the plasma membrane of the B cell. The body produces millions of different kinds of B cells. Each kind of B cell has a slightly different shape of antibody on its surface.

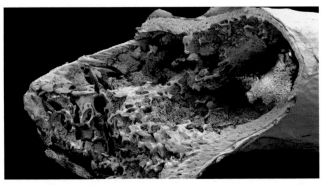

Figure 1 *Interior of a bone (coloured scanning electron micrograph). The bone marrow (red) is the site of blood cell production including B cells*

How B cells respond to antigens

The macrophages (Topic 5.1) move to the lymph nodes. Here, the macrophage 'displays' its antigens to all the different kinds of B cells. When a B cell with the right shape of antibody passes the macrophage, the antigen and antibody will fit together. This stimulates that particular B cell to divide repeatedly, making many identical copies of itself.

This process is called **clonal selection**. All the cells produced by the dividing B cell are identical, so they form a **clone**. It is called 'selection' because only one kind of B cell, from the huge number of different kinds, is chosen.

Types of B cell

Many of the cells, or clones, formed by the dividing B cell become **plasma cells**. These rapidly produce large amounts of their specific antibody. These antibodies are released from the plasma cell into the blood, where they bind to the antigens on the bacteria. This causes the bacteria to be destroyed.

However, some of the cells produced by the dividing B cell become **memory B cells**. These cells remain in the blood for a long time. They carry an **immunological memory** of the original antigen. This means that, if the same antigen enters the body again on another occasion, the memory B cells will be able to produce specific antibodies very quickly. This is called **active immunity**.

You can see this process in Figure 2.

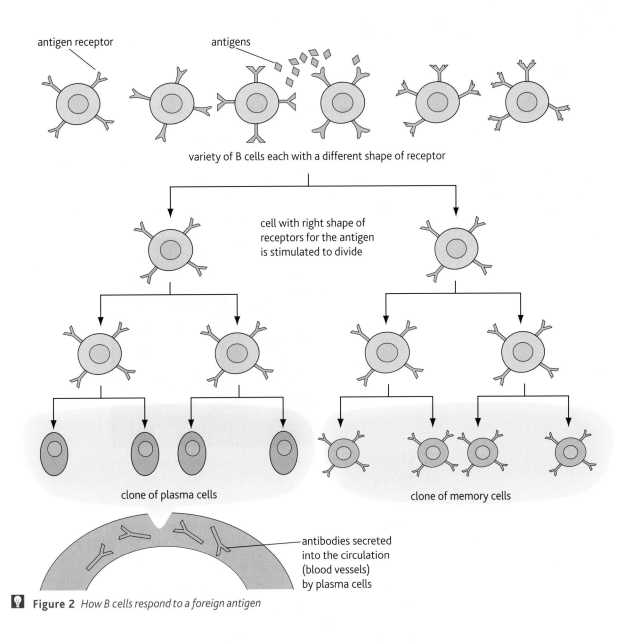

Figure 2 *How B cells respond to a foreign antigen*

Summary questions

1. A person who has had salmonella food poisoning will have antibodies against the *Salmonella* bacterium in their blood. However, this will not protect them against another bacterium, such as *Mycobacterium*. Explain why.

2. If a person has had measles, they are unlikely to ever suffer from measles again. Suggest why.

3. Colds are caused by a virus. Even if a person has already had a cold, they may have another infection later. Suggest a reason for this.

4. Plasma cells produce large amounts of antibodies. Name **two** organelles that will be present in a plasma cell in very large quantities.

5.3 T cells

Learning objectives:

- What are T cells?

- How are T cells stimulated?

- There are two types of T cells – killer T cells and helper T cells. What are their roles in fighting disease?

Specification reference: 3.1.5

T lymphocytes (called T cells) are another kind of white blood cell. They are another way that the body reacts to antigens. They are called T cells because they develop in the thymus gland behind the sternum (breast bone). After this, they move to the lymph nodes. T cells look just like B cells but they have a different function. Like B cells, there are many different kinds of T cell, each with a different receptor on its surface. These receptors look just like antibodies, but they are not called antibodies because they are never released from the plasma membrane.

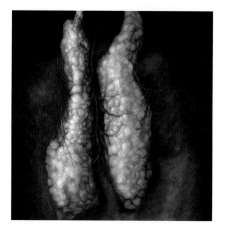

Figure 1 *T cells develop in the thymus gland behind the sternum*

Macrophages

You will remember from Topic 5.1 that macrophages engulf foreign material such as bacteria. They display the antigen from the bacterium on their plasma membrane. Cells that have been invaded by viruses may also have a viral antigen present on their surface.

Macrophages display this antigen to the many different T cells in the lymph nodes. One of the T cells will have the right shape of surface receptor to bind to the complementary antigen on the macrophage. When this happens, the T cell is stimulated. It divides many times to form a clone of cells. This is also known as **clonal selection**.

Types of T cell

Some T cells from this clone of cells become **killer T cells**. These cells have surface receptors that are complementary to the antigen. This means they bind to cells carrying the specific antigen and destroy them.

Other cells from this clone develop into **helper T cells**. These cells produce chemicals that:

- stimulate macrophages to engulf pathogens by phagocytosis,
- stimulate antibody production by B cells,
- activate killer T cells.

Both killer T cells and helper T cells produce their own type of **memory cells**. These remain in the blood in case the same antigen invades the body again. You can see this in Figure 2.

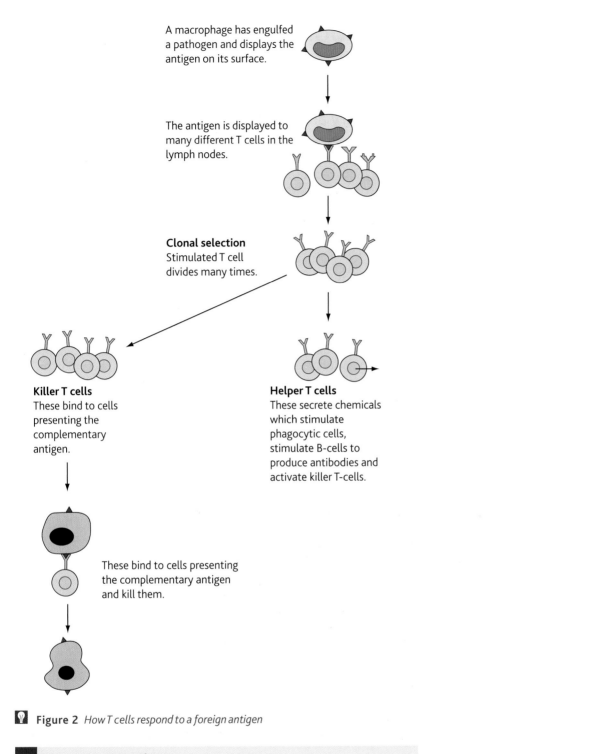

A macrophage has engulfed a pathogen and displays the antigen on its surface.

The antigen is displayed to many different T cells in the lymph nodes.

Clonal selection
Stimulated T cell divides many times.

Killer T cells
These bind to cells presenting the complementary antigen.

Helper T cells
These secrete chemicals which stimulate phagocytic cells, stimulate B-cells to produce antibodies and activate killer T-cells.

These bind to cells presenting the complementary antigen and kill them.

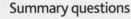 **Figure 2** *How T cells respond to a foreign antigen*

Summary questions

1 Look back at Topic 4.6. In which part of a virus would you find an antigen?

2 HIV infects helper T cells. Explain how this causes people with HIV to become more prone to infections.

3 Explain why the killer T cells that are produced in response to a specific antigen are called **clones**.

5.4 Antibodies and vaccination

Learning objectives:

- What are the roles of plasma cells and memory cells in producing the primary and secondary responses?

- What happens when a person is vaccinated against a disease?

- What is passive immunity?

Specification reference: 3.1.5

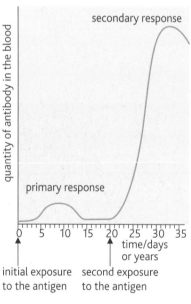

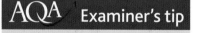

Figure 1 *Primary and secondary responses to an antigen*

Primary and secondary response

You learned in Topic 5.2 how B cells produce antibodies. There is a small time delay between getting infected with a pathogen and the production of antibodies against that pathogen. This is because it takes time for the antigen to be recognised, and for specific plasma cells to be produced. However, once a clone of plasma cells has been made, antibodies are produced in large amounts. You can see this in Figure 1. We call this the **primary response**, because it is the first time that the body has encountered this particular antigen.

Once the pathogen has been destroyed, the number of specific plasma cells goes down, and the number of specific antibodies in the blood falls. However, memory B cells remain. These survive for many years. If the person becomes infected with the same pathogen, the memory cells become activated rapidly. They start to produce large amounts of antibodies very quickly. This is the **secondary response** that you can see in Figure 1. Antibodies are produced in much larger numbers than in the primary response, and they are produced more quickly. They usually destroy the pathogen before the person is aware of any symptoms of illness.

Artificial immunity

This is what happens when a person is vaccinated against a disease. A vaccination is when a person is given antigens, either by injection or by mouth. The vaccine produces a primary response. As a result, the body produces memory B cells against the specific antigens. Later, if the person is infected by the real pathogen, the memory B cells will produce large numbers of antibodies in a secondary response. This will stop the person becoming ill.

Vaccines contain antigens, but there are different forms of vaccine.

- The vaccine may contain live microorganisms that have been repeatedly sub-cultured so that they no longer cause the disease. This kind of vaccine is called an **attenuated** vaccine.

- The vaccine may contain dead microorganisms. Heat or chemicals are used to kill the microorganism, but of course, the antigens will still be present on the surface of the dead microorganisms.

- The vaccine may contain isolated antigens. The antigen is produced using a genetically modified microorganism, and then purified.

Passive immunity

Active immunity is when the body produces its own memory cells. This can be as a result of catching a disease, or as a result of vaccination. **Passive immunity** is when a person is given ready-made antibodies.

Before a baby is born, a foetus receives antibodies from its mother's blood through the placenta. This protects the baby from pathogens before it is born, but it does not last for very long after birth.

Mothers can also pass antibodies on to their babies through breast milk. The milk formed in the first few days after birth is called colostrum, and this milk is especially rich in antibodies.

Antibodies may also be produced in an experimental animal, such as a horse. These antibodies can be purified and then injected into a human patient. This can be used to protect a person who has tetanus or diphtheria. It can also be used to give a person antibodies to protect them if they have been bitten by a poisonous animal, such as a venomous snake. This kind of immunity does not last long.

Applications and How science works

Mass vaccination – risks and benefits
Tuberculosis
You will remember from Topic 4.3 that tuberculosis (TB) is caused by the bacterium, *Mycobacterium tuberculosis*.

The main preventative measure against TB in the UK is vaccination. People in the groups most at risk of developing tuberculosis are offered vaccinations. Before vaccination, people are routinely tested to see if they are already immune to TB. This uses the **Mantoux test** (Figure 2). A needle is used to inject a substance called **tuberculin** into the skin. This is an extract from *Mycobacterium tuberculosis* that contains antigens from the bacterium. If the person is already immune to TB, the skin around the site of the injection will become red and inflamed. If the person gives a strong response to the Mantoux test, there is no need to vaccinate.

1. Explain why tuberculin does not cause the symptoms of TB.

2. Use your knowledge of the immune system to explain why the skin becomes red and inflamed if the Mantoux test is positive.

3. In some people, the response to the Mantoux test is very strong, and the skin becomes sore and blistered. In these cases a doctor will probably recommend a chest X-ray. Explain why.

The vaccination used in the UK to protect against TB is the **BCG** vaccine. BCG stands for Bacille Calmette-Guerin. This is an attenuated strain of *Mycobacterium bovis*. This was introduced into the UK in 1951 and reduced the incidence of TB.

4. What does 'attenuated' mean?

5. Suggest why *Mycobacterium bovis* can protect the body against infection by *Mycobacterium tuberculosis*.

The graph in Figure 3 shows that there has been a significant fall in the number of cases of TB in the UK over the past 100 years.

6. Is the BCG vaccination the main cause of this decrease? Explain your answer.

7. Suggest reasons for the decrease in cases of TB between 1910 and 1930.

8. Suggest reasons for the increase in incidence of TB between a 1930 and 1940 b 1990 and 2006.

Link

Look again at Topic 4.3 to check that you understand how TB is spread and how it can be treated.

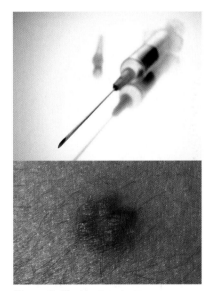

Figure 2 *The Mantoux test*

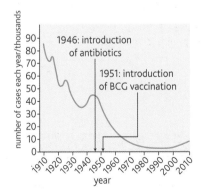

Figure 3 *Graph showing the number of TB cases in the UK during the period 1910-2006*

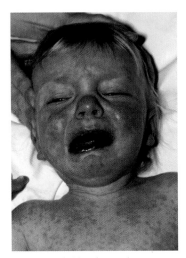

Figure 4 *A child with measles*

The MMR controversy

■ The MMR vaccination protects children from three different viral infections – mumps, measles and rubella.

■ Measles can kill children. About 5% of children who catch measles develop serious pneumonia. Measles can also cause serious brain damage.

■ Mumps very rarely kills children. However, 4% of children who catch mumps suffer some kind of hearing impairment afterwards. It can also lead to meningitis, although this is not usually severe.

■ Rubella is sometimes called German measles. It is not usually a dangerous disease for children or adults. However, if a pregnant woman catches rubella, the virus can cross the placenta and harm the foetus. The baby may be born with heart or brain defects, deafness or eyesight problems.

However, the MMR vaccination can also have side-effects.

■ 1 in 5 children develops a slight fever. A few children develop a high fever, but this is rare. 1 in 20 children develops a slight rash but serious reactions are extremely rare.

■ 1 in 1 000 000 children has a severe allergic reaction, causing them difficulty in breathing, but they always recover.

9 Using the information above, should a parent get their baby vaccinated against MMR? Give reasons for your answer.

10 Rubella does not cause a serious disease in men or boys. Suggest why the government still recommends that boys are vaccinated against rubella.

In 1998 Dr Andrew Wakefield of the Royal Free Hospital in London published a report. He claimed that this report showed that there is a link between the MMR vaccine and autism. Autism is a serious condition, affecting about 0.1% of all children. They have difficulty interacting with others and communicating. They also have narrow and unusual interests. The condition cannot be cured.

Figure 5 shows some data that Dr Wakefield used in his report. It showed the number of cases of autism in California in the USA, before and after MMR vaccination was introduced.

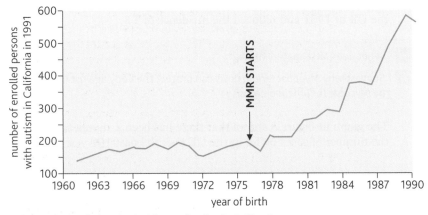

Figure 5 *Graph showing incidence of autism in California*

11 How does the evidence in Figure 5 support Dr Wakefield's theory that the MMR vaccination causes autism?

12 Does it prove that the MMR vaccination causes autism? Give reasons for your answer.

A Japanese scientist, Hideo Honda, also carried out a study to see whether there was a link between MMR vaccination and autism. He recorded the number of cases of autism per 100 000 of the population of Japan. His results are shown in Figure 6.

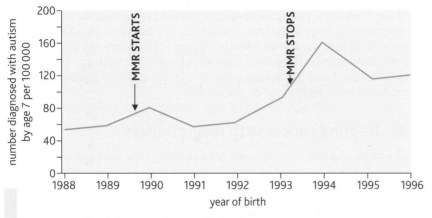

Figure 6 *Graph showing incidence of autism in Japan*

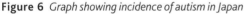

13 Do the data in Figure 6 support Dr Wakefield's theory? Give reasons for your answer.

14 Are there any other factors that might be affecting the results of these studies?

15 Consider all the information about the MMR vaccine on this page. Do you think that a parent should vaccinate their baby against MMR? Give reasons for your answer.

Applications and How science works

Cervical cancer

Cervical cancer is cancer of the cervix, i.e. the neck of the uterus. It is the first cancer in humans that seems to be caused almost entirely by an infectious microorganism. The cancer is caused by the Human Papilloma Virus, HPV. Cervical cancer is the second most common cause of cancer deaths in women worldwide. Several different strains of HPV cause cancer. The virus is spread by sexual contact.

Recently a vaccine has been developed that gives protection against two of the commonest strains of HPV. These two strains of HPV cause about 70% of cases of cervical cancer. The vaccine is being tested, but there is every indication that it is safe to use. Many people think that the vaccine should be given to girls before they are sexually active.

1 Give at least **one** argument for vaccinating girls against HPV, and at least **one** argument against.

2 Should boys be vaccinated against HPV as well as girls? Give reasons for your answer.

Summary questions

1 Copy and complete the table to summarise the different types of immunity.

	natural immunity	artificial immunity
passive		
active		

2 Explain why the immunity a foetus receives from its mother's antibodies via the placenta does not last long.

3 A person is given antibodies to protect them from a bite by a poisonous black widow spider. The vaccine contains antibodies made by a horse in response to an injection of spider venom. The doctor tells the person that they cannot be given this serum again if they get bitten by a black widow spider for a second time. Explain why.

5.5   Monoclonal antibodies

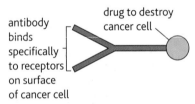

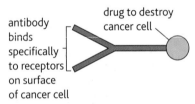

Learning objectives:

■ What is a monoclonal antibody?

■ How are monoclonal antibodies used to treat some forms of cancer?

■ What are the problems associated with monoclonal antibodies?

■ How are monoclonal antibodies used for medical diagnosis?

Specification reference: 3.1.5

By now, you should understand that antibodies are highly specific. They are exactly the right shape to fit on to one particular antigen, but not any others. Perhaps you can imagine how useful it would be, in medicine, to use specially made antibodies in applications such as treating disease.

Plasma cells that produce a specific antibody can be made using an experimental animal, such as a mouse. A way has been found to grow these plasma cells in artificial culture. This means that it is now possible to produce large amounts of a specific antibody. We call these **monoclonal antibodies** because they are identical antibodies, all produced by a single clone of plasma cells.

■ Treating cancer with magic bullets

Monoclonal antibodies are being used to treat some kinds of cancer. Drugs that kill cancer cells are usually very toxic. They are harmful to all the cells in the body, not just the cancer cells. This is why some cancer treatments have unpleasant side-effects.

Scientists can make monoclonal antibodies that bind specifically to the antigens on cancer cells. They then attach the cancer drug to the antibodies. You can see this in Figure 1. These antibodies are then injected into the person's blood. The antibodies travel in the blood until they reach the site of the cancer. Here, they bind to the cells. Conventional drugs are circulated in the blood and are present in cells throughout the patient's body, whereas drugs attached to monoclonal antibodies are targeted only at the cells that need to be destroyed. There are already a few treatments for cancer that involve monoclonal antibodies. One of them is herceptin®, a treatment for breast cancer. These monoclonal antibodies are sometimes called 'magic bullets' because they deliver toxic drugs only to the cells that need to be destroyed. This means they have far fewer side-effects than conventional cancer drugs.

Monoclonal antibodies are also being developed to inhibit the immune system after a patient has received an organ transplant. Another monoclonal antibody is useful in the treatment of heart disease. It inhibits blood clotting, to reduce the chances of a coronary thrombosis occurring after a person has received angioplasty (see Topic 6.6).

Figure 1 *Monoclonal antibody used to treat cancer*

antibody binds specifically to receptors on surface of cancer cell

drug to destroy cancer cell

⚠ Problems with monoclonal antibodies

The main problem with using monoclonal antibodies in this way is that mouse antibodies are seen by the immune system as 'foreign'. This means that there is an immune response to the monoclonal antibody, so that anti-mouse antibodies are made. These attach to the mouse antibodies and destroy them. They also join on to mouse antibodies, forming a complex that can cause kidney damage. One solution would be to produce human monoclonal antibodies rather than using an experimental animal. It is possible that genetic engineering technology would be useful here.

Diagnosis

Antibodies are also useful in diagnosis. Monoclonal antibodies can be used in test kits to detect specific antigens or antibodies that indicate disease. The tests are very specific and quick. Some test kits can be used by a GP, so a patient can receive a test result within a few minutes.

Prostate cancer is a cancer affecting the prostate gland, so it occurs only in men. One way to detect prostate cancer is to test blood serum to see whether it contains prostate specific antigen (PSA). If PSA is present, it is likely that the patient could have cancer and further investigations such as a biopsy would be carried out. The test is shown in Figure 2.

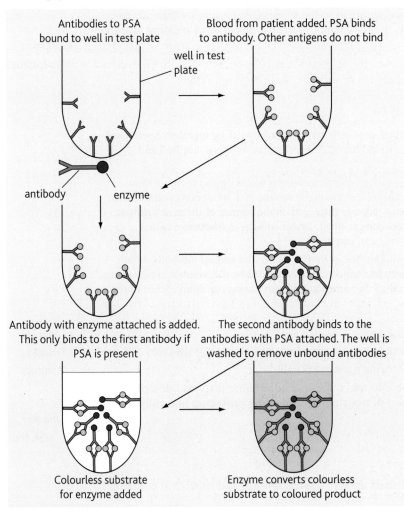

Antibodies to PSA bound to well in test plate

well in test plate

Blood from patient added. PSA binds to antibody. Other antigens do not bind

antibody   enzyme

Antibody with enzyme attached is added. This only binds to the first antibody if PSA is present

The second antibody binds to the antibodies with PSA attached. The well is washed to remove unbound antibodies

Colourless substrate for enzyme added

Enzyme converts colourless substrate to coloured product

Figure 2 *Using monoclonal antibodies to test for prostate cancer*

Another way that monoclonal antibodies can be used is in pregnancy testing kits. As soon as the embryo implants in the lining of the uterus, a placenta starts to form. This placenta secretes a hormone, human chorionic gonadotrophin (hCG). This hormone is excreted in the woman's urine. hCG is only produced by women who are pregnant, so finding it in a woman's urine is a reliable way to test for pregnancy. There are several different test kits on the market. You can see one in Figure 3.

The woman is instructed to dip the test stick into a sample of urine. If hCG is present in the urine there will be a colour change, or other display change. The required monoclonal antibodies are all present on the test stick.

Figure 3 *Pregnancy test – if the woman is pregnant, two blue lines will appear as shown. If she is not pregnant, only one line will appear. Different tests display the results in different ways*

Summary questions

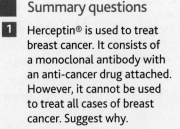

1. Herceptin® is used to treat breast cancer. It consists of a monoclonal antibody with an anti-cancer drug attached. However, it cannot be used to treat all cases of breast cancer. Suggest why.

2. Sketch a test kit, involving monoclonal antibodies, that could be used to test a patient's blood for TB antibodies.

3. Look at Figure 2.
   a Explain why the secondary antibody, with an enzyme attached to it, is needed in the test kit.
   b Explain the result you would obtain if the patient's serum did not contain PSA.
   c Explain why the well has to be washed after stage 2.

1 (a) (i) What is an antigen?

     (ii) Myeloid leukaemia is a type of cancer. Monoclonal antibodies are used in treating it. A monoclonal antibody will bind to an antigen on a myeloid leukaemia cell. It will not bind to other types of cell. Explain why this antibody binds only to an antigen on a myeloid leukaemia cell. *(4 marks)*

  (b) Calichaemicin is a substance which is very toxic and kills cells. Scientists have made a drug by joining calichaemicin to the monoclonal antibody that attaches to myeloid leukaemia calls. Explain why this drug is effective in treating myeloid leukaemia. *(2 marks)*

AQA, 2003

2 Read the following passage.

The body is protected by a large number of cells and molecules working together. Specialised cells, such as macrophages, travel around the body ingesting the antigens they find and fragmenting them into peptides.

Pieces of these peptides are then joined to special molecules which display them on the surface of the macrophage. Receptor molecules on the surface of T lymphocytes enable each T lymphocyte to recognise a different peptide displayed on the surface of the macrophages. T lymphocytes, activated by this recognition, divide and then secrete substances called lymphokines which boost the activity of B lymphocytes.

There are millions of types of B lymphocytes, each with a different surface antibody. When one type of B lymphocyte recognises and antigen, it is stimulated by the lymphokines to clone. Cloning produces many cells each with the same antibody-producing capability. Some of these cells are stored as memory B cells.

  (a) What is a vaccine? *(2 marks)*

  (b) Describe how a vaccine makes a person immune to a particular disease. *(3 marks)*

  (c) Explain the advantage of storing memory B cells. *(1 mark)*

  (d) A newborn infant is not able to make the sort of immune response described in the passage. Describe how a newborn infant might be protected naturally against infection. *(2 marks)*

AQA, 2002

3 MMR is the combined vaccine used aginst measles, mumps and rubella. It contains attenuated microorganisms.

  (a) What is an attenuated microorganism? *(1 mark)*

  (b) Vaccines protect against disease by stimulating the production of memory cells. Describe how memory cells protect the body from disease. *(3 marks)*

  (c) **Figure 1** shows the number of reported cases of whooping cough during the period 1950 to 1975.

     Describe and explain what **Figure 1** shows about the number of reported cases of whooping cough during the period 1952 to 1960. *(2 marks)*

  (d) The number of reported cases of whooping cough increased during the 1980s. Suggest one reason why. *(1 mark)*

AQA, 2001

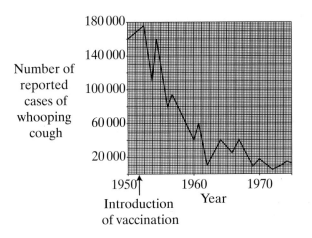

Figure 1

4   (a) Distinguish between active and passive immunity.   *(2 marks)*

    (b) There are many different forms of the Human Immunodeficiency Virus (HIV).
         Each form has slightly different proteins on its outer surface.

         Explain why this makes it difficult for scientists to develop a vaccine against HIV.   *(2 marks)*

    (c) The drawings in **Figure 2** show the changes in a B cell after stimulation by specific antigens.

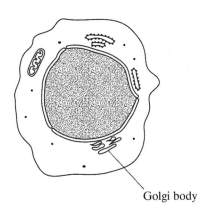

B lymphocyte before stimulation   B lymphocyte after stimulation

Figure 2

    (i)   Describe the role of macrophages in stimulating B cells.

    (ii) Explain how the changes shown in the drawings are related to the function of
          B cells.   *(5 marks)*

AQA, 2004

5   The box jellyfish produces a poison (venom) which enters the blood when a person
    is stung. A person who has been stung can be treated with an injection of antivenom.
    This antivenom is produced by injecting small amounts of venom from box jellyfish
    into sheep, then extracting antibodies from the sheeps' blood. These antibodies are
    then injected into the person who has been stung.

    (a) If a sheep is injected with the box jellyfish venom on more than one occasion a
         higher yield of antivenom is obtained. Explain why.   *(2 marks)*

    (b) Injecting antivenom does not give a person lasting protection against the venom
         of box jellyfish. Explain why.   *(2 marks)*

    (c) Explain one possible problem in injecting people with antivenom made in this
         way.   *(1 mark)*

AQA, 2006

6 Disease and lifestyle

6.1 The heart

Learning objectives:

- What is the structure of the heart and how does it relate to its function?
- What happens during the cardiac cycle?

Specification reference: 3.1.6

The heart is a muscular organ which pumps blood continuously around the body. It is actually divided into two halves, left and right. Each half acts as a separate pump. You can see this in Figure 1. The left side of the heart receives deoxygenated blood from the body via the venae cavae. The blood enters the right atrium, is pushed into the right ventricle, and then pumped to the lungs via the pulmonary arteries. At the same time, oxygenated blood from the lungs returns to the left atrium via the pulmonary veins. It is pushed from the left atrium into the left ventricle, from where it is pumped around the body via the aorta.

The walls of the atria are relatively thin and elastic. They do not have a lot of muscle as they do not need to generate much pressure to pump blood to the ventricles. The ventricles have much thicker, muscular walls to generate a higher pressure to pump blood to the lungs and body.

Blood in one side of the heart does not mix with blood in the other side. However, the two pumps beat in time with each other. There are valves in the heart that prevent the backflow of blood.

- The **atrioventricular (AV) valves** lie between the atria and the ventricles. They stop blood flowing back from the ventricles into the atria. They have strong fibres, the tendinous cords, to stop them turning inside out.
- **Semilunar valves** stop blood flowing back into the ventricles from the pulmonary artery and the aorta.

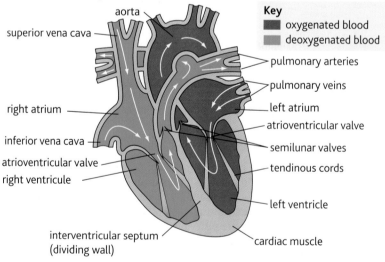

Key
- oxygenated blood
- deoxygenated blood

aorta
superior vena cava
pulmonary arteries
pulmonary veins
right atrium
left atrium
atrioventricular valve
inferior vena cava
semilunar valves
atrioventricular valve
tendinous cords
right ventricule
left ventricle
interventricular septum (dividing wall)
cardiac muscle

Figure 1 *Structure of the heart*

The cardiac cycle

The sequence of events that causes blood to be pumped around the body is called the **cardiac cycle**. You can see the events of the cardiac cycle in Figure 2.

In **diastole** the heart muscle is relaxed. Deoxygenated blood enters the right atrium from the venae cavae and oxygenated blood enters the left atrium via the pulmonary veins. As the atria fill with blood, the pressure in the atria rises. This pushes the atrioventricular valves open and allows blood to pass into the ventricles.

In **atrial systole** the walls of the atria contract. This pushes the blood remaining in the atria into the ventricles. The force of the atria contracting pushes the AV valves wide open.

In **ventricular systole** the walls of the ventricles contract. This increases the pressure inside the ventricles. This pressure forces the AV valves to close. You can see this in Figure 3. The pressure in the ventricles also forces the semilunar valves in the pulmonary artery and the aorta to open. Blood is forced out of the ventricles towards the lungs and around the body.

The AV and semilunar valves both work in a similar way. They are made of flaps of tough, fibrous tissue. They work a little like trapdoors that will only open one way.

The AV valves open when the pressure in the atria is higher than the pressure in the ventricles.

The AV valves close when the pressure in the ventricles is higher than the pressure in the atria.

The semilunar valves open when the pressure in the ventricles is greater than in the aorta (or pulmonary artery).

The semilunar valves close when the pressure in the aorta (or pulmonary artery) is greater than the pressure in the ventricles.

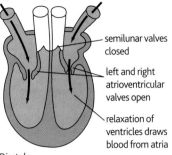

1 Blood enters atria and ventricles from pulmonary veins and venae cavae

- semilunar valves closed
- left and right atrioventricular valves open
- relaxation of ventricles draws blood from atria

Diastole
Atria are relaxed and fill with blood. Ventricles are also relaxed.

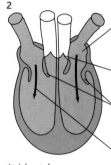

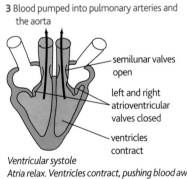

2
- atria contract to push remaining blood into ventricles
- semilunar valves closed
- left and right atrioventricular valves open
- blood pumped from atria to ventricles

Atrial systole
Atria contract, pushing blood into the ventricles. Ventricles remain relaxed.

3 Blood pumped into pulmonary arteries and the aorta
- semilunar valves open
- left and right atrioventricular valves closed
- ventricles contract

Ventricular systole
Atria relax. Ventricles contract, pushing blood away from heart through pulmonary arteries and the aorta.

▼ **Figure 2** *The cardiac cycle*

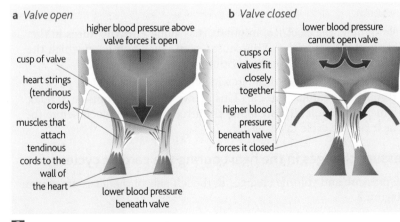

a *Valve open*

higher blood pressure above valve forces it open

- cusp of valve
- heart strings (tendinous cords)
- muscles that attach tendinous cords to the wall of the heart
- lower blood pressure beneath valve

b *Valve closed*

lower blood pressure cannot open valve

- cusps of valves fit closely together
- higher blood pressure beneath valve forces it closed

▼ **Figure 3** *Action of the AV valves*

Summary questions

1 Copy and complete the table to show when the valves in the heart are open and closed.

	diastole	atrial systole	ventricular systole
AV valves			
semilunar valves			

2 Explain why the wall of the left ventricle is thicker than the wall of the right ventricle.

3 In a foetus, there is a hole between the left and the right atria of the heart. Suggest why this is an advantage to a foetus.

4 In a few people, the hole in the heart, between the atria, does not close over properly at birth. People with this condition are said to have a 'hole in the heart'. Suggest the effects that this will have.

6.2 How the heart beats

Learning objectives:

▨ What is myogenic muscle?

▨ How is the cardiac cycle controlled?

▨ How do artificial pacemakers work?

Specification reference: 3.1.6

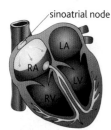

a *Wave of excitation spreads out from the sinoatrial node*

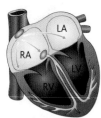

b *Wave spreads across both atria causing them to contract and reaches the atrioventricular node*

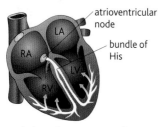

c *Atrioventricular node conveys wave of excitation between the ventricles to the Purkyne fibres*

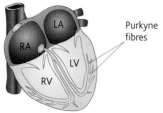

d *Wave of excitation is released by the Purkyne fibres and ventricles contract*

Figure 1 *Control of the cardiac cycle*

The heart is made of a special kind of muscle called **cardiac muscle**. It is different from other kinds of muscle because it is **myogenic**. This means that it does not need to be stimulated by a nerve impulse to contract. However, it is important that the cardiac muscle contracts in a coordinated way so that the cardiac cycle can occur, over and over again.

⚡ 💡 Controlling the cardiac cycle

A group of cells in the wall of the right atrium is called the **sinoatrial node (SAN)**. These cells start off the electrical activity that produces the cardiac cycle. For this reason, the SAN is sometimes called the **pacemaker**. You can see the electrical events that occur during the cardiac cycle in Figure 1.

Electrical impulses pass from the sinoatrial node through the walls of both atria, causing them to contract. This causes atrial systole.

▨ There is a ring of fibrous tissue between the atria and the ventricles that prevents electrical impulses passing directly to the ventricles. The electrical impulses pass to the **atrioventricular node (AVN)**. There is a short time delay here, allowing the atria to empty completely.

▨ The electrical impulses pass very quickly down some special muscle fibres called the **bundle of His**. This carries them to the bottom of the septum.

▨ From here, the electrical impulses pass along **Purkyne fibres** in the walls of the ventricles. This causes ventricular systole, in which the ventricles contract from the bottom up.

▨ There is a short time delay in which no electrical impulses pass through the cardiac muscle. This allows the cardiac muscle to relax, which is diastole. It also allows the atria to fill with blood before the next cardiac cycle takes place.

Pressure changes in the heart during the cardiac cycle

The pressure and volume changes in the left side of the heart are shown in Figure 2.

Artificial pacemakers

Sometimes a person's SAN does not send out electrical impulses quickly enough, or there might be a blockage in the conductive tissue in a person's heart. For these people, an artificial pacemaker may help.

Artificial pacemakers are electronic devices that are surgically implanted and use electrical impulses to regulate the beating of the heart. Some pacemakers have one lead, which can stimulate either the atria or the ventricles, depending on the problem. Other pacemakers have two leads, one inserted in the atria and the other in the ventricles. You can see this in Figure 3.

Modern pacemakers can be programmed to stimulate the heart in exactly the right place at the right time.

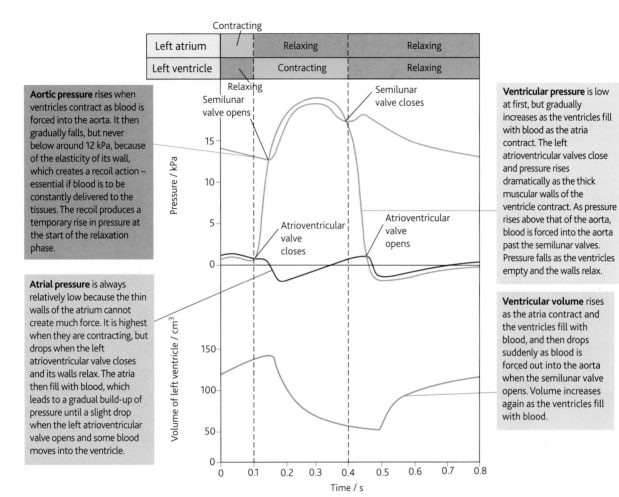

Aortic pressure rises when ventricles contract as blood is forced into the aorta. It then gradually falls, but never below around 12 kPa, because of the elasticity of its wall, which creates a recoil action – essential if blood is to be constantly delivered to the tissues. The recoil produces a temporary rise in pressure at the start of the relaxation phase.

Atrial pressure is always relatively low because the thin walls of the atrium cannot create much force. It is highest when they are contracting, but drops when the left atrioventricular valve closes and its walls relax. The atria then fill with blood, which leads to a gradual build-up of pressure until a slight drop when the left atrioventricular valve opens and some blood moves into the ventricle.

Ventricular pressure is low at first, but gradually increases as the ventricles fill with blood as the atria contract. The left atrioventricular valves close and pressure rises dramatically as the thick muscular walls of the ventricle contract. As pressure rises above that of the aorta, blood is forced into the aorta past the semilunar valves. Pressure falls as the ventricles empty and the walls relax.

Ventricular volume rises as the atria contract and the ventricles fill with blood, and then drops suddenly as blood is forced out into the aorta when the semilunar valve opens. Volume increases again as the ventricles fill with blood.

Figure 2 *Pressure and volume changes in the left side of the heart during the cardiac cycle*

Summary questions

1 Look at Figure 2.

a One cardiac cycle lasts 0.8 seconds in this person. Calculate the heart rate in beats per minute.

b How would you expect the pressure changes in the right atrium and ventricle to differ from those in the left atrium and ventricle? Explain your answer.

2 a Why is it important that there is a ring of fibrous tissue to stop waves of electrical activity passing directly from the atria to the ventricles?

b What is the advantage of a slight time delay at the AVN?

c Why is it an advantage for waves of electrical activity to pass through the bundle of His very quickly?

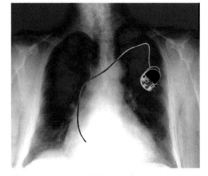

Figure 3 *An artificial pacemaker*

6.3 Blood vessels

Learning objectives:

- What is the structure of an artery, vein and capillary?

- How are the structures of the above blood vessels related to their function?

Specification reference: 3.1.6

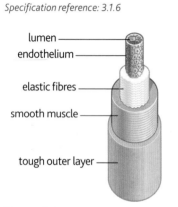

Figure 1 *Artery*

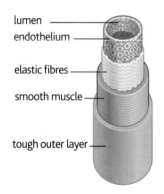

Figure 2 *Vein*

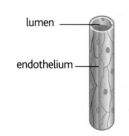

Figure 3 *Capillary*

From the heart, oxygenated blood is pumped in pulses through **arteries** and then through smaller vessels called **arterioles** to all organs of the body. Inside these organs, blood flows through microscopic blood **capillaries**. The blood in the capillaries supplies the organ with the substances it needs, such as oxygen and glucose, and removes waste products such as carbon dioxide. Deoxygenated blood leaves the organs in **venules**, which join together to form **veins**. These carry the deoxygenated blood back to the heart.

Arteries

Look at the diagram of an artery in Figure 1. You will see that it has a thick muscular wall with many elastic fibres. This allows the artery wall to stretch when the heart forces a pulse of blood at high pressure into it. The elastic wall then springs back, keeping the blood under pressure and smoothing out the pulses. We call this **elastic recoil**. There is an outer layer of tough collagen fibres to stop the artery bursting under pressure. The lumen (the space through which the blood flows) is relatively small, which keeps the blood under high pressure. The vessel is lined with a smooth layer called **endothelium**. This reduces friction as blood flows rapidly through.

Veins

Look at the diagram of a vein in Figure 2. You will notice that it has a much thinner layer of elastic tissue in its wall because blood in the veins is under much lower pressure than in the arteries. The muscle layer is also thin because it carries blood away from organs. Therefore this muscle cannot control blood flow to organs. However, veins have just as many collagen fibres as arteries. This is because the veins flow closer to the skin surface than arteries, and the collagen fibres protect the veins from injury. The lumen is wider than in the artery because blood is under lower pressure so it flows more slowly. However, the thin, smooth endothelium helps the blood to flow along without excessive friction. Veins also contain valves. These work like the semilunar valves in the heart. There are body muscles next to the veins, e.g. in the legs. When your muscles contract, they press against the blood inside the veins and make it move. The valves prevent backflow and keep the blood moving back towards the heart.

Capillaries

Look at the diagram of a capillary in Figure 3. It is actually much smaller than the artery and vein. Its lumen is very small – just the right size for blood cells to move through one at a time. It has no collagen, muscle or elastic fibres in its wall, which consists only of endothelium. This is a layer of thin, flattened cells that make the vessel permeable. They allow the capillary to exchange materials, including oxygen and carbon dioxide, with body tissues. Spaces between the endothelium cells allow white blood cells to escape from the capillaries into the tissues. You will learn more about capillaries in Topic 6.8.

Arteries, veins and capillaries are compared in Table 1.

Table 1 *Comparision of arteries, veins and capillaries*

Arteries	Veins	Capillaries
Thick muscular wall	Thin muscular wall	No muscle
Much elastic tissue	Little elastic tissue	No elastic tissue
Small lumen relative to diameter	Large lumen relative to diameter	Large lumen relative to diameter
Capable of constriction	Not capable of constriction	Not capable of constriction
Not permeable	Not permeable	Permeable
No valves	Valves throughout all veins	No valves
Transports blood from the heart	Transports blood to the heart	Links arteries to veins
Oxygenated blood except in pulmonary artery	Deoxygenated blood except in pulmonary vein	Blood changes from oxygenated to deoxygenated
Blood under high pressure	Blood under low pressure	Blood pressure reducing
Blood moves in pulses	No pulses	No pulses
Blood flows rapidly	Blood flows slowly	Blood flow slowing

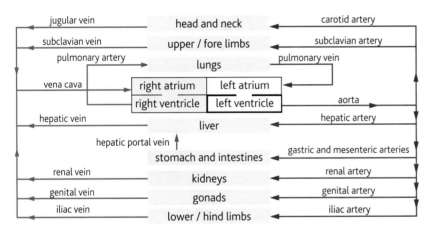

Figure 4 *Plan of the human circulatory system*

Summary questions

1 Copy and complete this table to compare the structure of arteries, veins and capillaries.

Feature	Artery	Vein	Capillary
lumen	narrower than vein		
endothelium layer	present		
elastic fibres		relatively thin	
collagen fibres	present		
valves			

Figure 5 *Artery(left) and vein*

2 Use Figure 4 to describe the route taken by a red blood call as it travels from the kidneys to the liver.

3 In Topic 5.1 you learned that when body cells and tissues are injured, they release certain chemicals. These cause the capillaries to become more 'leaky'. Explain the advantage of this.

4 In Figure 5 the artery looks approximately circular but the vein looks more oval. Use your knowledge of the structure of a vein to explain this difference.

6.4 Atheroma

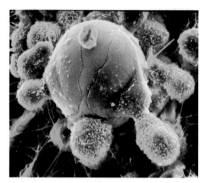

Figure 1 *Foam cells*

Atheroma is a fatty deposit that builds up inside the wall of arteries. It may take many years to develop. Eventually it can lead to coronary heart disease, such as strokes or heart attacks.

The development of atheroma

Atheroma is more likely to develop where the lining of an artery has been damaged in some way. This often happens where an artery branches, especially if the person has high blood pressure. Macrophages, a kind of white blood cell, engulf cholesterol droplets by phagocytosis. They start to appear white and foamy as a result of this, so they are known as 'foam cells'. You can see this in Figure 1.

The foam cells invade the artery wall and form fatty **plaques**. The plaque slowly builds up and starts to narrow the lumen. Apart from foam cells, the plaque also contains dead smooth muscle cells and fibres. You can see the atheroma building up in an artery in Figure 2. After many years, calcium is also deposited in the atheroma. This makes the artery wall much harder and less flexible.

You will see in Figure 2 that, as the atheroma builds up, the lining of the artery becomes uneven. The endothelium may split so that the artery lining becomes rough. This disturbs the blood flow through the artery. It becomes turbulent, making it more likely that a blood clot will form.

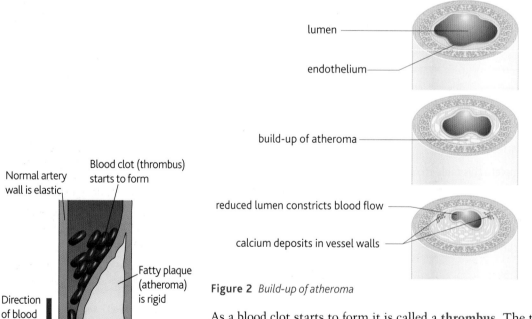

Figure 2 *Build-up of atheroma*

Figure 3 *Thrombus formation*

As a blood clot starts to form it is called a **thrombus**. The thrombus may become so large that it blocks off the blood supply through the artery. Alternatively, a piece of the clot may break off. This is called an **embolus**. This travels in the blood until it gets to another place where the artery is narrowed. Here it may cut off the blood supply to a particular tissue. When a thrombus blocks an artery, it causes a **thrombosis**. For example, if a coronary artery is blocked, it is called a coronary thrombosis. You can see how a thrombus forms in Figure 3.

Myocardial infarction

Cardiac muscle has to contract and relax continuously throughout life. This means it has a high rate of respiration. Look at Figure 4. This shows the **coronary arteries**. These branch off the aorta and supply the heart muscle with glucose and oxygen.

Sometimes these coronary arteries become blocked, either by atheroma or by a thrombosis (coronary thrombosis). If this happens, the heart muscle cannot obtain enough glucose and oxygen. The region of heart muscle beyond the blocked artery dies. This leads to a **myocardial infarction**, or heart attack.

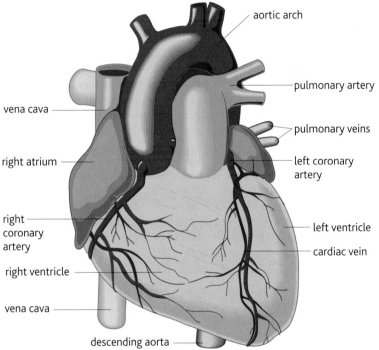

Labels: aortic arch, pulmonary artery, pulmonary veins, left coronary artery, left ventricle, cardiac vein, vena cava, right atrium, right coronary artery, right ventricle, vena cava, descending aorta

Figure 4 *The blood vessels supplying the heart muscle*

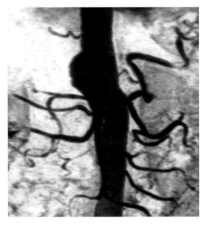

Figure 5 *An aortic aneurysm*

Angina

Atheroma can also lead to a condition called **angina**. Look again at Figure 2. You can see that, as atheroma builds up, the lumen of the artery becomes much narrower. This reduces the amount of blood that can pass the narrowed area. If this happens in a coronary artery, it reduces the supply of oxygen and glucose to the heart muscle. This condition is called angina.

People with angina experience severe chest pain when they start to exercise. The pain is usually felt in the left shoulder, chest and arm but sometimes the pain affects the neck or the left half of the face.

Aneurysm

Sometimes atheroma building up in the wall of an artery causes the artery wall to become weak. The pressure of blood in the artery pushes against the weakened artery wall, causing it to balloon out. This is an aneurysm. The artery wall may rupture, leading to a haemorrhage. This means that the organ being supplied by the artery will be short of blood. Sometimes an aneurysm forms in the aorta (Figure 5). The aorta is so big that if an aneurysm bursts, serious internal bleeding may result.

Summary questions

1. Explain why someone with angina is more likely to feel pain when they exercise than when they are relaxing.

2. Explain why atheroma makes an aneurysm more likely to form.

3. A stroke happens when there is a shortage of oxygen to part of the brain. It causes brain cells to die and may be fatal. Strokes are caused by a thrombosis in an artery leading to the brain, or a ruptured aneurysm in an artery leading to the brain. Explain how both of these result in brain damage.

6.5 Factors affecting coronary heart disease

Learning objectives:

- What is coronary heart disease (CHD) and how big a problem is it?

- What are the factors that cause CHD which we cannot control?

- What are the factors that cause CHD which we can control?

Specification reference: 3.1.6

Coronary heart disease (CHD) is a collective term for diseases of the heart and blood vessels, including angina, aneurysm and myocardial infarction. CHD kills more than 110 000 people in the UK every year. In the UK more than 1.4 million people suffer from angina and 275 000 people have a heart attack annually. CHD is the country's biggest killer.

Look at Figure 1. You can see that CHD causes different numbers of deaths in different countries. Studying statistics like this can help scientists to investigate the causes of CHD. If we can understand the factors that cause CHD, then we should be able to reduce the number of deaths. Even within a country, scientists have shown that CHD is more common in some regions, among some ethnic groups, and in some social classes. Factors that put some people at a higher risk of developing CHD can be divided into two groups: factors that we cannot control, and factors that we are able to control.

Factors that we are not able to control

- **Age.** The risk of developing CHD increases with age. Most deaths from CHD occur in people over 50 years old.
- **Gender.** Men are more likely than women to develop CHD. It may be that oestrogen has a protective effect against CHD in women. However, after the menopause, the risk of CHD in women increases. By the time they reach old age, women suffer from CHD as much as men do.
- **Genes.** Some people inherit genes that predispose them to CHD.
- **Ethnicity.** Some ethnic groups are more likely to develop CHD than others. For example, in the UK, people from Southern Asia have a higher rate of CHD than the caucasian population. The reason for this is not clear. It could be because of a genetic factor. Alternatively, a cultural factor, such as diet, may be responsible.
- **Diabetes.** People with Type 1 or 2 diabetes are more likely to develop CHD.

Factors that we can control

- **Smoking.** The greatest risk factor for CHD is smoking. Smoking increases blood pressure and makes the blood more likely to clot.
- **High blood pressure (hypertension).** This increases the risk of CHD because it leads to thickening and hardening of the walls of the arteries. It also causes damage to the lining of the arteries, making atheroma more likely to develop. Factors that increase blood pressure, apart from smoking, include **obesity**, lack of exercise and stress.
- **Diet.** High levels of saturated fats in the diet increase blood cholesterol levels and therefore increase the chances of developing CHD. High levels of salt in the diet increase blood pressure. However, some foods seem to reduce the chances of developing CHD. Omega-3 fatty acids, found in oily fish, seem to protect against CHD. Certain foods contain antioxidants, including vitamin C, vitamin D and carotene which also protect against CHD. Fresh fruit and vegetables are good sources of antioxidants.
- **Activity levels.** Aerobic exercise lowers blood cholesterol levels, lowers blood pressure and reduces obesity. These all reduce the chances of developing CHD.

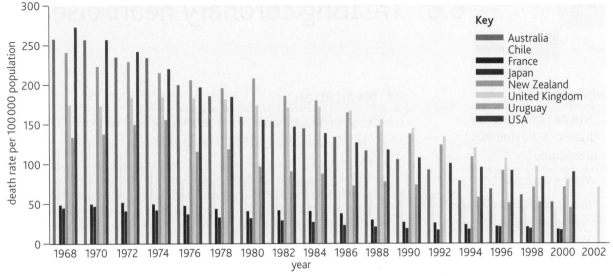

Figure 1 *Death rates from coronary heart disease for women aged 35–74 in various countries from 1968 to 2002*

Coronary heart disease and ethnicity

Scientists in Scotland carried out an investigation to find out whether people of some ethnic groups were more likely to develop CHD than people from a different ethnic group. They studied men and women who were living in Scotland and died from CHD. The table below shows some of the results from the men who were studied.

The expected number of deaths is the number of deaths from CHD that would occur if the death rate from CHD is the same in that group as it is in Scottish-born men.

$$\text{The standardised mortality ratio} = \frac{\text{number of deaths observed}}{\text{expected number of deaths}} \times 100$$

Country of birth	Number of deaths from CHD	Expected number of deaths from CHD	Standardised mortality ratio
Scotland	5 466	5 466	100
England and Wales	38 017	59 015	64.4
Northern Ireland	36	39	92.3
Republic of Ireland	54	50	108
India	23	17	135
Pakistan	19		158
China	1	3	33.3
Hong Kong	3	5	60

1 Explain why the standardised mortality ratio is calculated, rather than just looking at the number of deaths in each group.

2 Calculate the 'expected number of deaths from CHD' among men born in Pakistan.

3 Men born in Scotland have a greater chance of dying from CHD than people born in England and Wales who live in Scotland. Suggest some reasons for this.

4 One person looked at these data and concluded that people who were born in China and Hong King and live in Scotland have a much lower risk of dying from CHD than people born in Scotland. Is this a reliable conclusion? Give reasons for your answer.

Summary questions

1 Use your knowledge of water potential to explain why a person who eats a lot of salt in their diet is likely to have high blood pressure.

2 Use your knowledge of how atheroma develops to explain why high blood cholesterol levels increase your chances of developing CHD.

3 Nicotine in cigarette smoke decreases the diameter of blood vessels. Explain how nicotine increases the chances of developing CHD.

6.6 Treating coronary heart disease

Learning objectives:

- How can coronary heart disease be treated using medication?

- What is angioplasty?

- Under what circumstances is coronary bypass surgery carried out?

Specification reference: 3.1.6

Medication

A number of different kinds of medication can be used to treat CHD.

- **Statins** are drugs used to lower blood cholesterol levels.
- **GTN (glyceryl trinitrate)** is used to treat angina pains. It can be used as a tablet or a spray. Usually, people are advised to take a dose when required. The medication is placed under the tongue and is absorbed quickly into the blood. It works by relaxing the blood vessels which increases the diameter of the coronary arteries. People with angina are recommended to take a dose of GTN before exercise, e.g. before climbing the stairs.
- **Beta-blockers** are used to treat hypertension. In normal people, the heart is stimulated to beat faster when you exercise by the sympathetic nervous system. The sympathetic nerve releases the neurotransmitter, noradrenalin, into receptors at the SAN. This causes the SAN to send out impulses more quickly. Beta-blockers fit into these receptors on the heart muscle. This means that noradrenalin cannot fit into the receptors, so the heart rate cannot increase. By slowing the heart rate, blood pressure is reduced.

Angioplasty

Angina can be treated using **angioplasty**. First of all, doctors need to find out how much atheroma has built up in the coronary arteries. To do this, they carry out an angiogram. A special dye is inserted into a blood vessel in the groin, arm or neck. Then radiographs are taken as the blood flows through the coronary arteries. You can see this in Figure 1.

If the arteries are almost blocked, it is likely that an angioplasty will be carried out. A catheter (a hollow tube) is inserted into a blood vessel in the groin, arm or neck. The catheter is then threaded through the blood vessels until it reaches the blockage in the coronary artery. Inside the catheter is a tiny balloon. When the catheter is in the right place, the balloon is inflated. As the balloon inflates it pushes the artery wall outwards and makes the artery wider. Sometimes a tiny mesh tube called a **stent** is used. This holds the artery open and reduces the chance of it closing up again. You can see this in Figure 2. The balloon is then deflated and the catheter withdrawn.

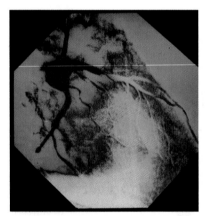

Figure 1 *Angiogram*

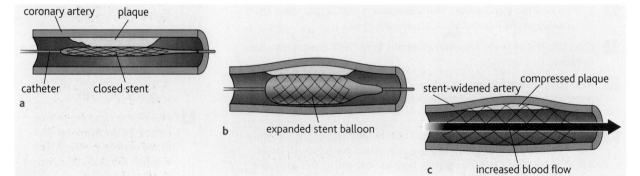

Figure 2 *Angioplasty*

Figure 2 labels: coronary artery, plaque, catheter, closed stent (a); expanded stent balloon (b); stent-widened artery, compressed plaque, increased blood flow (c)

🔧 Coronary bypass

Sometimes a coronary artery is so badly blocked that angioplasty cannot be used. In such cases, a bypass operation may be carried out. A piece of vein is taken, usually from the person's leg. This is then grafted on to the aorta at one end, and to the coronary artery below the blockage at the other end. This makes sure that oxygenated blood can reach all of the heart muscle. Sometimes more than one bypass has to be carried out. Figure 3 shows a triple coronary heart bypass.

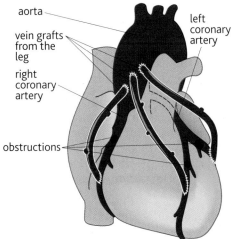

Figure 3 *Triple coronary heart bypass*

■ Applications and How science works

Beta-blockers and coronary heart disease

Scientists carried out an investigation to find out whether a beta-blocker would reduce the death rate among patients with CHD. Some patients were given a high dose of a beta-blocker, metoprolol. Some were given a lower dose of the beta-blocker. Another group was given a harmless substance, called a placebo.

Some of the data from this investigation are shown in the table.

Treatment of patient group	Number of people in group	Deaths/patient-years*/%
placebo	1845	10.8
metoprolol low-dose	604	8
metoprolol high-dose	1202	6.2

*Patient-year is a term that reflects the amount of time that each patient took the medication for. For example, patient A took the medication for 6 months and patient B took the medication for 15 months. Patient A contributes 0.5 patient-years to the calculation while patient B contributes 1.25 patient-years.

1   Explain why some people were given a placebo.

2   It was important that neither the patients nor their doctors knew which group they were in. Explain why.

3   The results are expressed as a percentage. Explain why.

4   Should a high dose of metoprolol be prescribed for people with CHD? Give reasons for your answer.

Summary questions

1   Beta-blockers are similar in shape to the neurotransmitter, noradrenalin. Use your knowledge of proteins in cell membranes to explain how they work.

2   When a coronary heart bypass is carried out, the piece of vein comes from the patient and not another person. Use your knowledge of the immune system to explain why.

6.7 Deep vein thrombosis

Learning objectives:

- What is deep vein thrombosis (DVT) and why does it occur?
- Which groups of people are at higher risk of having DVT?
- How can DVT be prevented?
- How can DVT be treated?

Specification reference: 3.1.6

A **deep vein thrombosis** (**DVT**) is a blood clot that forms in a deep vein in the body, usually in the lower leg. It can occur elsewhere, for example, in the arm. Usually, the blood does not clot unless the body is injured. However, if blood flow is slowed down, a clot may start to form. DVT usually happens when a person has been inactive for a long period of time.

If a small clot forms, this is usually not dangerous and the body slowly breaks the clot down over time. However, bigger clots may form and these can be more dangerous. Large clots can block the flow of blood through the vein, either partially or completely. You can see this in Figure 1.

If a large blood clot forms, there is a risk that a piece of the clot will break away. This is called an **embolus**. Sometimes the embolus can block a blood vessel in the lungs. This is called a **pulmonary embolism**. If a pulmonary embolism forms, the person will develop shortness of breath, coughing or chest pain. If the clot is quite large, a pulmonary embolism can be life-threatening.

Another risk is **post-thrombotic syndrome**. This is when the blood clot damages the valves in the leg vein. This means that the valves in the leg vein no longer work properly.

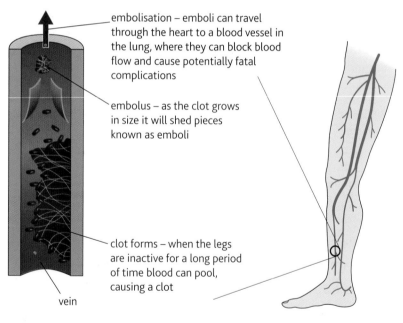

embolisation – emboli can travel through the heart to a blood vessel in the lung, where they can block blood flow and cause potentially fatal complications

embolus – as the clot grows in size it will shed pieces known as emboli

clot forms – when the legs are inactive for a long period of time blood can pool, causing a clot

vein

Figure 1 *How deep vein thrombosis forms*

Symptoms of DVT

- Swelling in the calf – this is not the same as the swelling that results from oedema (see Topic 6.8).
- Pain in the calf that becomes noticeable or worse when the person starts to walk.
- Leg warmth and redness.

Treating DVT

Once a doctor has diagnosed DVT the person is usually given an anticoagulant, a drug that prevents blood clotting. **Heparin** is often given, as this works immediately. Another drug, warfarin, is usually given as well. This stops the blood clotting over the next few days, but it works more slowly than heparin.

These drugs do not dissolve the blood clot. They simply stop more blood clots from forming. Usually, the body destroys the blood clot slowly over the next few days. However, a doctor may decide that the clot is very dangerous. In this case, a 'clot-busting' drug is given. These are thrombolytic drugs and are mostly enzymes, such as streptokinase.

Risk factors for DVT

DVT can occur in people of any age. However, the following groups of people are more likely to develop DVT:

- people over the age of 40,
- people with a past history of DVT,
- people who have a family history of DVT, or genetic factors that make their blood more likely to clot,
- women who are pregnant or have recently had a baby,
- people who are overweight,
- people who have recently had surgery,
- people who remain immobile for a long time, e.g. on a long-haul flight,
- women who are taking a contraceptive pill containing oestrogen,
- women who are taking hormone replacement therapy.

Preventing DVT

People who have had surgery are most at risk of DVT, but doctors will give these people medication to reduce the risk.

Some people worry about developing DVT as the result of a long-haul flight. The best way to reduce this risk is to:

- move or walk around at intervals. If you cannot do this, at least move your ankles and flex your muscles from time to time,
- drink plenty of water so that the blood-clotting factors do not become too concentrated in your blood,
- avoid drinking alcohol, as this can cause dehydration,
- wear 'flight socks' during the flight. These apply pressure to the lower leg, making it easier for blood to flow back upwards from the foot.

If you are at risk of DVT, ask your doctor to prescribe an anticoagulant, such as heparin, before the flight.

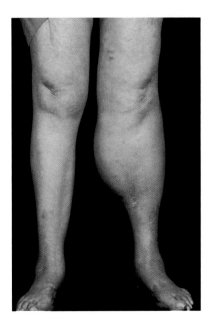

Figure 2 *Person with DVT*

Summary questions

1 A person who has had a DVT and suffered post-thrombotic syndrome will suffer from swelling in the legs. Explain why.

2 The thrombolytic drug, streptokinase, breaks down blood clots but does not damage blood cells. Use your knowledge of enzymes to explain why.

3 Sometimes, when a person is given streptokinase, the body makes antibodies against the drug. Explain why.

6.8 Capillaries and exchange

Learning objectives:

■ How is the structure of capillaries adapted for exchange of metabolites with the tissues?

■ What is tissue fluid and how is it formed?

■ How is tissue fluid returned to the circulatory system?

Specification reference: 3.1.6

You will remember from Topic 6.3 that capillaries are small blood vessels that supply oxygen and nutrients to tissues, and remove wastes. Look again at the structure of a capillary in Figure 3 on page 98.

Capillaries are adapted for efficient exchange with the tissues in the following ways:

■ Their walls are made of a single layer of thin, flattened endothelium cells. This means there is only a short distance for diffusion to occur.

■ There are many small capillaries in body tissues, providing a large surface area for exchange. There are so many capillaries that no cell in the body is very far from a capillary.

■ The lumen of a capillary is very small so that red blood cells can only squeeze through one at a time. As red blood cells squeeze through, they are flattened against the capillary wall, bringing them as close as possible to the cells that need oxygen.

■ There are tiny spaces between the endothelium cells in the capillary wall. This allows substances from the plasma, and white blood cells, to escape from the capillaries into the tissues.

Formation of tissue fluid

Although there are many tiny capillaries in body tissues, these cannot supply nutrients and oxygen to every individual cell. Capillaries exchange substances with every cell in the body by formation of **tissue fluid**.

Tissue fluid is a watery fluid formed from the blood plasma. It carries nutrients such as glucose and amino acids, and oxygen, to every cell in the body. It also collects waste products such as carbon dioxide from the cells, and eventually returns these waste products to the blood.

Tissue fluid is formed at the arteriole end of the capillary network. Here, the blood is under pressure because of the pumping action of the heart. The capillary, with its tiny spaces in the wall, is a little like a garden sprinkler. The pressure of blood in the capillary forces small molecules

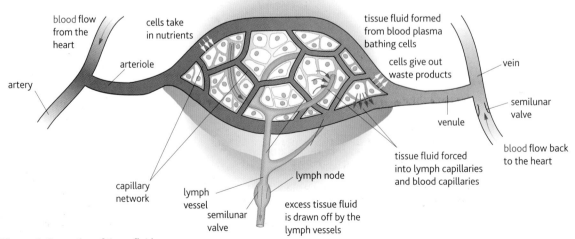

Figure 1 *Formation of tissue fluid*

through these spaces. This means that water from the blood plasma, together with nutrients, mineral ions and oxygen dissolved in it, is forced out of the blood into the tissues. However, blood cells, and large molecules such as plasma proteins, are too large to escape from the capillaries. These remain inside the capillary. The watery liquid that is squeezed out of the capillary is called tissue fluid. You can see this in Figure 1.

Once the tissue fluid has given up its nutrients and oxygen, and collected waste products, it needs to return to the blood system. This happens in two ways:

■ At the venule end of the capillary, blood pressure is lower because a lot of the water from the plasma has been squeezed out. However, plasma proteins remain. These plasma proteins lower the water potential of the blood. This means that water from the tissue fluid moves back into the venule end of the capillary by osmosis, down a water potential gradient. As this happens, dissolved substances are carried with it.

■ The rest of the tissue fluid drains into blunt-ended **lymph vessels**. Once the fluid has entered the lymph vessels, it is called **lymph**. Lymph is not pumped like blood, but it eventually enters the blood system at blood vessels in the neck region. Lymph vessels contain valves like those in veins. Lymph moves slowly through these vessels as it is squeezed by contraction of body muscles.

Oedema

Oedema is the medical name for a swelling in the tissues, caused by a build-up of tissue fluid.

Look at Figure 2. It shows a child with kwashiorkor. This is a protein deficiency disease that is very common among children in third world countries. Kwashiorkor develops when a child is weaned from breast milk, which has enough protein for the child's needs, to a diet that is almost completely based on carbohydrate. The swollen abdomen is the result of an accumulation of tissue fluid, or oedema. Tissue fluid is formed in the normal way, but the child lacks plasma proteins. This means that it is difficult for tissue fluid to re-enter the capillaries at the venule end of a capillary network. The lymph vessels cannot drain all the tissue fluid away and oedema results.

Figure 2 *A child with kwashiorkor*

Look at Figure 3. This person has a condition sometimes called elephantiasis. Oedema has developed in the leg, causing it to swell up. The reason for the oedema is filariasis – infection by a parasitic worm that lives in the lymph vessels. These worms cause blockages in the lymph vessels so tissue fluid cannot drain back into the lymph system effectively. Some of the tissue fluid drains back into capillaries, but this is not enough to prevent the oedema developing.

■ Summary questions

1 You will remember from Topic 1.2 that an efficient exchange surface should have a large surface area, a thin permeable surface and a large diffusion gradient. Use this to explain how the capillaries are adapted to their function of exchanging materials with body cells and tissues.

2 People with high blood pressure may develop oedema. Explain why.

3 Some people have a liver disease in which the liver does not make enough plasma proteins. These people may develop oedema. Explain why.

4 When people develop oedema, it is often most noticeable in the feet and legs. Explain why.

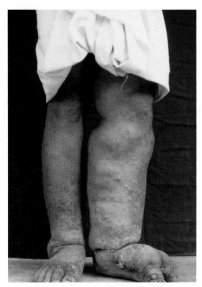

Figure 3 *A person with elephantiasis*

AQA Examination-style questions

1   (a) **Figure 1** shows a human heart.

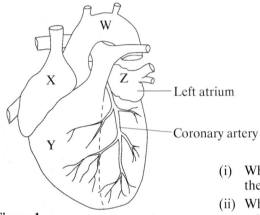

- (i)   Which of the letters W–Z represents the position of the sinoatrial node (SAN)?
- (ii) What is the function of the coronary artery?   *(2 marks)*

Figure 1

(b) Impulses spread through the walls of the heart from the SAN. The table shows the rate of conduction of impulses through various parts of the conducting tissue.

Part of pathway	Rate of conduction/ms^{-1}	Mean distance/mm
From SAN to atrioventricular node (AVN) across atrium	1.0	40
Through AVN	0.05	5
From AVN to lower end of bundle of His	1.0	10
Along Purkyne fibres in ventricle walls	4.0	–

- (i)   Calculate the mean time for an impulse to pass from the SAN to the lower end of the bundle of His. Show your working.
- (ii) Explain the advantage of the slow rate of conduction through the AVN.
- (iii) Suggest **one** advantage of the high rate of conduction in the Purkyne fibres which carry impulses through the walls of the ventricles.   *(5 marks)*

(c) How would cutting the nerve connections from the brain to the SAN affect the beating of the heart?   *(1 mark)*

AQA, 2003

2   **Figure 2** shows a section through a healthy coronary artery. **Figure 3** shows a section through a coronary artery from a person with atheroma.

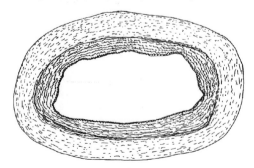

Figure 2

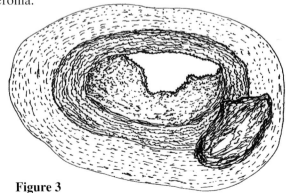

Figure 3

Give **two** ways in which the artery of the person with atheroma differs from the artery of the healthy person. *(2 marks)*

AQA, 2003

3 (a) Describe and explain how atheroma may form and lead to a myocardial infarction. *(6 marks)*

(b) The bar chart in **Figure 4** shows the number of males aged 19–64 admitted to English hospitals with a myocardial infarction within five days of the English football team losing to Argentina by penalty shoot-out in the 1998 World Cup.

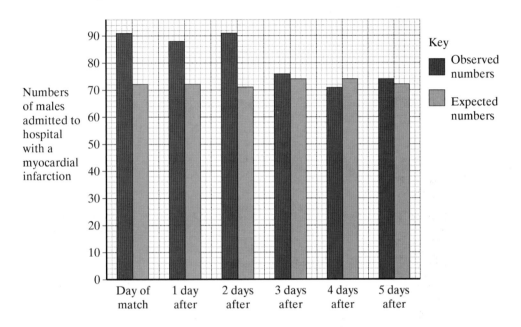

Figure 4

(i) Suggest how the expected number of admissions might have been calculated.

(ii) Describe the difference between the observed and expected numbers of males experiencing a myocardial infarction over the six days. *(4 marks)*

(c) Explain how repeated stress, such as that involved in a penalty shoot-out, may lead to a myocardial infarction. *(2 marks)*

AQA, 2004

4 (a) Deep vein thrombosis may occur in a person who has been sitting still for a long time. Explain how. *(3 marks)*

(b) Explain how wearing 'flight socks' can reduce the risk of developing deep vein thrombosis during a long-haul flight. *(2 marks)*

Unit 1 questions: The body and its diseases

1 (a) *Salmonella typhimurium* causes food poisoning in humans but not in other mammals. Suggest why these bacteria attach to human cells but not to the cells of other mammals. *(2 marks)*

(b) Salmonella bacteria release toxins that cause the body temperature to rise. Although a small increase in body temperature can be beneficial, a large increase can cause serious harm.

Explain how a large increase in a person's body temperature can cause harm. *(2 marks)*

(c) Washing hands with antibacterial soap reduces the risk of transmission of the bacteria that cause food poisoning. Tea tree oil is a plant extract used in soaps. It is claimed to have antibacterial properties. Outline a method for investigating this claim. *(4 marks)*

AQA, 2006

2 Describe and explain how the structure of the human breathing system enables efficient uptake of oxygen into the blood. *(6 marks)*

AQA, 2005

3 Coronary heart disease is a major cause of death in the western world.

Figure 1 shows an external view of a human heart with a blood clot in one of the main coronary arteries.

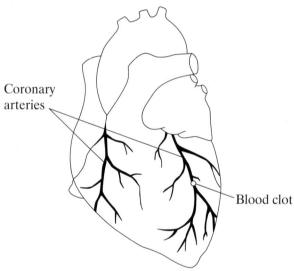

Coronary arteries

Blood clot

Figure 1

(a) Explain why a blood clot in a coronary artery is likely to result in a heart attack *(3 marks)*

(b) Three important risk factors associated with coronary heart disease are cigarette smoking, high blood pressure and a high plasma cholesterol level. Explain how each of these factors increases the risk of heart disease. *(6 marks)*

AQA, 2001

4   Read the following passage.

A study showed that a diet that scores low on the 'glycaemic index (GI)' helps overweight
people lose body fat. Food with a high GI score, like a biscuit, causes sharper peaks in sugar
levels than a low GI food, such as pasta. In a study of 189 overweight and obese adults, scientists
found that a diet high in either protein or carbohydrates, but with a low total GI score, brought
about the biggest reduction of body fat. They studied men and women aged 18 to 40. Subjects   5
were randomly assigned to one of four reduced-calorie and reduced-fat diets for 12 weeks. The
first diet was high in carbohydrate (55% of total energy) but scored low on the GI index. The
second was high in carbohydrate and had a high GI rating. The third was high in protein (25%
of total energy) with a high GI score, while the fourth was high-protein and low-GI. After three
months, all the volunteers lost a similar amount of weight: between 4.2% and 6.2% of body   10
weight. But those on the low GI diets lost the most body fat. For example, those on the high-
carb, low-GI diet lost about 80% more body fat than those on the high-carb, high-GI diet.

(a) What is a food's *glycaemic index*?   *(2 marks)*
(b) Explain why a biscuit has a higher GI score than pasta (line 2).   *(2 marks)*
(c) (i)   Explain why subjects were *randomly* assigned to one of four diets (line 6).
     (ii) Suggest how the subjects could be put randomly into groups.   *(3 marks)*
(d) Evaluate the reliability of the study mentioned in the passage.   *(4 marks)*
(e) The government is concerned that more people are becoming obese. Explain why.   *(3 marks)*

5   Read the following passage.

Finnish doctors say that giving babies 'friendly' gut bacteria during weaning can help reduce the
symptoms of atopic eczema. The doctors say this could be because they help change the gut's
ecosystem. However, UK experts have said that this study is not reliable. They say that parents
should not give babies probiotic bacteria.

Samples of faeces were taken from 21 babies who had already shown signs of atopic eczema   5
and were at a heightened risk of developing allergies. Those who were given probiotic bacteria
in their milk were found to have lower levels of harmful bacteria. Babies who were not given
supplemented milk had increased levels.
Babies with higher levels of harmful bacteria had a protein in their blood that is associated with
diseases such as hay fever, asthma and eczema. The Finnish doctors concluded that giving   10
babies probiotic bacteria prevents increases in levels of harmful bacteria.

(a) Some bacteria in the gut can have beneficial effects. Explain how.   *(4 marks)*
(b) The doctors examined samples of faeces from the babies. Explain why.   *(2 marks)*
(c) Explain why UK experts say this study is not reliable (line 3).   *(3 marks)*
(d) Suggest why UK experts are saying that parents should not give babies probiotic
     bacteria (line 4).   *(2 marks)*

6   **Figure 2** shows part of a capillary and some of the cells surrounding it.

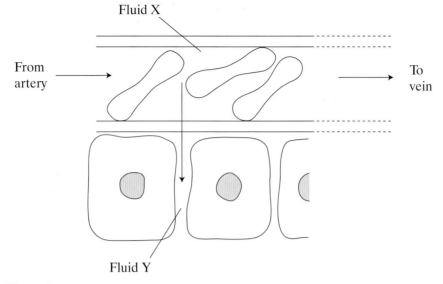

Figure 2

(a) Name:
   (i) Fluid X,
   (ii) Fluid Y. *(2 marks)*

(b) Describe and explain **one** way in which the composition of fluid Y differs from that of fluid X. *(2 marks)*

(c) Explain how fluid leaves the capillary at the arterial end. *(2 marks)*

AQA, 2006

7   **Figure 3** gives information about the effects of cigarette smoking, plasma cholesterol concentrations and high blood pressure on the incidence of heart disease in American men.

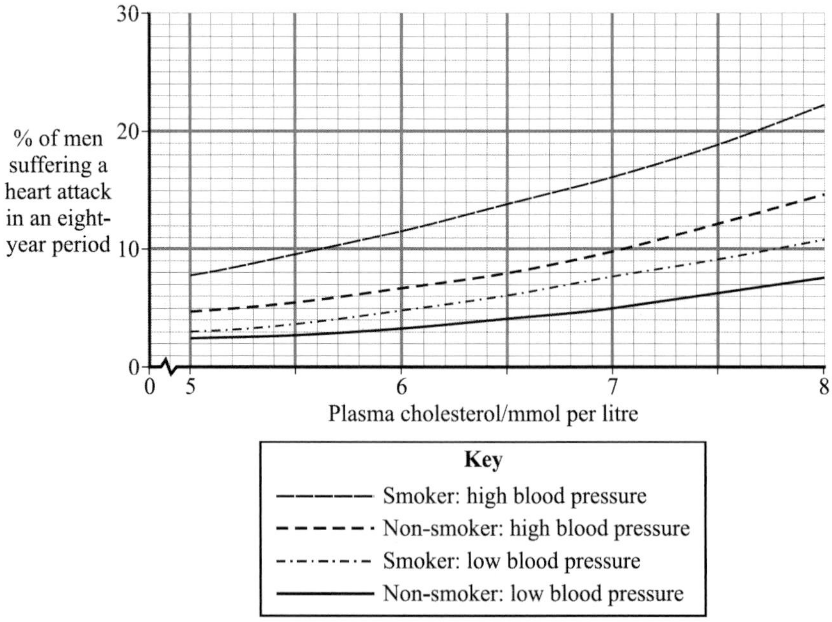

Figure 3

(a) A non-smoker with low blood pressure has a plasma cholesterol concentration of 5 mmol per litre. Over a period of time this concentration increases to 8 mmol per litre. By how many times has his risk of heart disease increased? Show your working. *(2 marks)*

(b) Two non-smoking men with low blood pressure both have plasma cholesterol concentrations of 5 mmol per litre. One of them starts to smoke and the plasma cholesterol of the other increases to 7 mmol per litre. Which man is now at a greater risk of heart disease? Explain your answer.

(3 marks)

AQA, 2001

8 (a) Explain why people who are lactose-intolerant may develop

    (i) bloating and stomach cramps

    (ii) diarrhoea. *(4 marks)*

One test for lactose intolerance involves giving the person some food containing lactose. The person's blood glucose level is measured several times over the next few hours.

Figure 4 shows the results of a lactose intolerance test on two people. One person was lactose intolerant and the other was not.

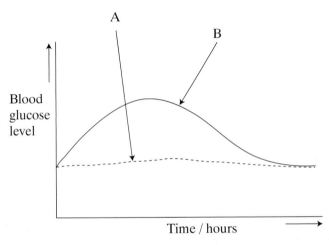

Figure 4

(b) Person A was lactose intolerant. Explain why the results for patient A are different from those for patient B.

(3 marks)

9 (a) (i) Give **two** symptoms of *Salmonella* food poisoning.

    (ii) Explain why the symptoms of *Salmonella* food poisoning do not usually appear until at least 6 hours after the contaminated food has been eaten. *(3 marks)*

(b) Explain the biological basis for each of the following rules of food hygiene:

    (i) Wash your hands after going to the toilet and before preparing food;

    (ii) Store raw meat at the bottom of the refrigerator. *(4 marks)*

Humans – their origins and adaptations

Chapters in this unit

Genetic information is copied and transmitted from generation to generation. It is the DNA molecule that holds the genetic information. Chapter 7 discusses the structure of DNA, the evidence that it is the hereditary material and how the information in it is translated into proteins.

How the genetic information is replicated in cells during cell division for growth and repair by mitosis is described in Chapter 8. Sometimes the regulation of cell division becomes faulty and cancer may result. Meiosis is the process where the genetic information is halved during cell division to produce the gametes or sex cells. Occasionally, there are errors in transmitting this information, which may lead to new forms of organisms.

The concept of a species, how organisms and named, and the evidence behind this is explored in Chapter 9. Species exist as one or more populations. There is variation in the phenotypes in a population due to genetic and environmental factors. Natural selection acts on phenotypes in a population, leading to differential survival. The best adapted individuals have a higher probability of surviving to reproduce and pass on their alleles to the next generation. This process leads to evolution and changes in the gene pool of a population. Over time, natural selection and evolution lead to a population becoming adapted to its environment. According to the theory of evolution, a population can evolve to the point where it becomes reproductively isolated from other populations. This is how a new species comes into existence. Humans have evolved from pre-existing species and the steps in this process are described here.

Humans have developed some unique adaptations that increase their chances of survival. These are social, behavioral and physical. These are explored in Chapter 10. Parasites are organisms that have adapted to living on other organisms. This chapter also explores the adaptations of some parasites to living on humans.

In addition, humans have changed their environment, for example, by clearing forests to yield farmland. Farming was an important step in the social development of humans. How and why people started to farm, how this step affected humans and our environment is discussed in Chapter 11.

What you already know

Whilst the material in this unit is intended to be self-explanatory, there is certain information from GCSE that will prove very helpful to the understanding of the content of this unit. A knowledge of the following elements of GCSE will be of assistance:

- Living organisms are interdependent and adapted to their environments.

- Variations within species can lead to evolutionary changes.

- Similarities and differences between organisms can be measured and classified.

- The ways in which organisms function are related to the genes in their cells.

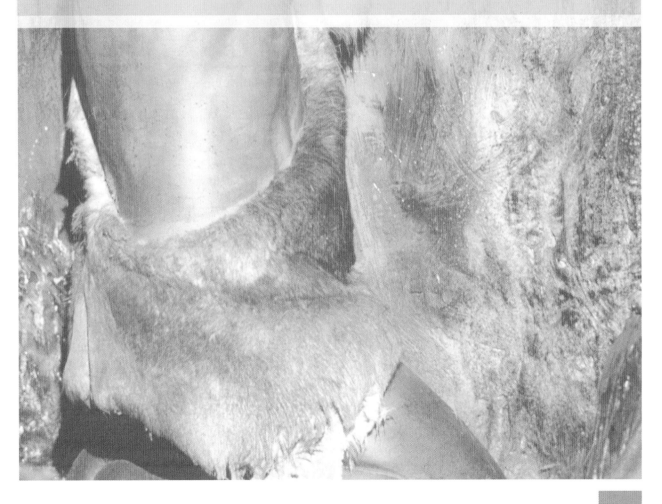

7.1 The structure of DNA

On 28 February 1953, Francis Crick walked into the Eagle pub in Cambridge with his colleague, James Watson. He announced 'We have discovered the secret of life!' In 1953, very few people had even heard of DNA. More than 50 years later, almost everybody knows about it.

The importance of DNA

DNA is the molecule that holds the genetic information of living things. Every cell of your body contains about 2 metres of DNA. All of your body cells contain exactly the same DNA because the DNA is copied exactly every time a cell divides. This means that just one cell of your body contains the genetic information to code for an entire human body. You will learn more about the DNA code at A2. At AS, you need to learn about the structure of DNA.

The structure of DNA

DNA stands for **deoxyribose nucleic acid**. It is a polymer made up of many repeated units called **nucleotides**. You can see the structure of a nucleotide in Figure 1. You will see that a nucleotide is made up of a five-carbon sugar, a phosphate group and an organic base. The five-carbon sugar in a DNA nucleotide is always deoxyribose. The organic base can be adenine, guanine, cytosine or thymine.

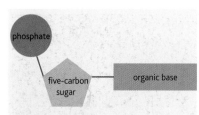

Figure 1 *Structure of a nucleotide*

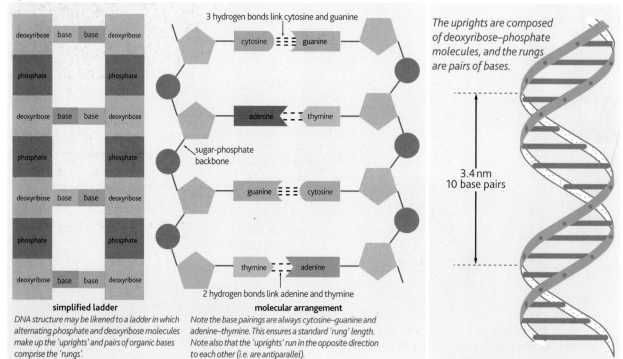

simplified ladder

DNA structure may be likened to a ladder in which alternating phosphate and deoxyribose molecules make up the 'uprights' and pairs of organic bases comprise the 'rungs'.

molecular arrangement

Note the base pairings are always cytosine–guanine and adenine–thymine. This ensures a standard 'rung' length. Note also that the 'uprights' run in the opposite direction to each other (i.e. are antiparallel).

3 hydrogen bonds link cytosine and guanine

2 hydrogen bonds link adenine and thymine

sugar-phosphate backbone

The uprights are composed of deoxyribose–phosphate molecules, and the rungs are pairs of bases.

3.4 nm
10 base pairs

Figure 2 *The basic structure of DNA*

Figure 3 *The DNA double helix structure*

The phosphate and sugars of adjacent nucleotides join together by condensation reactions to form a long **polynucleotide** strand (poly = 'many'). DNA is made of two polynucleotide strands, one upside-down relative to the other strand. The organic bases bond together by hydrogen bonds. However, they pair in a very specific way.

- Adenine will only pair with thymine.
- Cytosine will only pair with guanine.

You can see this in Figure 2. We call this **complementary base pairing**.

The two polynucleotide strands twist around each other, forming a shape called a **double helix**. It is rather like a twisted rope ladder. You can see this in Figure 3. The sugar-phosphate 'backbone' forms the upright part of the 'ladder', while the base-pairs form the 'rungs' of the ladder.

How science works

The discovery of DNA

In 1951, James Watson, an American who was working in Cambridge, saw a poor quality X-ray diffraction photograph of DNA that had been made by Maurice Wilkins, at King's College London. It did not give much information about the molecule, but Watson realised that it must have a fairly regular structure if it could be crystallised. Later that year, Rosalind Franklin, who was also working at King's College, produced some better quality X-ray diffraction photographs (Figure 4). James Watson saw these, but did not make very good notes. His colleague, Francis Crick, was proficient in interpreting X-ray diffraction photographs, but unfortunately the information that he obtained from James Watson was incomplete. The photographs indicated that DNA was a helix.

In November 1951, Watson and Crick built a model of DNA showing that it was a **triple** helix. They invited a number of people to view their model, including Franklin and Wilkins. Unfortunately, they had made a number of mistakes. In particular, they had placed the phosphate groups on the inside. The data showed that DNA had a very high water content, so the phosphate groups had to be on the outside.

In January 1953, Wilkins showed Watson a much clearer X-ray diffraction photograph of DNA that Franklin had actually made in May 1952. This showed Watson quite clearly that DNA is a helix. In the next few days, Crick and Watson learned more about Franklin's work, and realised that there must be two helices, one running the opposite way to the other. Another colleague explained the structure of the bases to Watson. From this, he could work out the base-pairing mechanism. At the end of that month, Watson and Crick started model-building, using all the information they had available to them.

On the 28 February 1953 Watson and Crick had a cardboard and metal model of DNA that fitted the data available (Figure 5). In April their proposed structure for DNA was published in a letter to the journal *Nature*, alongside papers about DNA by other authors including Wilkins and Franklin.

In 1962 Watson, Crick and Wilkins were awarded the Nobel Prize for Physiology or Medicine. Franklin had died of cancer in 1958. The Nobel Prize cannot be awarded posthumously (after death), but many people think she would not have been included, even if she had lived.

AQA Examiner's tip

It is very important that you remember the rules of complementary base-pairing. An easy way to remember that A pairs with T and C pairs with G is to think of peoples' initials. Can you think of someone with the initials AT or TA? Or someone with the initials CG or GC?

Figure 4 *Rosalind Franklin and her X-ray diffraction photograph*

Figure 5 *Watson and Crick with their model of DNA*

Summary questions

1. In a sample of DNA, 30% of the nucleotides contain thymine. What percentage of the nucleotides contain guanine?

2. Add the missing figures to the table below.

Source of DNA	Base composition/%			
	A	T	C	G
human	30.1			
sea urchin			17.5	

7.2 Evidence that DNA is the hereditary material

- Why is the structure of DNA related to its function?

- How can you analyse and interpret experimental evidence that DNA is the genetic material?

Specification reference: 3.2.1

We now know that DNA is the hereditary material, but this was not clear until the 1950s. Many people thought that DNA was too simple to be the hereditary material. You will remember from Topic 1.8 that proteins are made from 20 different amino acids, and they come in all shapes and sizes. They are much more complex than DNA. Many people thought that protein was a much more likely molecule to carry genetic information.

How the structure of DNA is related to its function

As DNA is the genetic material, it is very important that it can store all the information required without the information becoming corrupted. DNA has a number of features that make it ideally suited to its role of storing genetic information.

- The sugar–phosphate backbone makes the molecule stable.
- The molecule coils up so that it is compact, i.e. it can store a lot of information in a small space.
- The sequence of bases allows it to carry coded information for making proteins.
- It is a very long molecule so it can store a lot of information.
- Complementary base pairing allows the molecule to replicate itself accurately.
- The double helix makes the molecule stable, as the base pairs are on the inside of the molecule where they are less likely to be damaged.
- The bases are held together by weak hydrogen bonds, which allow the molecule to 'unzip' easily when it replicates.

Applications and How science works

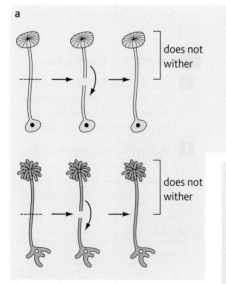

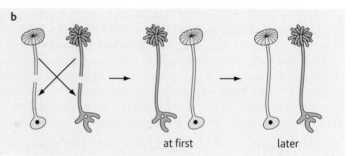

Figure 1 *Hammerling's* Acetabularia *investigations*

Hammerling's experiments

In the late 1930s, Hammerling worked with a single-celled organism called *Acetabularia*. He chose this organism partly because the cells have a particular shape, so he could tell one part of the cell from another part.

Look at Figure 1a). In this experiment, he cut the cells of two different kinds of *Acetabularia* in half. He found that part of the cell died but the other part regenerated into a whole new cell. He concluded that the information needed to regenerate the whole cell must be in the 'foot' of the cell. He looked at the cells under the miscroscope and noticed that the 'foot' of the cell contained a nucleus.

After this, Hammerling decided to investigate the information in the 'foot' of the cells. You can see his investigation in Figure 1b).

1 Why did Hammerling need to carry out the investigation shown in Figure 1a?

2 What could Hammerling conclude from the investigation in Figure 1b?

Link

Refer back to Topic 4.1 and check that you understand what a capsule is.

Applications and How science works

The work of Fred Griffith

A British scientist, Fred Griffith, carried out research in 1927. He worked with different strains of the bacterium *Diplococcus pneumoniae*. Some were **virulent** strains, meaning that they cause disease, but other strains were **non-virulent**. The virulent strains had a slimy capsule but the non-virulent strains did not.

Griffith's investigation is shown in Figure 2. He injected a virulent S-strain of the bacteria into some mice with the result that they died. He injected a non-virulent R-strain into some mice and they survived. Then, he killed some S-strain bacteria by heating them up. He injected these into some mice and they survived. Finally, he mixed the dead S-strain with some living R-strain bacteria. When he injected this mixture into mice, they died. He was able to extract living S-strain bacteria from the dead mice.

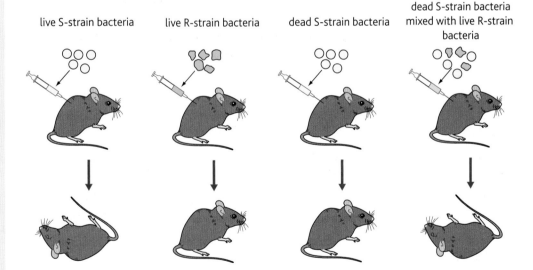

Figure 2 *Griffith's experiment*

Griffith knew that it was the capsule that caused the disease. However, he showed that injecting the capsule alone did not cause the disease. He knew that somehow the dead S-strain bacteria had 'transformed' the R-strain into the virulent S-strain, but he could not explain how this happened.

■ Link

Refer back to Topic 4.6 so that you remember what a virus is. Also look at Topic 4.1 to remind yourself about the structure of bacterial cells.

1 Why did Griffith need to carry out all four of these investigations?

2 How could Griffith show that the heat-killed S-strain bacteria really were dead?

Applications and How science works

Avery, MacLeod and McCarty

In 1944, Oswald Avery, Colin MacLeod and MacLyn McCarty published a paper that explained Griffith's results. They isolated DNA from the dead S-strain of bacteria. They purified the DNA so that no protein was present, and found that this extract would transform the non-virulent R-strain into the S-strain.

Next, they extracted deoxyribonuclease enzyme from dog and rabbit blood and used it to digest the DNA. The digested DNA would not transform the non-virulent R-strain into the S-strain. They concluded that DNA was the 'transforming principle'.

1 Why was it important that the DNA was purified so that no protein was present?

2 Explain why the DNA would not transform the bacteria after it had been digested by deoxyribonuclease enzyme.

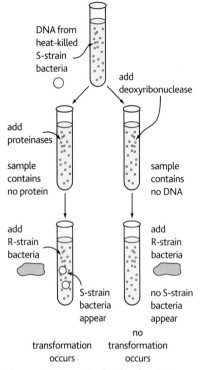

Figure 3 *Avery, Macleod and McCarty experiment*

Applications and How science works

Hershey and Chase

In 1952, just before Watson and Crick worked out the structure of DNA, Martha Chase and Alfred Hershey published the results of their work. This work also showed that DNA was the hereditary material. They worked with a kind of virus called a **bacteriophage**. Bacteriophages are viruses that only infect bacteria.

Look at Figure 4. This shows you how a bacteriophage (or 'phage for short) infects a bacterial cell and causes more 'phages to be made. Hershey and Chase knew that a 'phage contains a molecule of DNA surrounded by a protein coat called a capsid. It does not contain other molecules. They also knew that a 'phage attaches to a bacterial cell. The 'phage coat does not enter the cell, but something passes into the bacterial cell and causes it to make new 'phages.

Hershey and Chase carried out two parallel investigations. You can see this in Figure 5. In one investigation they grew 'phages for a long time in a medium containing radioactive phosphorus, ^{32}P. In the other, they grew 'phages for a long time in a medium containing radioactive sulfur, ^{35}S. You will remember that proteins contain sulfur but not phosphorus. Also, DNA contains phosphorus but not sulfur. This is crucial to this investigation. As a result, in one investigation the 'phage protein coats became 'labelled' with radioactive sulfur, and in the other investigation the 'phage DNA became labelled with radioactive phosphorus. Remember that the bacteria did not contain any radioactive atoms.

In each investigation, the labelled 'phages were added to bacteria. The mixture was then put into a blender. It strips off the 'phage

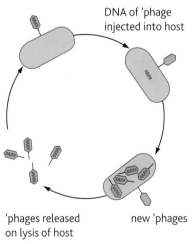

Figure 4 *The life cycle of a bacteriophage*

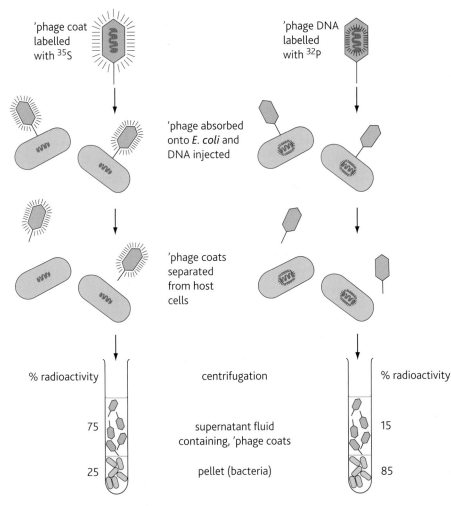

Figure 5 *The Hershey-Chase experiment*

coats from the bacterial cells. The mixture was then centrifuged – a centrifuge spins material at a very high speed. The denser bacterial cells form a pellet at the bottom of the tube, while the less dense 'phage coats form a layer at the top called the supernatant. Hershey and Chase tested each layer to find out which layer was radioactive.

1 How does this investigation provide evidence that DNA is the genetic material?

2 Why were both investigations necessary?

3 Suggest why radioactivity is found in both the pellet and the supernatant in each experiment.

■ Application and How science works

Erwin Chargaff

Chargaff was an Austrian scientist who spent most of his career in the USA. Chargaff analysed the composition of DNA. He isolated DNA from many sources and measured the amount of each of the four nitrogenous bases. Techniques were more advanced by the time Chargaff did his research in the 1940s. One of the techniques available to him was paper chromatography.

Chargaff famously commented that he found 'striking, but perhaps meaningless, regularities'. The following table shows some of Chargaff's results.

source of DNA	Approximate nucleotide composition/%			
	A	T	C	G
ox thymus	26	25	21	16
ox spleen	25	24	20	15
yeast	24	25	14	13
human sperm	29	31	18	18

1 Suggest how paper chromatography might have been useful to Chargaff in working out these results.

2 More recently, a scientist using advanced techniques measured the percentage of different nucleotides in the DNA of a particular kind of virus. His results are shown in the following table.

Nucleotide composition/%			
A	T	C	G
29	19	21	31

a Suppose that this organism was the only organism that Chargaff studied. What might Watson and Crick have concluded?

b Suggest an explanation for these data.

7.3 RNA

Learning objectives:

- What is the structure of RNA?
- What are the differences between RNA and DNA?
- What is the role of RNA in protein synthesis?

Specification reference: 3.2.1

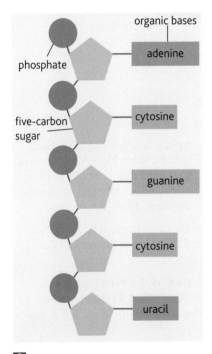

Figure 1 *The structure of RNA*

You have already learned about the structure of DNA. DNA is a type of nucleic acid. You will remember that it is a polymer of nucleotides. RNA is another kind of nucleic acid. Like DNA, it is also a polymer of nucleotides.

The structure of RNA

RNA stands for **ribonucleic acid**. Its nucleotides contain a different five-carbon sugar from DNA – it has ribose instead of deoxyribose. Its nucleotides contain adenine, guanine and cytosine, just like DNA does, but instead of thymine it contains a different organic base called uracil.

RNA is a single polynucleotide strand. You can see its structure in Figure 1.

Differences between RNA and DNA

Some differences between RNA and DNA are summarised in the table below.

Table 1 *Comparison of DNA and RNA*

DNA	RNA
double polynucleotide chain	single polynucleotide chain
five-carbon sugar is deoxyribose	five-carbon sugar is ribose
thymine present which would pair with adenine	uracil present which would pair with adenine
usually much longer than RNA	usually much shorter than DNA

The genetic code

You now understand the evidence that DNA is the genetic material. It carries the 'blueprint' to make a whole organism, which it does by coding for proteins.

The sequence of bases in a length of DNA carries genetic information. Three bases code for one amino acid. For example, GGG in DNA codes for the amino acid proline, and TAC codes for methionine. You will remember that a protein is made up of amino acids, so the sequence of bases in a length of DNA codes for the order of amino acids in the protein.

However, the DNA is in a long length inside the cell nucleus. You will remember from Topic 1.8 that proteins are made in the ribosomes in the cytoplasm. The role of RNA is in making proteins from the information in the DNA.

The role of RNA

A **gene** is a section of DNA that codes for one protein. The base sequence of the gene is copied into a molecule of RNA. Because this is single stranded and shorter than the DNA in the cell nucleus, it can pass through a pore in the nuclear membrane easily. It carries the information in the DNA to the ribosome. Next, RNA brings amino acids to the ribosome and joins them together in the right order. In this way the correct protein can be made. This process is summarised in Figure 2.

It is difficult to see how proteins can result in an organism as complex as a human being. However, you should remember that enzymes are proteins. Enzymes control most of the metabolic reactions in the body.

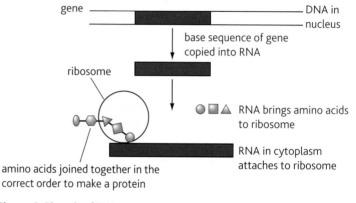

Figure 2 *The role of RNA*

Applications and How science works

The RNA world hypothesis

Scientists have different theories to explain how life began on Earth. A primitive living thing would need to have some kind of metabolism so that it could grow. This presumably means that it would need enzymes. It would also need to replicate itself, so it would need some kind of genetic material. So which came first, DNA or proteins?

Some scientists think that, early in the development of life, RNA carried out both of these functions. RNA can act like an enzyme, and it can also carry genetic information.

It is thought that DNA evolved later. DNA is a better genetic material than RNA. One reason for this is that the base cytosine can break down to form uracil. If this happens in DNA, DNA repair enzymes can 'spot' the error.

1. What features of RNA make it suitable for storing genetic information?

2. If cytosine changes to uracil in RNA the error cannot be 'spotted' by enzymes. Explain why.

3. Apart from this, what other features of DNA make it a better molecule than RNA for storing genetic information?

4. It is very difficult to prove or disprove the RNA world hypothesis. Explain why.

Summary questions

1. Draw a labelled diagram of an RNA nucleotide.

2. A protein contains 100 amino acids. What is the minimum number of nucleotides in the piece of DNA that codes for it?

3. Give **three** similarities between DNA and RNA.

7.4 Genes and proteins

Learning objectives:

■ What is a gene?

■ What is an allele?

■ How do genes control the phenotype of an organism?

Specification reference: 3.2.1

AQA Examiner's tip

Make sure that you know the difference between a gene and an allele.

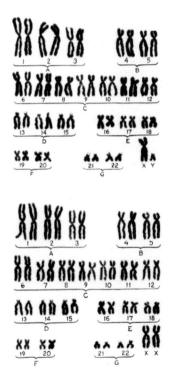

Figure 1 *Human chromosomes*

You learned in Topic 7.3 that genes code for proteins. These proteins may be enzymes. They can determine how an organism develops and what the structure of the organism is like.

Alleles

Human DNA is arranged in the form of chromosomes. Human body cells contain 23 pairs of chromosomes, making 46 chromosomes in all. We receive one set of chromosomes from our mother, and the other set from our father. You can see a photograph of human chromosomes in Figure 1.

Each cell has **homologous pairs** of chromosomes. A gene is a section of DNA that carries coded information about a characteristic. Genes occur at the same relative position (or **locus**) on homologous chromosomes. These paired chromosomes are not completely identical, but they carry the same genes. For example, the homologous pair of chromosomes in Figure 2 carries the gene for eye colour. However, one chromosome carries the code for blue eyes and the other carries the code for brown eyes.

This means that the gene for eye colour has two different **alleles** (or forms). One allele codes for blue eyes and the other allele codes for brown eyes. In this case, each of the homologous pair of chromosomes has a different allele for eye colour from the other.

In this way, genes influence the **phenotype** or characteristics of an organism. For example, one individual may have a phenotype with blue eyes and another may have a phenotype with brown eyes.

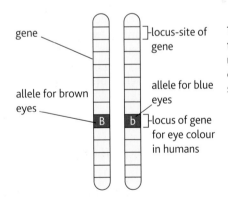

Figure 2 *A homologous pair of chromosomes*

How genes control characteristics

In Unit 1 you learned about cystic fibrosis. This is an inherited condition. Most people have an allele that codes for the normal CFTR protein. However, some people have two copies of the faulty allele that codes for a faulty CFTR protein. As you learned in Topic 3.7, this protein is a different shape.

The allele that codes for cystic fibrosis has three nucleotides missing. Otherwise, it is the same as the normal allele. These three nucleotides code for one amino acid. As a result, the CF allele produces a protein that is exactly the same as the normal protein, except for one amino acid. However, this one amino acid is very significant. You will remember from Topic 1.8 that proteins form a complex tertiary structure. Bonds form between different R-groups in the amino acids that hold the protein in a specific tertiary structure. The faulty CFTR protein produced by the CF allele is a different shape because just one amino acid is missing. This means it cannot function properly.

Many genes code for proteins that act as enzymes. In Topic 2.1 you learned that enzymes have a specifically shaped active site that enables it to catalyse reactions. The shape of the active site depends on the tertiary structure of the protein. This, in turn, depends on the order of amino acids in the protein. The order of amino acids is determined by the sequence of bases in the DNA molecule.

Different alleles have slightly different base sequences in the DNA. This means that they produce a protein with a slightly different sequence of amino acids, so that the enzyme has a slightly different tertiary structure. Often, an enzyme with a different tertiary structure has an altered active site and cannot form an enzyme–substrate complex with its substrate any more. However, in some cases the enzyme is still able to function, and may function more or less efficiently than the enzyme produced by a different allele.

Applications and How science works

Genetic diseases

Archibald Garrod was an English doctor, practising in the early 20th century. He studied a number of human disorders which seemed to be inherited. One of these disorders was **alkaptonuria**. People with this disorder cannot break down a substance called homogentisic acid (see Figure 3). Homogentisic acid accumulates in the tissues and is excreted in the urine. It is easy to detect because the molecule oxidises into a black product, which means that the urine is dark in colour. The black product also accumulates in places such as the sclera of the eye (see Figure 4), and the cartilage of the ear and nose.

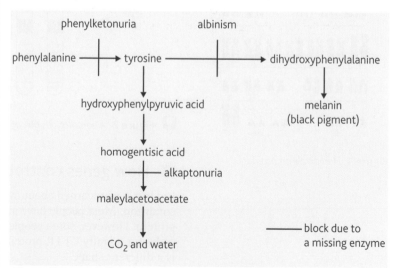

Figure 3 *A metabolic pathway that leads to phenylketonuria, alkaptonuria and albinism*

Garrod studied alkaptonuria by adding the amino acids phenylalanine or tyrosine to the diet. He noticed that homogentisic acid increased in the urine of people with alkaptonuria but not in normal individuals. Although Garrod did not know about genes and enzymes, he concluded that hereditary information controls chemical reactions in the body. He decided that the disorders he was studying were the result of faulty metabolism. Garrod published his first ideas in 1902 and his major piece of work in 1909.

We now know that people with alkaptonuria have an allele that produces a faulty enzyme. This means they cannot convert homogentisic acid to maleylacetoacetate.

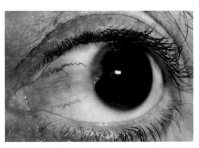

Figure 4 *Oxidised homogentistic acid (black) accumulates in the sclera of the eyes of alkaptonuria sufferers. Note the accumulation of dark pigment in the iris of the eye.*

1 Explain why people with alkaptonuria produce more homogentisic acid in their urine when they consume more phenylalanine or tyrosine in their diet.

2 Explain why normal people do not produce more homogentisic acid in their urine when they consume more phenylalanine or tyrosine.

3 Explain why it was important that Garrod studied the effects of increased phenylalanine and tyrosine on normal people as well as people with alkaptonuria.

4 Melanin is a black pigment that is present in skin. Albinism is a genetic condition in which an enzyme is not present (see Figure 3). Suggest the effect that albinism would have on an affected individual.

5 Phenylketonuria (PKU) was first described in 1934. It is a genetic condition that results in mental retardation. It occurs in about 1 in 11 000 births. Affected individuals cannot convert the amino acid phenylalanine to tyrosine (see Figure 3). Newborn babies are now routinely screened for PKU. If a child with PKU is fed on a low phenylalanine diet, mental retardation does not develop. Explain why.

Summary questions

1 Distinguish between a gene and an allele.

2 People with alkaptonuria produce an enzyme that cannot convert homogentisic acid to maleylacetoacetate. Explain why. Use the terms 'base sequence', 'tertiary structure' and 'active site' in your answer.

7.5 DNA replication

Learning objectives:

- What is the semi-conservative mechanism of DNA replication?

- What is the role of DNA polymerase in DNA replication?

Specification reference: 3.2.1

It is very important that DNA can copy itself accurately whenever a cell divides. When Watson and Crick published their paper about DNA structure in *Nature* in 1953, they added the words 'It has not escaped our notice that the specific pairing we have postulated immediately suggests a possible copying mechanism for the genetic material.'

Semi-conservative replication

DNA replicates by the **semi-conservative** method. 'Conserving' means 'keeping the same'. In this method, one strand of the old molecule is kept intact, and the other strand is newly made. You can see how DNA replicates in Figure 1.

1 *A representative portion of DNA, which is about to undergo replication.*

2 *The two strands of the DNA separate. The hydrogen bonds between the bases break.*

3 *Free nucleotides are attracted to their complementary bases.*

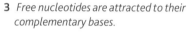
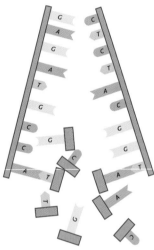

4 *Once the new nucleotides have lined up, they are joined together by the enzyme DNA polymerase.*

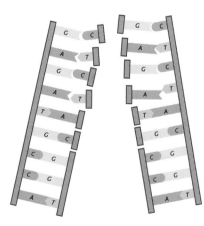

5 *Finally, all the nucleotides are joined to form a complete polynucleotide chain using DNA polymerase. In this way, two identical strands of DNA are formed. As each strand retains half of the original DNA material, this method of replication is called the semi-conservative method.*

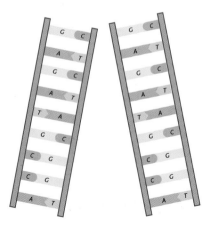

Figure 1 *Semi-conservative replication of DNA*

- The DNA molecule 'unzips' – the hydrogen bonds between the complementary bases break.
- New nucleotides align alongside their complementary base.
- An enzyme called **DNA polymerase** joins these new nucleotides together.
- You can see in Figure 1 that each new strand is **complementary** to the old strand, and that each of the new molecules formed is identical.
- DNA replication occurs during interphase, before the cell divides by mitosis. You will learn more about this in Topic 8.1.

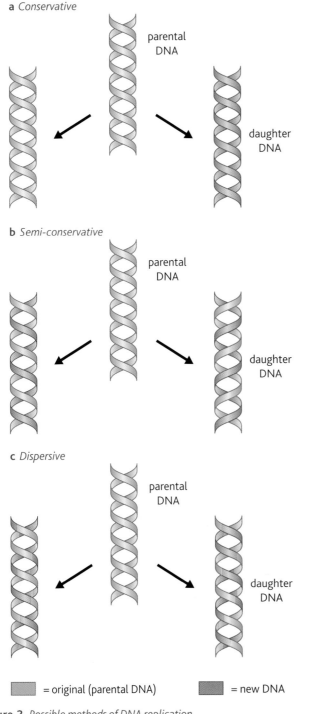

a *Conservative*

parental DNA

daughter DNA

b *Semi-conservative*

parental DNA

daughter DNA

c *Dispersive*

parental DNA

daughter DNA

▬ = original (parental DNA)   ▬ = new DNA

Figure 2 *Possible methods of DNA replication*

Evidence for the semi-conservative method

Watson and Crick's idea that semi-conservative replication of DNA occurred was only one theory. There were actually three theories, which you can see in Figure 2 on the previous page.

■ Semi-conservative replication is described above.

■ Conservative replication proposed that the original DNA molecule stayed intact and that a new molecule, exactly the same as the first, would be built up entirely from new nucleotides.

■ Dispersive replication suggested that the original DNA molecule would break down. Nucleotides would be replicated, then two new identical molecules would be assembled. Each daughter molecule would be a mixture of 'old' and 'new' nucleotides, randomly distributed between them.

Two American scientists, Matthew Meselson and Franklin Stahl, solved the problem in a classic experiment they carried out in 1958. Their investigation is summarised in Figure 3.

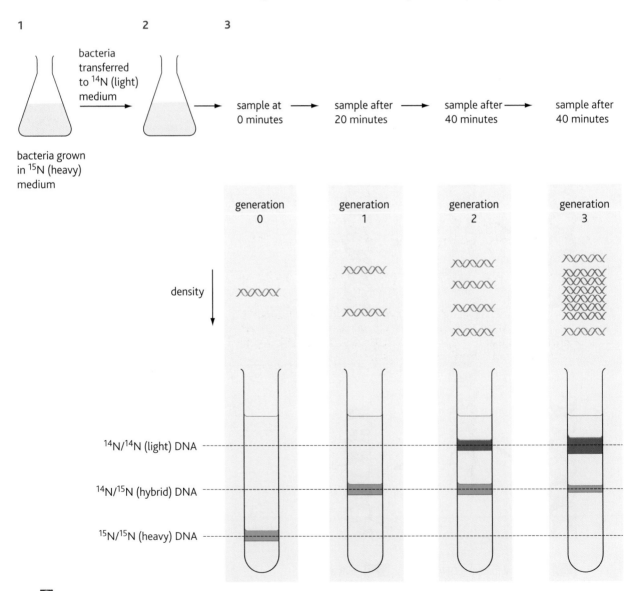

Figure 3 *The Meselson-Stahl experiment*

▨ They grew the bacterium *Escherichia coli* for many generations on a medium in which the nitrogen atoms were the heavy isotope, ^{15}N. (Heavy isotopes contain more neutrons than the normal atom so have a greater mass.) This meant that the nitrogen atoms the bacteria used to make their new DNA would all be of the heavier ^{15}N kind. This was called generation 0.

▨ The bacteria were then transferred into a medium in which the nitrogen atoms were all of the normal ^{14}N kind. This meant that any new DNA formed would contain normal ^{14}N.

▨ After the bacteria had divided just once on the ^{14}N medium, a sample was taken and the DNA extracted. It was centrifuged. DNA containing a lot of ^{15}N is denser than DNA containing a lot of ^{14}N, so it forms a band lower down in the centrifuge tube. This was called generation 1.

▨ After the bacteria had divided twice on the ^{14}N medium, another DNA sample was extracted and centrifuged as before. This was called generation 2.

▨ This was repeated again when the bacteria had divided three times on the ^{14}N medium. This was called generation 3.

The results of this investigation showed that DNA replicates semi-conservatively.

▨ The DNA from generation 1 forms a band midway between the position of 'light' and 'heavy' DNA. This shows that the molecules have one 'heavy' and one 'light' strand.

▨ The DNA from generation 2 shows a 'midway' band and a 'light' band.

Summary questions

1 What part of the DNA molecule contains the nitrogen atoms?

2 In generation 3, the bands of DNA are in the same position as the bands of DNA from generation 2, but the 'light' band is much wider. Explain why.

3 Explain the results that Meselson and Stahl would have obtained if DNA replication had been a conservative, b dispersive.

4 Meselson and Stahl used a bacterium in this investigation. One reason for this is that DNA is much easier to extract from a bacterial cell. Think about the structure of a bacterial cell, which you did in Topic 4.1. Suggest why DNA is easier to extract from a bacterial cell.

1   **Figure 1** shows a short section of a DNA molecule.

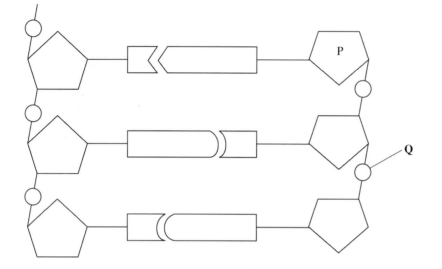

   Figure 1

   (a) (i)   How are the two strands of DNA held together?
       (ii) What do the letters **P** and **Q** represent?   *(3 marks)*
   (b) A sample of DNA was analysed and 27% of the nucleotides were found to
       contain adenine. Calculate the percentage of nucleotides which contained
       guanine. Show your working.   *(2 marks)*

AQA, 2004 & 2005

2   (a) Describe how DNA replicates.   *(4 marks)*
     (b) Give **two** differences between the structure of DNA and RNA   *(2 marks)*

3   (a) Explain what is meant by semi-conservative replication of DNA.   *(2 marks)*
     (b) In an investigation into DNA replication, bacteria were grown for many
         generations in two forms of nitrogen.
         Those in tube **1** were grown in a light nitrogen medium (^{14}N).
         Those in tube **2** were grown in a heavy nitrogen medium (^{15}N).
         Those in tube **3** were grown in a ^{15}N medium and then transferred to a medium
         containing ^{14}N and allowed to divide once.
         The DNA was then extracted and centrifuged.

         Figure 2 shows the results.

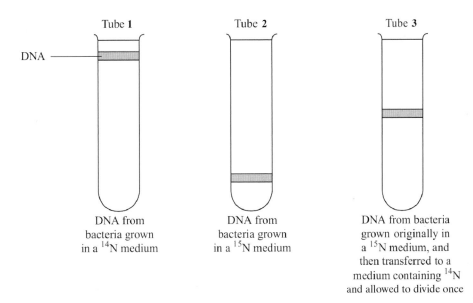

Figure 2

Explain what these results show. *(3 marks)*

AQA, 2006

4   Part of the sequence of DNA bases needed for the synthesis of a particular enzyme is shown below.

TCTATACCAGAAAGAATACCA

(a) What percentage of this section of DNA is cytosine?   *(1 mark)*

(b) Give the RNA sequence which would be complementary to this strand.   *(1 mark)*

(c) Explain the difference between a gene and an allele.   *(2 marks)*

AQA, 2005

5   **Figure 3** shows the replication of a molecule of DNA.

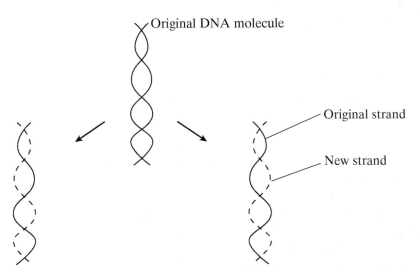

Figure 3

(a) Explain why DNA replication is described as *semi-conservative*.   *(1 mark)*

(b) (i)   What is meant by *specific base pairing*?

(ii) Explain why specific base pairing is important in DNA replication.   *(3 marks)*

(c) Describe **two** features of DNA which make it a stable molecule.   *(2 marks)*

AQA, 2003

Cell division

8.1 Mitosis and cell division

Cells need to divide for growth and tissue repair. Whenever a cell divides, it is important that the daughter cells receive exactly the same genetic information as the parent cell. Cells divide to give exact copies of themselves by a process called **mitosis**.

Learning objectives:

- How is DNA organised in the cell?

- How does DNA replication relate to the events of the cell cycle?

- What happens during the cell cycle?

- Why is mitosis important?

Specification reference: 3.2.2

Chromosome structure

In eukaryotic cells, the DNA is organised into chromosomes. You learned in Topic 7.1 that a human cell contains about 2 metres of DNA, but this is divided up into 46 chromosomes. When a cell is not dividing, you cannot see any chromosomes. This is because the DNA is 'unwound' and spread out in the nucleus. A cell that is not dividing is said to be in **interphase**. The DNA forms long threads, wound around protein molecules called **histones**. You can see this in Figure 1. We call this complex **chromatin**.

DNA replicates during interphase (see Topic 7.5). However, you cannot see anything happening in the cell at this stage.

When a cell starts to divide by mitosis, the chromatin coils up and folds to form **chromosomes**. The first stage of mitosis is called **prophase**. Figure 2 shows the structure of a chromosome as it appears in prophase. You will notice that it is made up of two **chromatids**, held together by a centromere. The reason it consists of two chromatids is that the DNA replicated during interphase. In other words, one of the chromatids is an exact copy of the one joined to it.

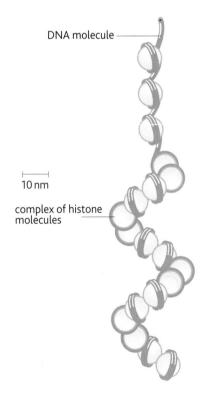

DNA molecule

10 nm

complex of histone
molecules

Figure 1 *Structure of chromatin*

The cell cycle

Cells do not divide all the time – they are mostly growing and carrying out their functions. The time when cells are not dividing but are active in carrying out their functions is called interphase. During this period proteins are made, cell organelles are replicated and respiration occurs. DNA replication also occurs during interphase – specifically the S, or synthesis, phase. This happens between two growth phases. You can see this in Figure 3.

The importance of mitosis

As you already know, mitosis is important because it produces genetically identical copies of the parent cell. This is important for:

- **Growth.** A sperm and an ovum fuse together to produce a single fertilised cell, or **zygote**. This cell is **diploid** because it has one set of chromosomes from each parent. These chromosomes carry all the genetic information needed to form a whole new organism. The zygote divides by mitosis so that all the cells in the new organism have exactly the same information. In other words, all the cells in the organism contain exactly the same alleles.

Repair. If cells die, or are damaged, new cells need to be produced. It is important that these new cells have exactly the same genetic information as the cells that they are replacing.

Asexual reproduction. Humans do not reproduce asexually, but some organisms, particularly plants that are useful to us as food plants, can. Asexual reproduction means that only one parent is needed. All the offspring produced are identical to the parent. This can be an advantage when the environmental conditions are not changing. It enables one organism to produce many offspring very quickly. Examples of vegetative propagation are growing new plants from bulbs, tubers or cuttings.

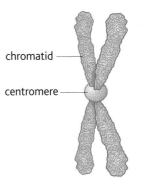

Figure 2 *Structure of a chromosome*

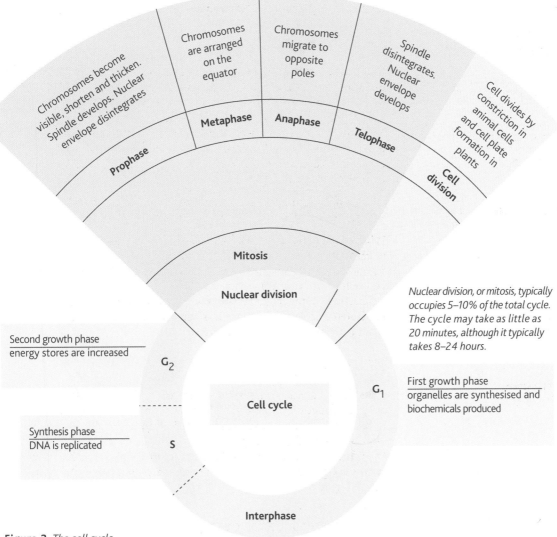

Nuclear division, or mitosis, typically occupies 5–10% of the total cycle. The cycle may take as little as 20 minutes, although it typically takes 8–24 hours.

Second growth phase energy stores are increased

First growth phase organelles are synthesised and biochemicals produced

Synthesis phase DNA is replicated

 **Figure 3** *The cell cycle*

Summary questions

1 Explain the difference between a chromatid and a chromosome.

2 Explain why chromosomes cannot be seen in a cell during interphase.

3 All the cells in an organism have exactly the same alleles because they are produced by mitosis. However, cells lining the epithelium of the respiratory tract look very different from nerve cells. Suggest why.

8.2 The stages of mitosis

- What are the stages of mitosis?

- What happens to the chromosomes at each stage?

Specification reference: 3.2.2

💡 Mitosis is the part of the cell cycle in which the nucleus divides. Mitosis is actually a continuous process, but it is helpful to divide it up into stages. You can see these stages in Figure 1.

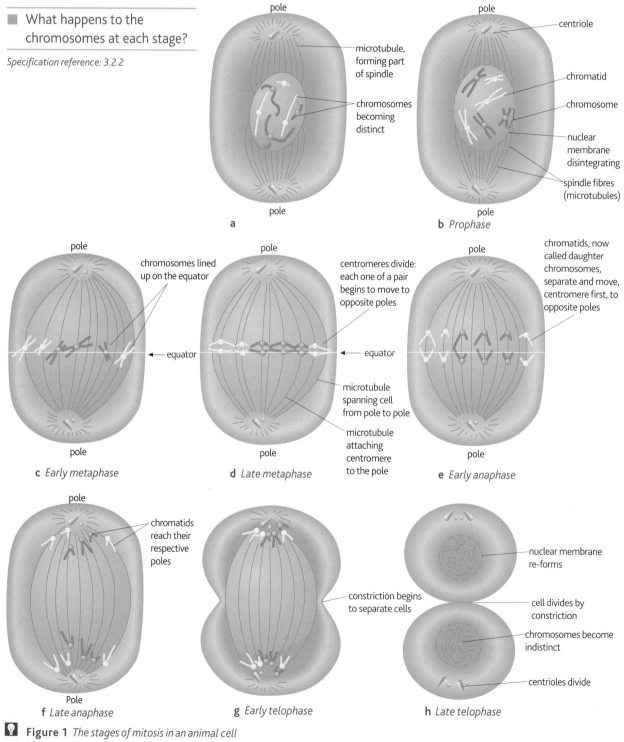

💡 **Figure 1** *The stages of mitosis in an animal cell*

Prophase (see Figure 1b). The chromosomes start to become visible. They begin as long, thin threads that shorten and thicken. It can be seen that each chromosome consists of two chromatids. This is because the DNA replicated during interphase. There are two organelles called **centrioles** in the cell. These move to opposite ends, or **poles** of the cell. The centrioles start to send out a system of tiny fibres called **microtubules** which stretch across the cell. Together they form a system of microtubules called the **spindle**. At the very end of prophase the nuclear membrane breaks down. This means the chromosomes are now free in the cytoplasm.

Metaphase (see Figures 1c and d). The centromeres of the chromosomes attach to the equator of the spindle. At the end of metaphase, the centromeres divide. Once this happens the chromatids can be called daughter chromosomes.

Anaphase (see Figures 1e and f). The microtubules attached to the centromeres contract. The daughter chromosomes are pulled to opposite poles of the cell.

Telophase (see Figures 1g and h). Once the daughter chromosomes have reached the opposite poles of the cell, they start to unwind again and get longer and thinner. Eventually they disappear altogether. The spindle fibres break down. The nuclear membrane re-forms around each group of chromosomes. Each centriole divides so that each daughter cell has two centrioles. The cytoplasm constricts, separating the cell in two.

Mitosis in photographs

Look at Figure 2 which shows photographs of mitosis occurring under a microscope. The main difference here is that you cannot see the spindle fibres. These are very thin and so they do not show up clearly under a light microscope.

In an exam you may be given diagrams or photographs, so you need to be able to understand both.

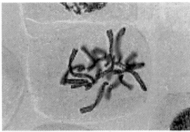

a *prophase*

b *metaphase*

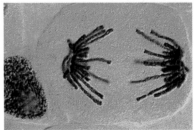

c *anaphase*

d *telophase*

Figure 2 *The stages of mitosis seen under a light microscope*

Summary questions

1 The graph in Figure 3 shows changes in the amount of DNA in a cell during the cell cycle.

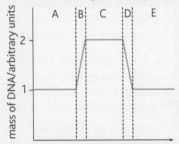

Figure 3 *Graph showing changes in the amount of DNA in a cell during the cell cycle*

   a Name the stage of the cell cycle that is occurring at B.

   b In which of the stages, A to E, is metaphase occurring?

   c What is happening during stage D?

2 Some of the events in the cell cycle are listed below. Put them in the correct order.

   A: centromeres divide

   B: chromosomes become visible

   C: chromosomes align at equator

   D: chromatids separate

   E: cytoplasm divides

   F: nuclear membrane breaks down

8.3 Cancer

Learning objectives:

- What is the difference between a benign and a malignant tumour?
- How is cell division controlled?
- What are the causes of cancer?

Specification reference: 3.2.2

Figure 1 *A benign tumour*

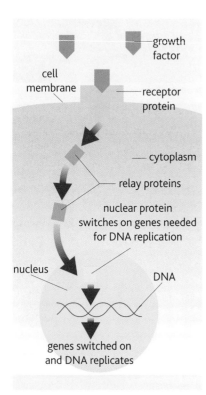

Figure 2 *Normal cell receiving signals from growth factors that tell it when to divide*

Normal body cells only undergo mitosis for growth or repair. There are genes that control cell division so that mitosis does not occur too often. However, these processes that regulate cell division may go wrong. When this happens, a tumour may result.

Types of tumour

A **tumour** is a mass of cells that have divided too many times. Some tumours may be **benign**. Benign tumours tend to be slow-growing and stay within one tissue. They do not spread to other parts of the body, and are not usually life-threatening. They may cause damage, e.g. by pressing on an important nerve or blood vessel. However, when they are removed they do not usually grow back. You can see a benign tumour in Figure 1.

Other tumours are **malignant**. These usually grow rapidly. They invade surrounding tissues and they also have cells that break off from the main tumour. These can spread around the body in blood or lymph vessels and form a new tumour somewhere else. These are life-threatening unless they are treated at an early stage.

Controlling cell division

Genes called **proto-oncogenes** stop cells dividing by mitosis too often. They work in one of two ways. This is illustrated in Figure 2.

- Some proto-oncogenes code for **receptor proteins** in the cell membrane. When these are activated by a specific **growth factor**, they activate the genes that stimulate cell division.
- Other proto-oncogenes produce the growth factors that stimulate cell division.
- However, changes can occur in the base sequence of these proto-oncogenes. A change in the base sequence is called a **mutation**. When a proto-oncogene mutates, it can become an **oncogene.** Oncogenes cause uncontrolled cell division in one of two ways:
- Some oncogenes produce a different form of the receptor protein that stimulates cell division, even when the growth factor is not present.
- Other oncogenes produce uncontrolled amounts of growth factors.

Cells also contain **tumour suppressor genes**. These genes code for proteins that stop cells dividing. They also cause cells with damaged DNA to die. If a tumour repressor gene mutates, the cell may carry on dividing uncontrollably, passing on its damaged DNA to its daughter cells.

Our cells have many proto-oncogenes and tumour repressor genes. Usually, several of these must mutate before cancer develops.

Primary and secondary tumours

Look at Figure 3. You can see that a tumour begins as an abnormal mass in one tissue of the body. As it grows larger, it develops its own blood and lymph vessels. However, it is still in one place. We call this a **primary tumour**. If the tumour is detected and removed at this stage it is very likely that it will not return.

As the primary tumour grows, some of its cells break off and spread into blood or lymph vessels. These cells travel around the body and can set up new tumours in other parts of the body, called **secondary tumours**. This spreading of tumour cells is called **metastasis**. Another name for a secondary tumour is a **metastasis.**

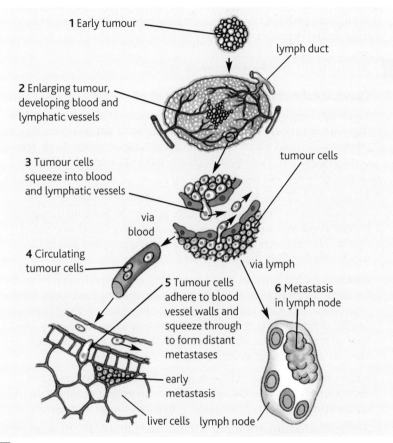

1 Early tumour

lymph duct

2 Enlarging tumour, developing blood and lymphatic vessels

tumour cells

3 Tumour cells squeeze into blood and lymphatic vessels

via blood

4 Circulating tumour cells

via lymph

5 Tumour cells adhere to blood vessel walls and squeeze through to form distant metastases

6 Metastasis in lymph node

early metastasis

liver cells   lymph node

Figure 3 *How an early primary tumour can develop and spread to form secondary tumours*

Causes of cancer

There are many different kinds of cancer, each caused by different factors. Some kinds of cancer are genetic, but other cancers are caused by environmental factors. Some of these causal factors are listed below.

- **Genetic factors.** Some people have proto-oncogenes that are more likely to mutate than others. This is why some kinds of cancer are more common in certain families. For example, there are two genes called BRCA1 and BRCA2 that increase the chance that a person will get breast cancer.

- **Age.** People are more likely to suffer from cancer as they get older. This is partly because they have had more years of exposure to environmental factors that cause cancer, such as ionising radiation and cancer-causing chemicals. It is also because they have had more chance to accumulate damage to their DNA.

- **Ionising radiation.** This includes X-rays and alpha- and beta-radiation. Ionising radiation contains a great deal of energy, so it can penetrate body cells and break bonds in DNA molecules.

- **Ultraviolet radiation.** This has less energy than ionising radiation, but it does have enough energy to penetrate skin cells. It breaks bonds in the DNA of skin cells and can cause skin cancer.

Chemicals. Many chemicals can cause cancer. These are called **carcinogens**. Cigarette smoke contains several different carcinogens. Asbestos fibres, some pesticides and diesel exhaust can also cause cancer.

Viruses. Some viruses can cause cancer. The best known example is Human Papilloma Virus, HPV, some kinds of which can cause cervical cancer. This is because these types of HPV carry the code for a protein that interferes with a tumour suppressor gene. HPV is passed on during sexual intercourse.

Application and How science works

Cervical cancer vaccine for girls aged 12

From 2008, girls as young as 12 will be vaccinated against a virus that causes cervical cancer. It is thought that a national vaccination programme could prevent 70% of cervical cancer cases. Each year cervical cancer is diagnosed in about 2800 UK women and more than 1000 die from the disease.

All girls aged 12 and 13 could receive the vaccine in three doses over a 6-month period. The vaccine protects against the sexually transmitted human papilloma virus (HPV), which causes most cases of cervical cancer. The vaccinations would not be compulsory, and parents would decide whether their daughter should have the vaccination.

Experts say that it could be 20 years before the first health benefits are seen. The vaccines are also expensive, costing more than all the immunisations each child currently receives put together. However, campaigners say that the vaccines represent value for money given how effective they are in combating HPV, which is common among sexually active young women.

Some campaigners and religious groups have expressed concerns about providing a vaccination to children to protect against a sexually transmitted infection. They think it may encourage promiscuity.

Cervical screening will need to continue for at least 20 years, particularly for those women who have the vaccine after the onset of sexual activity. This group may not derive as much benefit as those who are vaccinated before they start having sex.

Other experts think that giving the vaccination to boys should be considered.

Adapted from an article by David Rose in The Times. © *David Rose, NI Syndication Limited, 21 June 2007.*

1. Use your knowledge of the immune system to explain why girls will be given three vaccinations over 6 months.

2. Explain why the vaccination is being offered to children aged 12–13, rather than waiting until they are older.

3. Why will it be 20 years before the first health benefits are seen?

4. Cervical testing is used to detect cervical cancer at an early stage. Give as many reasons as you can to explain why it will need to be continued for at least 20 years.

5. Some people do not think that this programme should be started. What possible reasons might they have?

6. Boys cannot suffer from cervical cancer. Why do some people think that boys should be vaccinated?

Application and How science works

Evaluating the causes of cancer
Lung cancer and smoking
Figure 4 shows the cigarette consumption of men between 1900 and 1980, as well as the incidence of lung cancer.

1. Describe the evidence from this graph that smoking causes lung cancer.

2. Explain why the lung cancer deaths are calculated per 100 000 people.

3. Do these data prove that smoking causes lung cancer? Explain your answer.

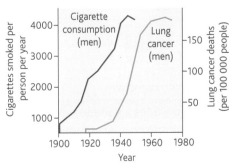

Figure 4 *Graph showing incidence of smoking and lung cancer in men between 1900–1980*

Colorectal cancer
Figure 5 shows the incidence and mortality rates of colorectal cancer in Ontario between 1964 and 2001.

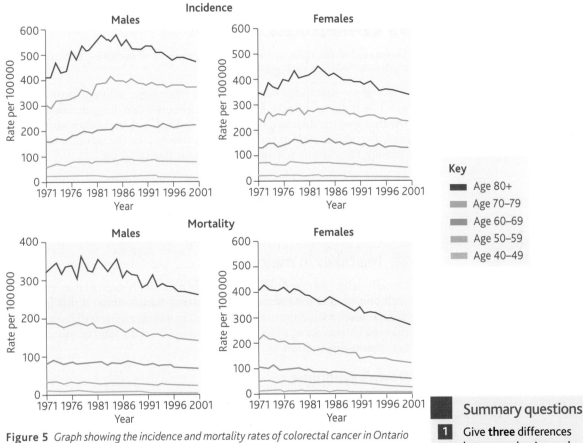

Figure 5 *Graph showing the incidence and mortality rates of colorectal cancer in Ontario between 1971 and 2001*

4. Suggest **two** reasons why men have higher rates of colorectal cancer than women.

5. People with colorectal cancer living in Ontario have a better chance of surviving in 2001 than in 1971. Explain the evidence from the graph that supports this statement.

Summary questions

1. Give **three** differences between a benign and a malignant tumour.

2. Some women have the BRCA1 or BRCA2 allele, but they do not develop breast cancer. Suggest reasons why not.

3. Explain why cancer is more likely to be cured if it is detected early.

8.4 Meiosis

Learning objectives:

- How does a gamete have half the normal number of chromosomes?

- What are the stages of meiosis?

- What happens when meiosis goes wrong?

- What is Down's syndrome?

Specification reference: 3.2.2

In Topic 7.4, you learned that human body cells contain 46 chromosomes. These chromosomes are in homologous pairs. In other words, each body cell has 23 pairs of chromosomes, one set from each parent. Homologous chromosomes have the same genes but not necessarily the same alleles. A cell with homologous pairs of chromosomes is said to be **diploid**. In humans, the diploid number of chromosomes is 46. We can also write this as $2n = 46$.

Each individual develops from a single fertilised cell, or zygote, by mitosis. This means that the gametes must each have half the normal number of chromosomes. A cell with just one set of chromosomes is said to be **haploid**. Human gametes contain 23 chromosomes. We can write this as $n = 23$.

🔍 💡 The process of meiosis

Gametes, or sex cells, are made by the process of **meiosis**. You can see an outline of meiosis in Figure 1.

You will see that the DNA replicates in interphase, before meiosis starts, just like it did in mitosis. However, meiosis is a two-stage division. In the first meiotic division, two cells are formed, but the chromosomes still have two chromatids at the end of this division. In the second meiotic division the chromatids divide, giving four haploid cells.

Meiosis is important because it produces haploid gametes. This means that the full diploid number is restored at fertilisation. If gametes were not haploid, the chromosome number would double with every new generation.

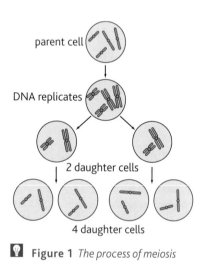

parent cell

DNA replicates

2 daughter cells

4 daughter cells

💡 **Figure 1** *The process of meiosis*

▪ Mistakes in meiosis

Occasionally, mistakes can occur during meiosis. A gamete may end up with one extra chromosome or one missing chromosome. If this faulty gamete fuses with a normal gamete, the resulting zygote will have a missing chromosome or an extra chromosome. This kind of mistake is called **non-disjunction**.

Down's syndrome

One kind of non-disjunction involves chromosome 21. This is a very small chromosome. If a gamete with an extra chromosome 21 fuses with a normal gamete, the resulting individual will have three chromosome 21s. Their chromosome number will be 47 instead of 46. A person with this condition has **Down's syndrome**. You can see how this happens in Figure 2.

Down's syndrome children account for one in every 800–1000 births. The risk of having a child with Down's syndrome increases with the age of the mother, although they may be born to mothers of any age. Table 1 shows how the risk increases with age.

Age of mother/ years	Risk of Down's syndrome
20	1:1700
25	1:1400
30	1:900
35	1:400
40	1:100
45	1:35

Table 1 *Risk of having a child with Down's syndrome by age of mother*

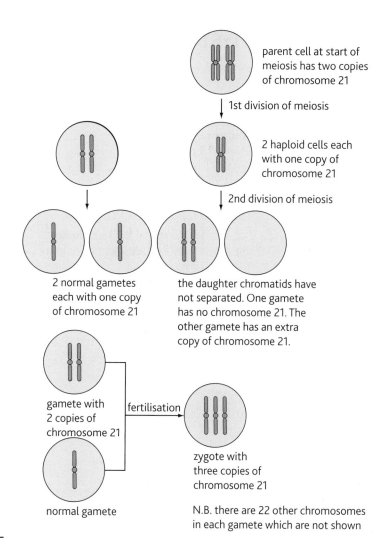

parent cell at start of meiosis has two copies of chromosome 21

1st division of meiosis

2 haploid cells each with one copy of chromosome 21

2nd division of meiosis

2 normal gametes each with one copy of chromosome 21

the daughter chromatids have not separated. One gamete has no chromosome 21. The other gamete has an extra copy of chromosome 21.

gamete with 2 copies of chromosome 21

fertilisation

zygote with three copies of chromosome 21

normal gamete

N.B. there are 22 other chromosomes in each gamete which are not shown

Figure 2 *How Down's syndrome can occur*

Figure 3 shows a person with Down's syndrome. They tend to have a flatter head than normal, smaller ears and a protruding tongue. They are shorter than average and their hands have a single fold across the palm. They may have other problems, such as heart defects. All people with Down's syndrome have a degree of learning difficulty, but this may range from moderate to severe.

Children with Down's syndrome usually have a very happy disposition and are very affectionate. Some adults are able to enter employment and lead independent lives, although others will need lifelong care. Many Down's syndrome individuals live into old age, and the average life expectancy is about 60 years.

Figure 3 *A person with Down's syndrome*

Examiner's tip

Make sure you spell meiosis and mitosis correctly in answers to exam questions. Spelling mistakes are usually marked wrong. For example, a candidate who writes 'meitosis' has not made it clear which kind of cell division they are referring to!

Summary questions

1 Explain the meanings of the words haploid and diploid.

2 Explain why homologous chromosomes have the same genes but may not have the same alleles.

3 A normal body cell in an organism contains 4.8 units of DNA. In the testes of one individual, where meiosis was occurring, some cells were found to have 9.6 units of DNA, while others had 4.8 or 2.4 units of DNA. Explain why.

1   The bar chart in **Figure 1** shows the effects of smoking and alcoholic drinks on the risk of developing mouth cancer.

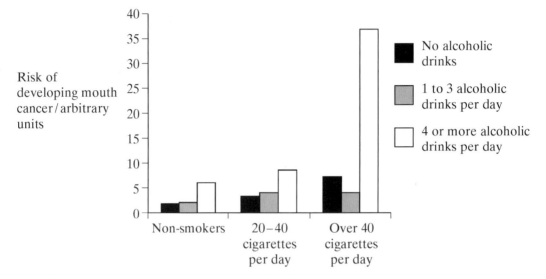

Figure 1

(a) Describe the effects of smoking and drinking on the risk of developing mouth cancer.   *(4 marks)*

(b) Suggest **one** reason why people who neither drink nor smoke sometimes develop mouth cancer.   *(1 mark)*

AQA, 2004

2   (a) Describe what happens to the chromosomes during each of the following stages of mitosis.
     Prophase
     Metaphase
     Anaphase
     Telophase   *(4 marks)*

(b) Give **one** difference between mitosis and meiosis.   *(1 mark)*

AQA, 2003

3   Read the following passage.

Body cells have elaborate control systems that regulate their division. If these control systems break down, cells start to grow and divide in an unregulated way and produce a tumour. Some tumours are benign and some are malignant. Cancer is not caused by a single mutation to the genes controlling cell multiplication but rather by between 3 and 20 mutations of these genes in a single cell. It is for this reason that cancer is more common in older people. Cancer cells differ in appearance and function from non-cancerous cells from the same tissue. Cancer cells are less well differentiated, produce only a few proteins and cannot perform the usual functions of healthy cells.

Use information from the passage and your own knowledge to answer the following questions.

(a) Cancer is more common in older people. Explain why.   *(2 marks)*

(b) During which stage of the cell cycle does DNA replication occur?   *(1 mark)*

(c) Describe the similarities and differences between benign and malignant tumours.   *(6 marks)*

AQA, 2006

4 Lung cancer, chronic bronchitis and coronary heart disease (CHD) are associated with smoking. **Tables 1** and **2** give the total number of deaths from these diseases in the UK in 1974.

Table 1 Men

Age/years	Number of deaths in thousands		
	Lung cancer	Chronic bronchitis	CHD
35–64	11.5	4.2	31.7
65–74	12.6	8.5	33.3
75+	5.8	8.1	29.1
Total (35–75+)	29.9	20.8	94.1

Table 2 Women

Age/years	Number of deaths in thousands		
	Lung cancer	Chronic bronchitis	CHD
35–64	3.2	1.3	8.4
65–74	2.6	1.9	18.2
75+	1.8	3.5	42.3
Total (35–75+)	7.6	6.7	68.9

(a) (i) Using examples from the tables explain why it is useful to give data for men and women separately.

(ii) Data like these are often given as percentages of people dying from each cause. Explain the advantage of giving these data as percentages. *(4 marks)*

(b) Give **two** factors, other than smoking, which increase the risk of coronary heart disease. *(2 marks)*

AQA, 2004

5 (a) Explain the importance of meiosis. *(2 marks)*

(b) Describe how non-disjunction can lead to Down's Syndrome. *(4 marks)*

6 **Figure 2** shows a photograph of all the chromosomes in the cell of one male individual. This individual has a particular genetic condition.

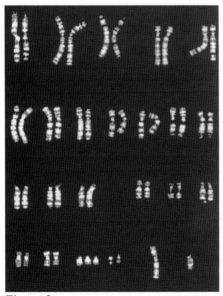

(a) (i) Name the genetic condition shown in **Figure 2**. *(1 mark)*

(ii) Describe how this genetic condition occurs. *(3 marks)*

(b) During which stage of mitosis were these chromosomes photographed? Explain your answer. *(2 marks)*

Figure 2

9 Where we fit in the world

9.1 The concept of a species

Learning objectives:

■ What is a species?

■ How are species named?

■ What is phylogenetic hierarchy?

Specification reference: 3.2.3

Biologists classify organisms into groups, based on the relationships between organisms. The basic unit of classification is the **species**.

■ The definition of a species

A species is a group of similar organisms that have certain features in common.

■ They are capable of interbreeding to produce fertile offspring.

■ They have very similar genes so members of a species are very similar, both anatomically and biochemically.

New species have developed from existing species by the process of natural selection.

■ Applications and How science works

Mules

Horses and donkeys belong to separate species. However, they can interbreed and produce offspring. The offspring are called mules. This does not mean that horses and donkeys belong to the same species, because mules are almost always infertile. This means that the genes of horses and donkeys do not mix.

■ Naming species

Organisms are given two names by biologists. This is called the **binomial system**. It was devised by a Swedish biologist called Carl Linnaeus (1707–1778). The names are based on Latin, and are used by biologists all over the world. For example, the tiger is called *Panthera tigris*. The first name, *Panthera*, tells you the genus to which the organism belongs. This is a little like a person's surname. You share your surname only with close relatives. The second name, *tigris*, indicates the species to which the organism belongs. This is a little like your first name which identifies you from your close relatives. Notice that the genus always has an upper case (capital) letter, and the species a lower case letter. It is written in italics, or underlined if you are writing by hand.

You may think that these Latin names are more complex than ordinary names. Look at Figure 1.

Which photograph shows a robin? Most people in the UK would choose photograph (b). However, if you were from the USA you would probably choose photograph (a). If a scientist from the USA were to talk to a British scientist about his work on robins, the British scientist might relate the conversation to the wrong organism. However, by using the

a *Turdus migratorius*

b *Enthacus rubecula*

Figure 1 *Which of these birds is a robin?*

Latin binomial names, it means there can be no confusion because the American robin and the British robin have very different binomial names. This tells you that they are not closely related to each other.

Classifying organisms

Originally, classification systems were based on observable features. For example, plants with similar leaf shapes or animals with the same number of legs were classified together. However, this does not mean that the organisms are related. For example, whales and sharks are both large organisms that live in the sea. We now know that whales are mammals, while sharks are fish. They have some similarities in appearance but they are not closely related to each other.

The system of classification that biologists now use is sometimes described as a **phylogenetic hierarchy**.

- A **hierarchy** means that big groups are subdivided into smaller groups with no overlap.
- **Phylogenetic** means that organisms are placed in groups with other organisms that have close evolutionary relationships with them.

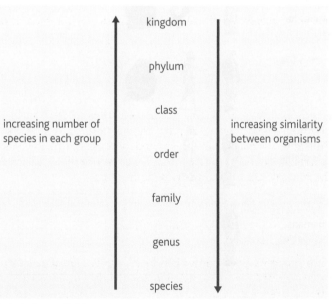

Figure 2 *A phylogenetic hierarchy*

You can see the hierarchy of groups that biologists use in Figure 2. The biggest group of all is the **kingdom**. Currently, biologists usually divide living organisms into five kingdoms: Prokaryotae, Protoctista, Fungi, Plantae and Animalia. Kingdoms are subdivided into phyla, then into classes. Classes are subdivided into orders, then into families. Families are subdivided into genera, and finally into species. As you go down the hierarchy, there are fewer organisms in each group, and the organisms have more features in common.

Classifying humans

You can see how humans are classified in Figure 3. The binomial name for humans is *Homo sapiens* which means 'wise man'. There are no other living organisms that share our genus, but there are extinct organisms in this category. You will learn more about them later in this chapter.

AQA **Examiner's tip**

You need to remember the groups used to classify organisms, and the order they come in. The order of groups is Kingdom – Phylum – Class – Order – Family – Genus – Species. It is useful to make up a mnemonic to remember this, such as 'King Philip Came Over For Green Spinach'.

Kingdom	Animalia	Humans are multicellular organisms. Their cells have nuclei and no cell walls.	
Phylum	Chordata	Humans are animals with backbones.	
Class	Mammalia	Humans have hairy skins and produce milk to feed their young.	
Order	Primates	Primates have flat faces, forward-facing eyes and opposable digits. They have adaptations for living in trees.	
Family	Hominidae	These are human-like creatures.	
Genus	*Homo*	Humans are the only living member of this genus.	
Species	*sapiens*	All modern humans belong to this species.	

Figure 3 *How humans are classified*

Summary questions

1. Copy and complete the table to show the classification of the tiger.

	Animalia
phylum	Chordata
	Mammalia
	Carnivora
	Felidae
genus	
species	

2. The binomial names of three different members of the family Felidae are listed below.

Cheetah – *Acinonyx jubatus*

Tiger – *Panthera tigris*

Lion – *Panthera leo*

What do their binomial names tell you about how these species are related to each other?

9.2 Evidence used in classification

Learning objectives:

■ How are different forms of evidence used to classify organisms?

Specification reference: 3.2.3

You learned in Topic 9.1 that biologists classify organisms into groups that reflect their evolutionary relationships. However, there are several different sources of evidence that biologists need when they classify organisms.

■ Biochemical evidence

Although there is an enormous variety of life on Earth, you learned in Chapter 1 that all living organisms are made up of the same basic molecules. Recently, scientists have developed techniques that allow us to compare molecules from different organisms in detail. Usually proteins and DNA are studied.

One protein, called **cytochrome *c***, has been studied in detail. Cytochrome *c* is found in mitochondria. It is an important protein used in cellular respiration. This molecule contains 104 amino acids in most chordates (animals with backbones), and slightly more in most other organisms.

Look at Table 1 which compares the structure of cytochrome *c* in different organisms. It shows the number of amino acids that are different in other organisms, compared to human cytochrome *c*.

Table 1 *Comparing the number of amino acid differences in cytochrome c between humans and some other organisms*

Organism	Number of amino acid differences
human	0
chimpanzee	0
rhesus monkey	1
rabbit	9
dog	10
penguin	11
moth	24
yeast	38

Scientists can see that cytochrome *c* has changed very little over millions of years of evolution. For example, the evidence shows that humans and monkeys diverged from a common ancestor 20 million years ago, yet there is only one amino acid different in their cytochrome *c*. Yeast and humans are very distantly related indeed, yet their cytochrome *c* differs by only 38 amino acids.

One way of studying biochemical differences between organisms is by DNA hybridisation. DNA is taken from two different species. 'Unzipped' strands of DNA are then mixed together. They pair up with each other wherever they have complementary base sequences. This is called hybridisation. The greater the degree of hybridisation, the more similar the DNA of the two organisms. Scientists can tell how much hybridisation there is by slowly heating up the hybrid DNA molecules. The more heat that is needed to separate the DNA strands, the more matches there are.

Very recently, scientists have been able to find the sequence of bases in the whole of the DNA of an organism. For example, the base sequence of human DNA has been worked out, as well as the sequence of bases in the DNA of chimpanzees.

■ Anatomical evidence

Organisms with similar anatomy are believed to be closely related. For example, the **pentadactyl** (five digit) limb is a structure seen in all vertebrates from amphibians to mammals. This can be seen in Figure 1 on the next page.

Scientists have used this evidence to classify organisms. For example, although a dolphin looks very different from a horse or a monkey, we can see that its flipper has the same basic structure as the limbs of the

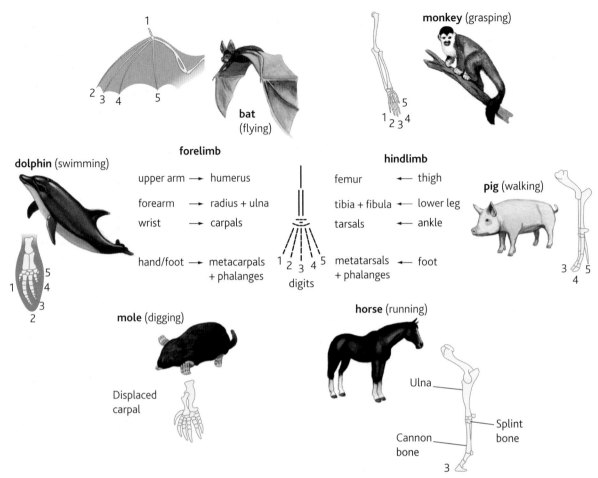

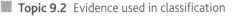

Figure 1 *The pentadactyl limb in different organisms*

monkey and horse. This tells us that they are much more closely related to these animals than to fish. The fin of a fish is very different from the flipper of a dolphin.

You saw in Topic 9.1 that humans are classified in the order Primates. This is because they have anatomical features that they share with other primates such as apes, monkeys and lemurs:

■ grasping limbs with opposable thumb,

■ brachiation – the arm can swing through 180°,

■ large brains with a highly developed cerebral cortex that allows them to learn complex skills,

■ two forward-facing eyes allowing stereoscopic vision which means they can judge distance accurately,

■ nails to protect the ends of fingers and toes.

■ Embryological evidence

Look at Figure 2. This shows stages in the development of the embryos of three different vertebrates.

You will see that the early embryos look very similar. It is only in the later stages of development that the embryos look different. For example, all vertebrate embryos have a tail-like structure early in their development, but only some of them have a tail in the later stages.

Tortoise

Chick

Rabbit

Figure 2 *Stages in the development of three different vertebrate embryos*

This is evidence that they have evolved from a common ancestor. There would be no other reason for a vertebrate such as a human, to have a tail-like structure early in embryonic development if the structure is not present in the adult.

Immunological evidence

You learned in Topic 5.1 that proteins can act as antigens when they enter the blood of another animal that does not normally have this protein. The animal that receives the foreign antigen produces antibodies specific to the antigen. The antibodies bind to the antigen.

Human serum (blood plasma without blood clotting proteins) can be injected into rabbits. The rabbit responds by producing antibodies specific to the human serum proteins. After a time, some serum is removed from the sensitised rabbit and added to a test tube. Human serum is added to the rabbit serum. Antibodies in the rabbit serum bind to the antigens in the human serum. These form a complex that settles out as a precipitate. The amount of precipitate can be measured.

More samples of the rabbit serum that contains antibodies specific to proteins in human serum can be taken and put into more test tubes. Samples of serum from different animals can be added to these test tubes. The amount of precipitate formed can be measured. An example of this technique is illustrated in Figure 3.

The results show that humans are very closely related to chimpanzees, less so to baboons, and even less so to spider monkeys. Humans are only distantly related to dogs.

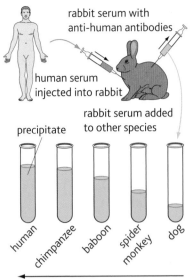

The results show that humans are very closely related to chimpanzees, less so to baboons and even less so to spider monkeys. Humans are only distantly related to dogs.

Figure 3 *Immunological comparisons of human serum with that of other species*

Behavioural evidence

Scientists can also study the behaviour of organisms. This can help them to work out the relationships between them. For example, humans are classified as primates. All primates show certain behavioural characteristics:

- increased period of dependency of the young on its mother, giving a longer period of parental care,
- most live in social groups and bond with each other by grooming behaviour,
- higher primates communicate by vocalisation and facial expression.

Summary questions

1. What is the evidence in Table 1 that rabbits are more closely related to humans than penguins are?

2. Name the bonds in the DNA molecule that are broken when DNA is heated.

3. The more closely related two organisms are, the more heat is needed to separate the hybrid DNA into two strands. Explain why.

4. Explain how finding the sequence of bases in the DNA of different organisms can help scientists to classify living things.

5. Scientists inject human serum into rabbits to carry out immunological studies. They wait for a time before they take serum from the rabbit to use in their investigations. Use your knowledge of the immune system to explain why.

9.3 Lamarck and Darwin

Learning objectives:

- What was the theory of evolution proposed by Lamarck?

- What was Darwin's theory of evolution?

- What is natural selection?

Specification reference: 3.2.3

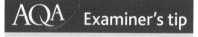

AQA Examiner's tip

You only need to know the theories of Lamarck and Darwin – but you should be aware that there are other theories.

Lamarck believed that giraffes originally had short necks. However, they 'needed' longer necks to reach food and gradually stretched their necks over their lifetimes. They passed this characteristic on to their offspring. Eventually all giraffes had long necks.

Figure 1 *How the giraffe developed its long neck – Lamarck's theory*

Until almost 200 years ago, most people believed that species had been specially created. They would use religion to explain the variety of life forms on Earth, and to explain where they had come from. Archbishop Ussher (1581–1656) used the scriptures to calculate the date of creation as 23rd October, 4004 BC. Later, Le Compte de Buffon (1701–1788) realised that many different kinds of animals were found in different continents. He proposed that animals could change into new forms under the influence of local conditions. He also realised that the Earth must be at least 75 000 years old.

Jean-Baptiste Lamarck (1744–1829)

Lamarck proposed a theory of evolution in 1809. He believed that the power to change was a natural property of an organism. He proposed that the environment caused the need for change, and that the organism changed in response to this. Organisms developed new characteristics because of an 'inner need'. These characteristics that an organism had acquired in its lifetime were then inherited by its offspring. For example, a blacksmith would develop stronger muscles than most people as a result of his work. Lamarck believed that the blacksmith's son would inherit these strong muscles. Although we no longer accept Lamarck's theory, it was a theory that did not require a creator.

Charles Darwin (1809–1882)

Charles Darwin spent many years as a naturalist on board HMS Beagle, 5 years of which was spent travelling round the world. He studied fossils in South America, and in particular was impressed by the enormous variety of life in the Galapagos Islands. This gave him considerable evidence for his theory of evolution, and the mechanism of natural selection that was behind it. In 1856 Darwin wrote an essay about his ideas, in preparation for publishing a book.

Another biologist, Alfred Russell Wallace (1823–1913) wrote to Darwin with his own ideas about evolution. Without knowing anything about Darwin's theory, he had come to the same conclusion himself. They decided to present their ideas together. They both published short papers in 1858. Shortly afterwards, Darwin published his book *'On the Origin of Species by Means of Natural Selection'*. It is usually Darwin who is remembered for his theory of evolution, while Wallace is largely forgotten.

Darwin's theory of evolution

Darwin's theory of evolution is based on three facts and two conclusions.

- **Fact 1** – all organisms over-reproduce. All female organisms produce far more gametes than can ever be fertilised and survive to maturity. For example, a female cod lays about 85 million eggs in a season, and an orchid produces about 1.7 million seeds in a year.

- **Fact 2** – despite this, the number of organisms of each species remains roughly stable from year to year, as a result of competition for resources such as food, water or light availability. This is observable. Populations do fluctuate but they always remain approximately constant.

- **Conclusion 1** – the continuous competition between individual organisms for environmental resources creates a 'struggle for existence'.
- **Fact 3** – there is variation of detail between the members of a species.

Darwin studied many organisms and noticed that there were small differences between them. He noticed that when people selectively bred pigeons, they could produce pigeons with a variety of features. You can see these in Figure 2.

- **Conclusion 2** – some individuals with particular variations will be more suited to survive and reproduce.

Any variation, however small, that gives one organism an advantage over another organism acts as a selective advantage in the 'struggle for existence'. The variation might be physical, behavioural or physiological. Darwin did not know anything about DNA and genes. We now realise that variation results from different combinations of alleles. Those organisms with favourable variations that make them well adapted to survive in their environment will pass on their alleles to their offspring. Organisms with unfavourable variations will not survive, so their alleles will not be passed on to their offspring. This is what is meant by **natural selection**.

Figure 2 *Variation in pigeons. A number of different types of pigeon can be bred from the ancestral rock pigeon (top)*

Application and How science works

The germ plasm theory

Weismann was a German biologist. Although he did not know about DNA and genetics, he developed the **germ plasm theory**. He believed that characteristics were inherited only by means of germ cells, i.e. the male and female gametes. He believed that body (or somatic) cells were not important in heredity.

Weismann carried out a famous experiment which is sometimes said to have 'proved' that Lamarck's theory of evolution was wrong. Weismann cut off the tails of hundreds of mice. He then bred them for 22 generations. Each baby mouse born had a normal tail.

a *Darwin believed that the ancestors of giraffes all had short necks, but their necks varied in size.*

> **1** Does this experiment prove that Lamarck was wrong? Explain your answer.

Comparing Lamarck's theory with Darwin's theory

One way to compare these two theories of evolution is to look at their different explanations for how the giraffe gained its long neck, see Figures 1 and 3.

b *Those giraffes who, by chance, had slightly longer necks were able to reach more food. They survived better and reproduced more, passing on their alleles to their offspring.*

> ### Summary questions
>
> **1** Swimming birds, such as ducks, have skin between the digits of their feet. These 'webbed feet' enable them to swim effectively. Suggest how Lamarck and Darwin would explain how ducks' feet became webbed.
>
> **2** Figure 2 shows a variety of features that can be seen when pigeons are selectively bred. However, these features are very rarely seen in wild pigeons. Use Darwin's theory to explain why.

c *Eventually all giraffes had long necks.*

Figure 3 *How the giraffe developed its long neck – Darwin's theory*

9.4   Natural selection in action

Learning objectives:

- ◼ How can you tell natural selection is happening in a population?

- ◼ How is a new species formed?

Specification reference: 3.2.3

Figure 1 *Industrial melanism in the peppered moth. Each photograph shows a speckled and a melanic moth*

Natural selection can be seen at work over quite a short period of time. This is shown by changes in the peppered moth, *Biston betularia* population during industrialisation of Manchester.

Applications and how science works

Industrial melanism

Look at Figure 1. This shows the peppered moth, *Biston betularia*. Up until the middle of the 19th century, the only known form of this moth was the speckled kind. In 1845, a single black form of *Biston betularia* was found near Manchester. By the end of the 19th century, 98% of the peppered moths in the Manchester area were of the black, or melanic, kind.

The change in these moths happened at the same time as the growth of heavy industry in Manchester. Before the industrial revolution, the air around Manchester was clean and the tree trunks were covered in lichen. Against tree trunks like this, the speckled kind is well camouflaged and less likely to be eaten by a bird. You can see this in the top photograph in Figure 1. However, with the growth of heavy industry in Manchester, the air became polluted and the lichens died. Tree trunks became blackened with soot. In this environment, the melanic moth was much better camouflaged, as you can see in the bottom photograph in Figure 1.

This is a simple example of natural selection in action. In a polluted environment the speckled moths are more likely to be eaten, so few would survive to pass on their alleles. By contrast, the melanic form is better camouflaged. Therefore it is more likely to survive and breed, passing on its alleles to its offspring.

In the 1950s, Bernard Kettlewell carried out experiments to prove that natural selection caused the change in frequency of the two kinds of moth. He bred very large numbers of the speckled and melanic forms of the moth. He marked them and released them in two different areas. One area was polluted Birmingham, where 90% of the peppered moths were melanic. The other area was unpolluted Dorset where no melanic moths had been found.

Kettlewell filmed birds, such as robins and hedge sparrows, feeding in the two areas. He found that they fed more often on the moths that were not camouflaged against the background.

He also recaptured as many as possible of the moths that he released. He counted the number of moths of each kind. The table shows some of his results.

Site		Non-melanic	Melanic
Dorset 1955 (unpolluted)	released	496	473
	recaptured	62	30
	% recaptured		
Birmingham 1953 (polluted)	released	137	447
	recaptured	18	123
	% recaptured		

1 Calculate the missing figures on the table above.

2 Can you suggest any improvements to Kettlewell's investigation?

3 Does Kettlewell's investigation prove that natural selection is responsible for the change in frequency of the different kinds of peppered moth? Give reasons for your answer.

Speciation

You will remember from Topic 9.1 that a species is a population of similar organisms that are able to interbreed and produce fertile offspring. New species arise from pre-existing species by a very slow process of evolution.

Speciation is the development of new species. This happens when different populations of the same species evolve in different ways. Speciation is normally thought to happen by a gradual process.

- Part of the population becomes isolated in some way that prevents them breeding with the rest of the population. This is usually because of a physical barrier such as a river or a range of mountains. We call this **geographical isolation**.

- The word **phenotype** is used to describe the features that an organism has as a result of its alleles and the effects of the environment. The environment experienced by the two separated populations will be different. This means that phenotypes that are advantageous in one environment may not be advantageous in the other environment. As a result, natural selection favours different phenotypes in each environment. Gradually, the frequency of different alleles in the two populations becomes different.

- You will remember from Topic 8.3 that a mutation is a change in the base sequence of DNA. By chance, a new allele may occur because of a mutation. Mutations are not normally beneficial, but occasionally they are. The new allele may code for a feature that gives an organism a selective advantage. This organism will survive, reproduce and pass on its alleles. Gradually, the new allele becomes more common in the population.

- Over a long time, the genetic differences in the two populations become much greater. Eventually, one population has changed so much that it can no longer interbreed with the other population. For example, one group may now have a slightly different courtship ritual from the other group, or they may reproduce at different times of the year. This is called **reproductive isolation**. Now that the two groups cannot interbreed, they can be called new species.

Darwin's finches

Figure 2 shows some birds that Darwin studied in the Galapagos Islands. They are often called 'Darwin's finches'.

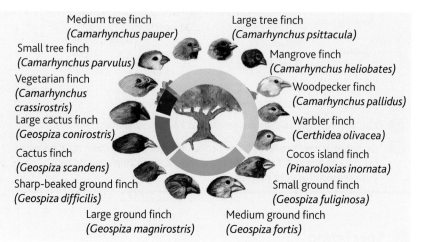

Key

- mainly insects
- mainly seeds
- cactus seeds and parts
- buds and fruits

Medium tree finch
(*Camarhynchus pauper*)

Large tree finch
(*Camarhynchus psittacula*)

Small tree finch
(*Camarhynchus parvulus*)

Mangrove finch
(*Camarhynchus heliobates*)

Vegetarian finch
(*Camarhynchus crassirostris*)

Woodpecker finch
(*Camarhynchus pallidus*)

Large cactus finch
(*Geospiza conirostris*)

Warbler finch
(*Certhidea olivacea*)

Cactus finch
(*Geospiza scandens*)

Cocos island finch
(*Pinaroloxias inornata*)

Sharp-beaked ground finch
(*Geospiza difficilis*)

Small ground finch
(*Geospiza fuliginosa*)

Large ground finch
(*Geospiza magnirostris*)

Medium ground finch
(*Geospiza fortis*)

Figure 2 *Different kinds of finches found in the Galapagos Islands*

The finches are all adapted to the environment on different islands, where different food sources are available. Darwin believed that these finches had all evolved from a common ancestor that came from the mainland and ate seeds.

The ancestral population of finches arrived on the islands. They showed **variation**.

Environmental conditions were different on the different islands, e.g. different food sources were available. The finch populations were geographically isolated. Those individuals with phenotypes most suited to the conditions on each island survived, reproduced, and passed on their alleles to their offspring.

Mutations arose, producing new alleles. For example, some mutations may have resulted in a finch with a better beak shape for obtaining its food. Finches with the new allele would survive and reproduce, so that the frequency of this allele increased.

Eventually mutations occurred that affected the reproduction of the finches, for example, their courtship rituals. This meant that now the populations on the different islands could no longer interbreed. They were now separate species.

Summary questions

1 Soon after penicillin was first discovered, it was found that penicillin did not kill some bacteria as easily as before. Some bacteria were developing resistance to penicillin. The penicillin resistance was the result of a mutation. The mutated allele carried the code for penicillinase, an enzyme that breaks down penicillin. Explain how natural selection caused the development of penicillin-resistant bacteria.

2 Scientists think that a clouded leopard found on the islands of Borneo and Sumatra is a different species from the clouded leopard found on the mainland.

The two kinds of clouded leopard have different skin markings. Scientists estimate that the two kinds of clouded leopard have evolved separately for 1.4 million years. They also found 40 differences when they compared the DNA of the two populations.

a Use this information to explain what is meant by geographical isolation.

b Use your knowledge of natural selection to explain how the two populations of clouded leopard have developed differences.

c Suggest why scientists believe that these populations are different species.

9.5 Fossil evidence

Learning objectives:

- What are fossils?

- How does the fossil record provide evidence for evolution?

- How can we date fossils?

- How can we use fossil evidence?

Specification reference: 3.2.3

Fossils are any form of preserved remains from a living organism. You can see some examples in Figure 1. Fossils may consist of whole organisms, preserved in ice, amber, bogs, or rocks. Fossils may also consist of imprints such as footprints and trails, part of the organism, or fossilised faecal pellets. When most organisms die, they usually decompose, or get eaten by a scavenger. Fossilisation is therefore rare. This is why we do not have a perfect fossil record showing all stages in the evolution of many species, such as humans. Even when fossilisation does occur, the soft parts of the organism may decompose. An impression of the organism may remain on fine-grained sediments, or hard parts of the organism may be trapped in sediments. The sediments gradually turn to rock. The hard parts of the organism may be gradually replaced by mineral deposits, or they may slowly dissolve and be replaced by fine materials that slowly harden to rock over time. Sometimes great detail is preserved in this way.

People were aware of fossils before there were any theories of evolution. There were several different theories offered. Some people thought they were creatures that died during Noah's flood; some thought they were earlier creations.

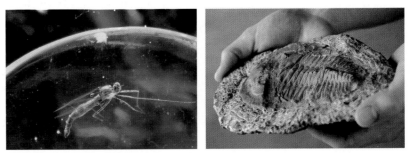

Figure 1 *Some examples of fossils*

💡 Dating fossils

In general, older rocks have fewer kinds of fossils, and they are simpler in structure. Fossils also give us evidence that many species used to exist but are now extinct. We know that environmental conditions changed enormously on Earth in the past, so natural selection would account for the evolutionary change seen in these fossils.

Some methods for dating fossils depend on the rate of decay of radioactive isotopes. Isotopes are different forms of the same atom. Radioactive atoms slowly decay over time and scientists know the rate at which they decay. It is measured in terms of a 'half-life'. The half-life of an isotope is the time taken for half the radioactive atoms present to decay. This provides a reliable 'clock' that is not affected by temperature, pressure or water availability.

Carbon dating can be used to date organic materials. A small amount of radioactive carbon, ^{14}C, is present in carbon dioxide molecules in the air all the time. This is taken in by plants in photosynthesis, so the ^{14}C becomes incorporated in molecules in the plants. Animals will gain ^{14}C when they eat the plants. Living organisms have a fairly constant amount of ^{14}C. When an organism dies no more ^{14}C is incorporated and the ^{14}C

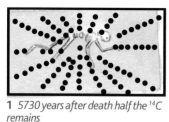

1 *5730 years after death half the* ^{14}C *remains*

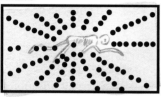

2 *16 704 years after death one-eighth remains*

3 *70 000 years after death almost all has disappeared. But sophisicated* ^{14}C *dating can find the age of even older organic objects.*

Figure 2 *Carbon dating*
A dead body loses ^{14}C *by radiation at a measurable rate by which the body's age can be determined. The margin of error increases with the time span.*

starts to decay. The half-life for ^{14}C is about 5700 years. By measuring the ratio of ^{14}C to normal ^{12}C in a sample, scientists can work out its age. The half-life of ^{14}C is fairly short. After 30 000 years there is only about 3% of the original ^{14}C left in a sample. Carbon dating is not normally used to date samples more than 40–50 000 years old, although sophisticated methods can find the age of even older samples.

Potassium-argon dating. Potassium-40 (^{40}K) decays into argon-40 (^{40}Ar) and calcium-40 (^{40}Ca) at a known rate. The half-life of ^{40}K is approximately 1.25 billion years. Scientists can work out the age of a sample by measuring how much ^{40}Ar it contains. ^{40}K is only found in significant amounts in volcanic rocks, so this method is really only useful to date volcanic rocks. However, fossils are usually found in sedimentary rocks. Nevertheless, the method can still be used to date fossils. This is done by **stratigraphy**.

Stratigraphy is the study of layers in the rock. Generally, new rock forms on top of older rocks. This means that, in general, the lower down a fossil is found, the older it is. Look at Figure 4. A fossil is found in sedimentary rocks, sandwiched between two layers of volcanic rock. Using potassium-argon dating, we know that the volcanic layer underneath the fossil is 1.7 million years old, and the volcanic layer above the fossil is 1.5 million years old. This tells us that the fossil is between 1.5 and 1.7 million years old.

However, a skilled geologist is needed to date fossils by stratigraphy. This is because earthquakes, fault lines and volcanic eruptions may split the rocks, or bend and tilt them. When this happens, it is possible to find older fossils on top of newer ones. Sometimes fossils are washed out of their layer by weathering and heavy rain. Look at Figure 5. A fossil is found at A. However, it was washed out of the layer of rock at C. Palaeontologists, who study fossils, need to investigate rock layer C if they wish to find more fossils related to the fossil at A.

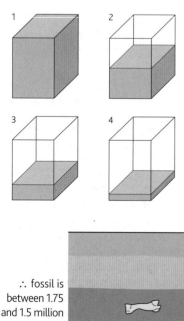

∴ fossil is between 1.75 and 1.5 million years old

volcanic ash
1 500 000 years B.P.

sedimentary rock

volcanic ash
1 750 000 years B.P.

Figure 3 *Potassium-argon dating.*
Potassium-40 decays into argon-40 and calcium-40 at the rate shown in this diagram,
1 *The mass of potassium-40 in newly formed volcanic rock*
2 *The proportion of potassium-40 remaining after one half life (1310 million years)*
3 *the proportion left after another 1310 million years (two half lives)*
4 *The proportion left after another 1310 million years (three half lives).*

Fossil is found at A because it has been washed out of the sedimentary rock layer at C. It does not come from the layer of sedimentary rock at B.

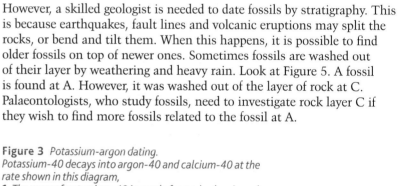

Figure 4 *Dating a fossil in sedimentary rock using potassium-argon dating*

Figure 5 *A problem with stratigraphy*

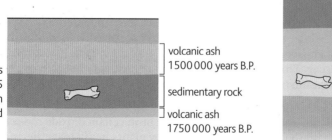

Using fossil evidence

We have already seen that fossilisation is rare, and of course, many fossils will never be found. This means that it is difficult to obtain a clear fossil record showing how organisms evolved. One of the best fossil records that we have is for the horse. This can be seen in Figure 6. It shows how the modern horse evolved from a small animal called *Hyracotherium* that lived about 54 million years ago.

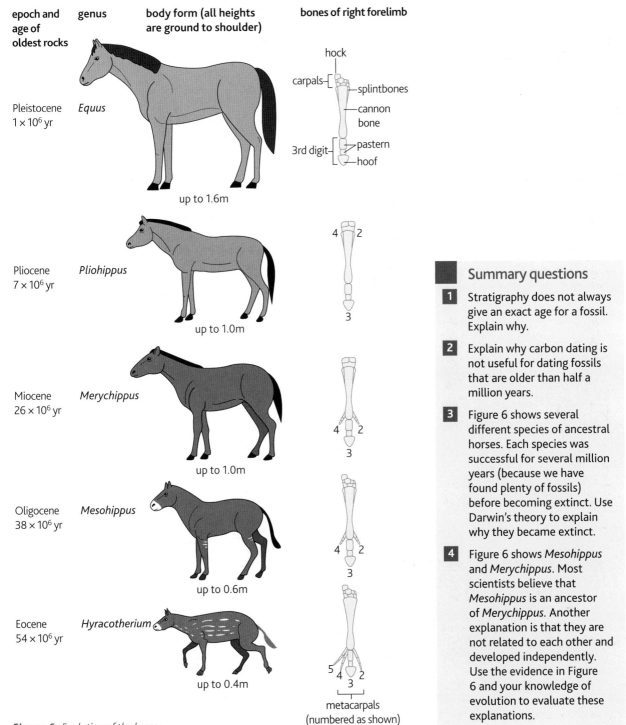

Figure 6 *Evolution of the horse*

Summary questions

1 Stratigraphy does not always give an exact age for a fossil. Explain why.

2 Explain why carbon dating is not useful for dating fossils that are older than half a million years.

3 Figure 6 shows several different species of ancestral horses. Each species was successful for several million years (because we have found plenty of fossils) before becoming extinct. Use Darwin's theory to explain why they became extinct.

4 Figure 6 shows *Mesohippus* and *Merychippus*. Most scientists believe that *Mesohippus* is an ancestor of *Merychippus*. Another explanation is that they are not related to each other and developed independently. Use the evidence in Figure 6 and your knowledge of evolution to evaluate these explanations.

9.6 Evolution of humans

Learning objectives:

- How might humans and apes be related?

- How can we tell from fossils whether an animal was bipedal?

- How can we estimate the size of a fossil animal's brain and what its diet was?

Specification reference: 3.2.3

In Topic 9.5 you saw that we have good fossil evidence for the evolution of the horse. However, tracing the evolution of humans using the fossil record is much more difficult. We have found very few fossils of early humans and human ancestors, and the fossils we have are often incomplete. As a result, scientists have different interpretations of the evidence. New fossil finds sometimes mean that we have to change our previous views.

Hominids

You learned in Topic 9.1 that humans are in the order Primates. Other primates include monkeys, apes, lemurs and tarsiers. These are all animals that are adapted for living in trees. Scientists believe that humans and apes diverged from monkeys about 25 to 30 million years ago. Apes and humans diverged between 5 and 10 million years ago. This means that humans are thought to have evolved from a tree-dwelling ancestor.

The word **hominid** is used to describe members of the family Hominidae. Traditionally, humans were considered to be the only living members of this family, although there are extinct species that also belonged to Hominidae. Biochemical evidence now shows such close similarities between humans and the great apes (gorillas, chimpanzees and orang-utans) that many experts classify the great apes as Hominidae as well.

Note that humans and apes share a common ancestor, believed to have existed between 5 and 7 million years ago. Darwin did not say that humans evolved from apes, although this is a common misconception. Two of the most important changes that happened as humans evolved were a change to walking on two legs (bipedalism) and an increase in brain size.

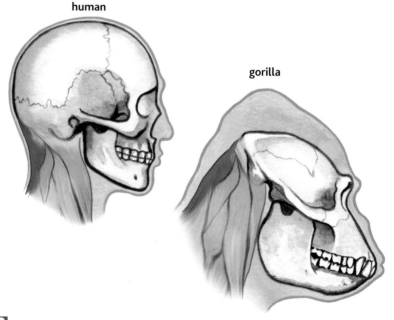

Figure 1 *Comparing a human and a gorilla*

How can we tell if a fossil animal was bipedal?

Look at Figures 1 and 2 which show the neck and skull of a human and a gorilla. A gorilla is an ape, and it walks using four limbs in a style called 'knuckle-walking'. Humans are bipedal.

You will see that the human's head is well-balanced on its backbone. The backbone meets with the skull through a hole in the skull called the **foramen magnum** ('large hole'). In humans, the foramen magnum is underneath the skull. Because the head is balanced on the backbone, the muscles that hold the head in place are small and attached to the skull low down.

By contrast, the gorilla's skull has a foramen magnum at the back. It needs large, strong muscles to hold the skull in position. These muscles are attached high up on the skull. You can tell where muscles are attached to the skull because there are bumps and ridges present.

Humans have a short, broad hipbone giving a basin-shaped pelvis. This shows that they are bipedal because it supports the body organs immediately above them. The gorilla has a long, narrow hip bone.

In humans, the thigh bone (femur) is straight, with a long neck so it can fit into the hip bone. The knees are directly underneath the pelvis, and the knee joint locks when the leg is straightened. This allows the human to stand upright for long periods of time without expending too much energy. The gorilla cannot straighten its legs. The knees bend outwards from the pelvis.

The human foot is arched, and the big toe is parallel with the others. This means that the foot is adapted for walking. Gorillas have a flat foot with an opposable big toe, adapted for grasping.

Humans have a vertebral column with two slight curves, making it S-shaped. This means that the head is directly above the centre of gravity. The gorilla has an arched vertebral column which supports the weight of the body while knuckle-walking.

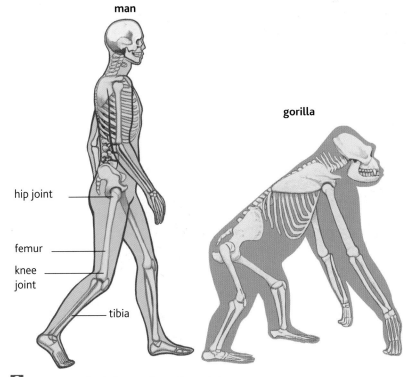

man

gorilla

hip joint

femur

knee joint

tibia

Figure 2 *The skeletons of a gorilla and a human*

How can we tell the size of the brain?

We have already seen that when organisms die, the soft parts usually decay. This means that we will not find a fossil with a brain. However, we do find fossil skulls. We know that the brain fits snugly into the skull of a living organism, so we can estimate the size of the brain by finding the volume inside the skull. This is called the **cranial capacity**. One way to do this is to tip the skull upside down and pour dry sand into the foramen magnum. When the skull is full of sand, it is carefully tipped out into a measuring cylinder. The volume of sand collected is an estimate of the volume of brain that was inside the skull.

How can we tell what food it ate?

The teeth of an organism can tell you something about the kind of food it ate. Teeth are hard and so they are often preserved.

- Teeth with thick enamel are adapted for eating hard foods like hard seeds and dry nuts. Thinner enamel is associated with a softer diet, like fruit.
- Teeth can be examined under the microscope for scratches called **microwear**. Hard, tough food sources like dry nuts and tough roots would leave more scratches than a softer diet.
- Animals with large jaws and bony crests on skulls would have had strong jaws with powerful muscles to move them. This would mean that the animal could eat tough, fibrous food. Smaller jaws with less powerful muscles are seen in animals that eat softer food.
- Apes have fairly large canine teeth. However, this does not mean that they only eat meat. Canines are particularly large in male apes. They are used to display aggression. Therefore, canine teeth cannot tell you anything about the diet of human ancestors. However, hominids had smaller canines than apes, and this change meant that the jaw could develop more side-to-side grinding movements. This is useful for chewing.
- Ape jaws are U-shaped but human jaws are more parabolic in shape. You can see this in Figure 3.

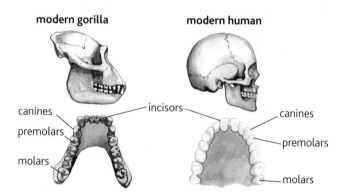

Figure 3 *The teeth of an ape and a human*

Summary questions

1 Suggest why we have found very few fossil remains of human ancestors.

2 Biochemical evidence suggests that the great apes are closely related to humans. Give examples of what this evidence might be.

9.7 Australopithecines

Learning objectives:

- What are the characteristics of *Australopithecus* thought to be?

- What is the evidence that supports *Australopithecus*?

Specification reference: 3.2.3

The **Australopithecines** were early hominids. They evolved in Africa about 5 million years ago, and survived until about a million years ago. No fossils of this genus have been found outside Africa. Several different species of *Australopithecus* have been found, but scientists believe that many of these were not human ancestors. It is thought that Australopithecines lived side by side with early *Homo* for about a million years.

The earlier Australopithecines were small creatures about the size of a chimpanzee. They seem to have evolved later into other species which were much bigger and more muscular, as well as giving rise to our genus, *Homo*. Their brain size, compared to their body size, was only a little bigger than an ape's. They had ape-like heads with a flat face, flat nose, no chin and powerful jaws. They also walked upright, but probably with a slightly more 'rolling gait' than modern humans.

Australopithecus afarensis

Figure 1 shows a skeleton discovered in 1974 in Ethiopia, nicknamed Lucy, and an artist's impression of what she would have looked like.

Australopithecus afarensis is thought to have lived between 4 and 2.5 million years ago. Scientists believe that they lived in family groups and ate mainly plant food. They had fairly long arms compared to their legs, and there is evidence of ape-like wrists and curled fingers. It is thought that they lived in treed savannah. This would be grassland with trees, and it is likely that they were still very able at climbing trees, to escape predators and find food. They may have slept in trees at night. They almost certainly gave rise to the other australopithecines and to humans.

Other Australopithecines

Figure 2 shows the skull and teeth of a fossil *Australopithecus boisei*. It is thought that this species lived between 2.5 and 1 million years ago. Most scientists believe that it is not a human ancestor.

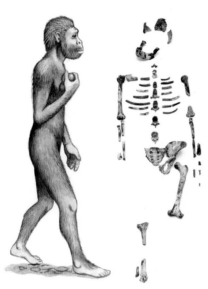

Figure 1 *(a) Skeleton of Lucy and (b) Reconstruction of* Australopithecus afarensis

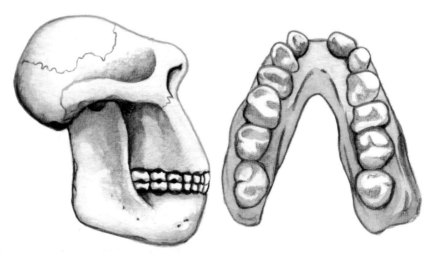

Figure 2 *Skull and teeth of* Australopithecus boisei

Figure 3 *The Laetoli footprints*

The Laetoli footprints

Figure 3 shows the Laetoli footprints, a set of fossil footprints found in 1976 at Laetoli in Tanzania. The footprints are 3.6 million years old and are believed to have been made by *Australopithecus afarensis*.

The footprints appear to have been made by two Australopithecines, one large and one small, walking upright through volcanic ash. Some people think a third australopithecine was following behind, stepping in the adult's footprints. Shortly afterwards, another layer of volcanic ash was laid down, preserving the footprints. By studying these footprints, we can see that the creatures walked by hitting the ground with their heel first, and then used their toes to push off at the end of the stride. This is how modern humans walk. It is also possible to tell that the big toe was in line with the rest of the foot, not at an angle as an ape's toe would be.

Summary questions

1 We do not have a complete skeleton of Lucy (Figure 1). What is the evidence that she walked upright?

2 Figure 1 shows an artist's idea of what Lucy looked like. Which aspects of this reconstruction are factual, and which are intelligent guesses?

3 How would the Laetoli footprints have been dated?

9.8 The first humans

Learning objectives:

- What was *Homo habilis* like?
- What sort of tools did *Homo habilis* use?
- How did *Homo habilis* use the tools?

Specification reference: 3.2.3

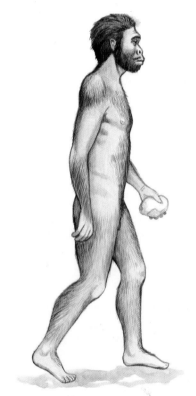

Figure 1 *Reconstruction of* Homo habilis

Homo habilis

Homo habilis means 'handy man'. It lived between about 2 and 1.5 million years ago, and was no more than 1.5 metres tall. Scientists currently believe that this was the first member of our genus, *Homo*. *Homo habilis* had a larger brain than the australopithecines, although it was still half the size of a modern human brain. It had a smaller, less projecting face. You can see this in Figure 1.

The teeth of *Homo habilis* show a more parabola-shaped jaw and narrower back teeth than the australopithecines. Finds near its bones suggest that it made simple stone tools. Scientists believe that it hunted small, and maybe larger, animals, as well as scavenging meat from carcasses killed by carnivores. It probably gathered plant foods and built simple shelters.

The brain of *Homo habilis* was larger than an australopithecine's, but more importantly, bulges inside the skull suggest that the brain had a well-developed Broca's area. Broca's area is important in speech production. However, the larynx may not have been capable of making the range of sounds that a modern human can make.

The first tools

Early humans were weaker than the big carnivores, but they made up for this by making tools. The very first tools were probably pieces of bone or sharp sticks that were used temporarily and then discarded. Remains of these tools will not be found. However, stone tools remain. We have found remains of simple stone tools in Ethiopia dating from about 2.5 million years ago. These show that early humans hit one rock as a hammer against another to make sharp flakes. These were probably used to cut up meat. The remaining pebble made a jagged chopper-like tool that could have been held in the hand, although some scientists think that this was only a waste product, and the sharp flakes were the real tools. You can see how these tools were made in Figure 2. This is called the **Oldowan culture**, after the Olduvai Gorge in Tanzania where many of these tools were found.

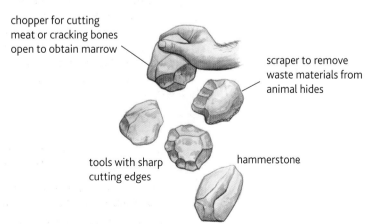

chopper for cutting meat or cracking bones open to obtain marrow

scraper to remove waste materials from animal hides

tools with sharp cutting edges

hammerstone

Figure 2 *Making early stone tools*

How do we know how stone tools were made and used?

Stone tools can be examined carefully under the microscope, so we can see how flakes were removed from a core stone. We can try to make tools ourselves, and see whether we can reproduce the stone tool we have found.

Sometimes tiny pieces of stone are found in animal bones that are excavated. This is evidence that stone tools were used to cut up meat. Some animal bones show the teeth marks of large carnivores, with cut marks from stone tools over the top. This tells us that a large carnivore killed the animal, but an early human with a stone tool later scavenged the carcass for meat.

We can also make stone tools like the ones that we find, and then try them out to see what we can use them for.

Use of the hands

Homo habilis had hands that were more like a modern human. The joint at the base of the thumb was more mobile, giving an **opposable thumb**. This means that the thumb can grip objects against any of the other digits. As a result, *Homo habilis* had two different grips, like modern humans:

- a **power grip** (e.g. gripping a walking stick)
- a **precision grip** (e.g. holding a pencil).

You can see this in Figure 3.

Figure 3 *Power and precision grips*

Summary questions

1. *Homo habilis* may have developed simple language. Suggest the advantages of developing speech.

2. Some scientists think that the australopithecines used tools. Suggest reasons why we cannot be certain about this.

3. If we make replica stone tools and find things that we can do with the tools, does this tell us how *Homo habilis* made and used the tools?

9.9 *Homo erectus*

Learning objectives:

■ What are the characteristics of *Homo erectus*?

■ What sort of tools did *Homo erectus* use?

■ How would *Homo erectus* use fire?

■ When did *Homo erectus* start to migrate out of Africa?

Specification reference: 3.2.3

By 1.6 million years ago, *Homo habilis* had given way to *Homo erectus*. This means 'upright man'. This species of human colonised new parts of the world and had a bigger brain, developing better technology. By 200 000 years ago, however, it had become extinct.

■ Features of *Homo erectus*

Homo erectus had a brain that was a little larger than *Homo habilis*. Its skeleton was like that of a modern human, although it was a little heavier. Its height was also similar to that of modern humans. You can see a reconstruction of *Homo erectus* in Figure 1.

The main difference between *Homo erectus* and modern humans is the skull, which was very different from ours. The cranium was flat, with large brow ridges. There were larger chewing muscles, and a big bump on the back of the skull where large neck muscles attached. Their teeth and jaws were larger than modern humans' because they ate a largely unrefined diet. However, they ate more meat than their ancestors and were able to soften food through cooking. *Homo erectus* was able to use fire. They also had language, though their larynx was not as well developed as a modern human's.

There is evidence that *Homo erectus* were not simply plant gatherers and scavengers, but active hunters as well. It is thought that they worked in groups to plan and carry out hunting expeditions. One site shows that they used fire to drive large herds of migrating animals into a gully in a steep-sided valley.

Figure 1 *Reconstruction of* Homo erectus

■ Stone tools

Homo erectus developed new tool-making techniques. They made more different kinds of stone tools, including hand-axes, cleavers, scrapers and flakes. This type of tool is called the **Acheulian culture**. You can see how these tools were made in Figure 2. They were slimmer and had straighter cutting edges than earlier tools.

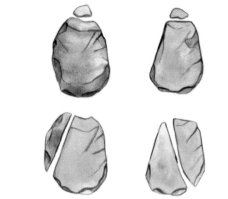

Figure 2 *Acheulian culture*

■ The use of fire

Scientists are more or less certain that *Homo erectus* could use fire, probably repeatedly using embers from natural forest fires. This is because they have found ash and charcoal from fires, along with burnt animal bones, in caves alongside *Homo erectus* remains. At some stage early humans would have learned how to make fire.

Using fire would have been very important to early humans:

- It produced warmth, which was useful for those migrating out of Africa.
- It was a source of light, allowing them to extend their day and occupy the deeper parts of caves.
- It protected them from wild animals.
- It enabled them to cook food. This meant that fibrous or tough food that could not be eaten raw was available as a source of food. It also meant that eating was a communal activity.

■ Migration

Most scientists agree that *Homo erectus* populations migrated out of Africa around a million years ago. Fossil forms of *Homo erectus* have been found in other continents, including Asia and Europe. Some of these fossils look different from the African fossils because of natural selection in the different environments.

Summary questions

1 Scientists believe that *Homo erectus* hunted animals rather than scavenging carcasses that had been killed by predators. Suggest how they could work this out from the remains of animal bones.

2 Scientists believe that *Homo erectus* ate their food together, around a fire. Suggest the advantages of this.

3 Fire provided light, so *Homo erectus* could extend day-length. Suggest the advantages of this.

9.10 The Neanderthals

Learning objectives:

■ How were *Homo neanderthalensis* related to modern humans?

■ What are the characteristics of *Homo neanderthalensis* and how did they live?

Specification reference: 3.2.3

Homo neanderthalensis are named from the Neanderthal Valley in Germany where many fossils were found. They lived mainly in Europe between 70 000 and 40 000 years ago. They were highly adapted to life in cold northern Europe, and they had a highly developed culture. However, most experts believe that they are not ancestors of modern humans and they became extinct by about 30 000 years ago. Some people believe that they interbred with modern humans. However, most people think they died out because of competition with modern humans.

■ Neanderthal man

You can see a reconstruction of *Homo neanderthalensis* in Figure 1.

You will see that the Neanderthals had skulls rather like those of *Homo erectus* with heavy brow ridges and a sloping forehead. They also had a bump on the back of the head where powerful neck muscles attached. Neanderthals were very muscular and strong, with large joints and hands. Their brains were a little larger than modern humans, although their brain: body mass ratio was a little lower. They seem to have been very well adapted to the cold environment that they lived in, as winters in northern Europe were very cold at this time.

Neanderthal tools

The Neanderthals made sophisticated tools. Their tool culture is called **Mousterian** from Le Moustier in France where many tools were found. You can see some of their tools in Figure 2.

They made stone flakes by breaking flakes off a stone core, but they then used a softer hammer of bone or antler to refine the flake. After this, they used a technique called pressure-flaking to sharpen the knife edge.

Figure 1 *Homo neanderthalensis*

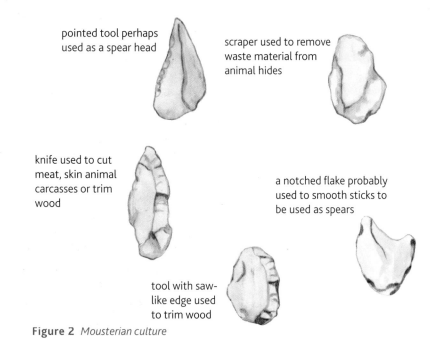

pointed tool perhaps used as a spear head

scraper used to remove waste material from animal hides

knife used to cut meat, skin animal carcasses or trim wood

a notched flake probably used to smooth sticks to be used as spears

tool with saw-like edge used to trim wood

Figure 2 *Mousterian culture*

Hunting

The Neanderthals were highly successful hunters. In the cold winters of the Ice Age they would have relied on meat for food. The remains of animal bones that we find show that they mainly ate large animals like bison, wild cattle, woolly mammoths, etc. They would have used the bones, fur and sinews of the animals for clothing, shelters, tools, etc. Although we cannot be sure how they killed their prey, they must have worked together in large groups. They would have planned their hunting expeditions very carefully. They probably used fire to drive herds of animals over cliffs, and they probably built traps. While the men went hunting, the women and children would have gathered plant foods like berries and roots, and smaller animals like lizards, insects and rodents, from nearer their home base.

Homes and clothing

In some places, groups of up to 40 Neanderthals lived in caves. Remains of such communities have been found in France. In one place, the remains of a posthole have been found, suggesting that they built a wall of skins to keep wind and rain out of the cave. In other places, the Neanderthals built shelters using wood, animal skins and heavy mammoth bones. The remains of hearths show that they used fire to warm their homes, and that they used iron pyrites to create sparks that would set fire to dried bracket fungi.

Although clothing has not survived, scientists have found tools that would have been used to sew furry animal skins together with sinews.

Neanderthal culture

Neanderthals were the first people to bury their dead. Graves have been found, showing that dead people were deliberately placed in the grave. Many had grave goods with them, such as flowers, meat and stone tools. It seems likely that they may have had a religion and a belief in an afterlife. The remains of an old man have been found in Iraq. He was half blinded, had a withered arm and was crippled by arthritis. He could not have survived to old age unless he had been cared for by others.

There is evidence that Neanderthals used dyes to paint their bodies, but very few examples of Neanderthal art have been found. In 2003 a flint was found in a cave in France that had once been used by Neanderthals. You can see this in Figure 3. A bone has been pushed through the flint to look like eyes. The flint has been worked to make it more face-like.

animal bone wedged in hole by flint flakes

flint worked to improve its likeness to a face

10.5 cm

Figure 3 *Neanderthal 'face'*

Summary questions

1 Suggest how scientists can find out what animals Neanderthals ate.

2 Some people think that Neanderthals interbred with modern humans. Other people think that the two populations remained separated. Suggest ways in which scientists might investigate these theories.

9.11 Modern humans

Learning objectives:

- What were the early modern humans like?
- How did early modern humans live?
- What were the competitive advantages of modern humans over the Neanderthals?

Specification reference: 3.2.3

The first remains of fully modern humans, *Homo sapiens*, were found at Cro-Magnon in France. These remains date back to 40000 years ago. Although it is thought that modern humans are closely related to Neanderthals, most experts think that Neanderthals were not ancestors of modern humans.

There are three theories:

- *Homo sapiens* and *Homo neanderthalensis* developed independently and modern humans gradually replaced earlier forms.
- *Homo sapiens* evolved in Africa, and then migrated out of Africa about 100000 years ago. They gradually replaced the earlier forms of *Homo sapiens*.
- Modern humans arose in one place and then interbred with the older forms of human to produce the different races of humans that we have today.

Homo sapiens

The early modern humans, often called the Cro-Magnons, were taller and less powerful than the Neanderthals. Look at Figure 1. You can see that the Cro-Magnons had a more rounded braincase, an upright forehead, and very small brow-ridges. The face does not protrude forward and there is a well-developed chin.

Cro-Magnon stone tools

Cro-Magnons used flaked stone tools and weapons like the Neanderthals. However, they developed a very efficient technique to make stone tools called indirect percussion. You can see this in Figure 2.

Figure 1 *Cro-Magnon man*

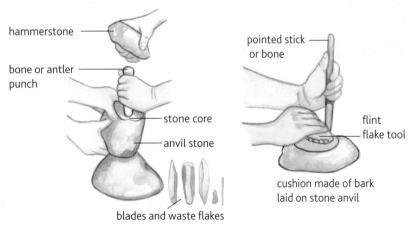

Figure 2 *Cro-Magnon tools*

First they made a punch from stone, wood, bone or antler. They hit the punch against a stone to split off a narrow, sharp-edged flake. They then made the blade edge on the flake even sharper by pressure-flaking. This meant pressing a pointed tool along the sharp edge, breaking off tiny flakes. They could make more tools, with much finer blades, from just one stone than any other human ancestor.

The Cro-Magnons also made a greater variety of tools than any previous hominids. They used antler, bone and ivory as well as wood and stone. They made tools such as needles for sewing, handles, fish hooks and harpoons.

Cro-Magnon hunting

Cro-Magnons had better tools and hunting techniques than the Neanderthals. They developed tools for throwing spears, so that they could aim a spear from a greater distance. This meant that they did not need to get so close to their prey, so the prey was less likely to be aware of their presence. They developed harpoons for killing fish, which became an important part of the diet in many areas. They also built traps and snares to kill birds, wolves and larger animals such as bison.

The Cro-Magnons were aware of the migration of animals and they would move to different sites when the animals moved.

Homes and clothing

Like the Neanderthals, Cro-Magnons sometimes lived in caves. Some built shelters of wood, animal skins, stones and animal bones. Many of these homes were seasonal as they moved on when the food supply ran out.

We have some evidence of the clothing used by Cro-Magnons. This is not because it has survived, but because the Cro-Magnons produced carvings and cave drawings. These show that they made clothing out of animal skins, including close-fitting hoods, boots, mittens and trousers.

Art and culture

Small, carved objects have been found from about 30 000 years ago. Cave paintings have also been found from about 25 000 years ago. You can see some examples in Figure 3.

The Cro-Magnons, like the Neanderthals, buried their dead. The graves often contain elaborate grave goods, such as necklaces of bones, shells and teeth, spears, and clay figurines. The dead figures were often covered with red ochre. This indicates they had some kind of religious belief and perhaps believed in an afterlife.

Figure 3 *Examples of Cro-Magnon art*

Summary questions

1. The Neanderthals were well adapted to cold northern Europe, yet they became extinct and modern humans survived. Suggest reasons why Cro-Magnons were able to compete successfully with Neanderthals.

2. Figure 4 shows a graph of total tooth area compared to body weight for a number of different organisms.

   a Describe the trends shown by the graph.

   b Explain what these data show about the diet of the different organisms.

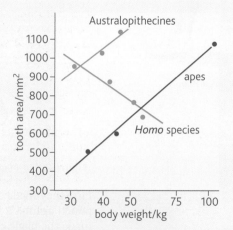

Figure 4 *Total tooth area compared to body weight for several different organisms*

9.12 The hominid chronology

Learning objectives:

- What are the relationships between the different hominids?

- Why is the hunter-gatherer lifestyle important?

- How did human social groups develop and why are they advantageous?

Specification reference: 3.2.3

As you have seen, it is very difficult to work out the relationships between different kinds of hominids. Experts disagree about how to interpret the evidence. Also, we have limited fossil evidence for many of these stages. Table 1 summarises the evidence.

Table 1 *Hominid chronology*

Time/million years ago	Living hominids
0.15	*Homo sapiens* evolved, probably in Africa. They migrated out of Africa 100 000 years ago. They gradually replaced the Neanderthals, maybe because they made better tools and had a more developed culture.
0.4–0.03	*Homo neanderthalensis* was present throughout Europe. They made tools and buried their dead.
1.8–0.5	*Homo erectus* had a larger brain than *Homo habilis* and had a similar skeleton to modern humans, although his skull was still primitive with heavy eyebrow ridges. They made better tools and learned to control fire.
2.3–1.7	*Homo habilis* had a larger brain than the australopithecines. He made simple stone tools. Some robust species of australopithecine co-existed with *H. habilis* but they are not thought to be human ancestors.
3–2.2	*Australopithecus africanus* had a small brain, though a more human-like skeleton and teeth. This species may not be a human ancestor.
4–3	*Australopithecus afarensis* was bipedal but small-brained.
4.4	*Australopithecus ramidus* – the earliest known hominid. It was bipedal and had a small brain.
8–4.4	There are no fossils available from this period, but at some time in this period the first hominids appeared.

The hunter-gatherer lifestyle

You have seen that our ancestors were mainly hunter-gatherers. The earliest hominids gathered plant food and perhaps insects and small animals. They may also have scavenged carcasses killed by large carnivores but they would not have done much hunting. However, once the genus *Homo* appeared, hunting became more evident.

Hunting was important for members of *Homo* species. They were bigger brained, so they needed more energy in their diet. Meat is high in energy, but plant foods are very low in energy. However, gathering plant foods, insects, rodents and so on would have supplied a large part of their food.

In some parts of the world hunter-gatherers moved around. They might not have been able to have a settled permanent home-base because food was not available in one place all year round. This might have been because of animal migrations, and little plant food being available in winter. There is evidence that the Neanderthals and the Cro-Magnons built temporary shelters as they moved from place to place.

Hunting and gathering meant a division of labour. Women and children would stay close to the home base, where they gathered food. The men would go off to hunt in groups. This involved cooperation. The food that was hunted and gathered was shared by the whole group.

■ Social groups

Chimpanzees and gorillas are the closest living relatives of humans. These primates live in social groups, but these are different from the groups in which modern humans live. In a chimpanzee group, there is a hierarchy among the males. This is achieved through displays of aggression. The alpha male is the head of the group, and the other males respect his position.

The reproductive cycle of female apes (the oestrous cycle) is physiologically exactly the same as the human menstrual cycle. However, the female ape's behaviour is very different. The time of ovulation is the period of **oestrus**. This is the only time in the cycle when the female is receptive to mating. Also, the fact that the female is in oestrus is clear to the males, because she gives off a scent, has swollen genitalia and reddened skin around the vagina. The alpha male will mate with her several times over the few days of oestrus. Other males may mate with her, but only if they can do this without the alpha male noticing. After this time, there is no relationship.

In chimpanzee groups, only the females care for the young. Sometimes another female, such as an older sister, may help but the males play no part. Similarly, all the chimpanzees forage for their own food. If a female cannot find enough food for herself and her baby, she will not be helped by the baby's father.

Humans have a different reproductive cycle that is not shared by any other primate. Although the human female, like the chimpanzee, is fertile for only a few days in a month, there is no period of oestrus. A human female is receptive to a male throughout the cycle.

Some scientists think that this behaviour evolved as humans evolved bigger brains. They believe that the earliest hominids almost certainly lived in social groups like those of apes. However, as humans developed bigger brains, there was a need for a higher energy diet. A pregnant female, or a mother with a baby, might have difficulty gathering enough food for herself and her infant. However, a male is not likely to help her feed the infant unless he is fairly certain that the baby is his.

It has been suggested that a pair-bond might be established, in which the male offered gifts of food to the female. In return, she would mate with him regularly. Once the pair-bond was established, this would involve two adults in the care of their infants. This would increase the survival of the species. One family on its own, however, would not have been as successful as a group in which there were several family groups.

It is impossible to tell at which stage over the evolution of hominids that this change in behaviour occurred.

■ Application and How science works

Piltdown Man

Piltdown Man is one of the best-known hoaxes in the scientific world. It was found in Sussex in 1912. At the time, very little was known about human evolution. People imagined that there must have been some sort of ape-man. They thought the 'missing link' would have a big brain like a human but would have other ape features. Charles Dawson discovered the first skull in 1912. He named it *Eoanthropus dawsoni*. He found fragments of a skull and jawbone. Piltdown Man was everything he had expected. It had a large-brained skull like a modern human, but a jaw like an ape's. You can see the skull that was reconstructed from these fragments in Figure 1.

A few people were sceptical of the find. In the 1920s, Franz Weidenreich, an anatomist, examined the fragments. He correctly identified them as a modern human skull and an orang-utan jawbone with filed-down teeth. However, he was ignored.

The fossil was finally recognised as a hoax in November 1953. A professor from Oxford University showed that it was made up of fragments of a medieval human skull, the lower jaw of an orang-utan and chimpanzee fossil teeth. The bones had been stained to give them an ancient appearance. When the teeth were examined under the microscope, file-marks were seen. The forger had tried to make the teeth look more human. Dating methods also showed that it was a hoax.

Most scientists were pleased that it was revealed to be a hoax, as by 1953 they had found other fossil humans and Piltdown Man did not fit with them.

Why did the hoax succeed so well? One reason is that the scientists at the time thought that a big brain had evolved before the modern omnivorous diet. Also, it was British. Fossil humans had been found in Germany and France, and British scientists wanted some fossils of their own.

Figure 1 *Piltdown Man reconstructed from the fossil fragments*

Summary questions

1. Suggest why we have not yet found fossil hominids older than 4.4 million years.

2. Human ancestors who lived as hunter-gatherers in social groups would have better chances of survival than their ancestors. Explain why.

9.13 *Ramapithecus*

Learning objectives:

■ How was the evidence related to *Ramapithecus* interpreted?

Specification reference: 3.2.3

Very often, scientists studying evolution have very little fossil evidence. The extinct primate called *Ramapithecus* is a good example of this. It lived about 9–12 million years ago.

■ Different evidence

The fragments of *Ramapithecus* that were found were described as having the following features:

■ The canines were small, not large like those of the great apes. This is a feature of hominids. This would allow more sideways movement of the jaw, so it could chew.

■ The jaw is shorter and pointed at the front in a V-shape, or is more parabola-shaped like a human's.

■ The teeth are set in a deep jaw. They are flattened and have much larger biting surfaces than the apes. The enamel of the teeth is very thick. This means it probably lived in open woodland where it would eat tough, dry vegetation, including hard seeds and dry nuts. This was a feature that was thought to be similar to humans.

As a result of studying the appearance of fossil bones, scientists decided that the relationships between humans, *Ramapithecus* and the other great apes were as shown in Figure 1a. They believed that humans must have split away from gorillas and chimps at least 9 to 12 million years ago, because *Ramapithecus* had more in common with humans than they did.

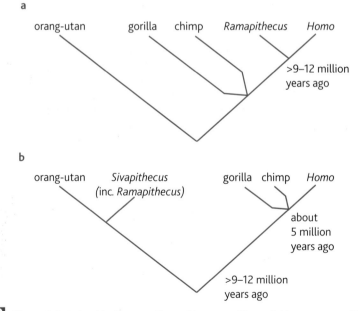

■ **Figure 1** *Relationships between Ramapithecus, gorillas and chimpanzees, and humans*

Later, work was done using immunological methods (see Topic 9.2). They showed that humans had so many similarities with gorillas and chimps that they could not have diverged so long ago. In fact, this evidence indicated that humans diverged from gorillas and chimps only 5 million years ago. This meant that humans could not be more closely related to *Ramapithecus* than to gorillas and chimps. Immunological evidence suggested that the relationships between humans, *Ramapithecus* and the great apes were more like the diagram shown in Figure 1b. In other words, there was a big difference between the fossil evidence and the immunological evidence.

Looking at the evidence again

This led the scientists to look more closely at the fossil evidence.

- Although the canines were small, scientists realised this could be because the fossils came from a female. In many kinds of ape, the female has much smaller canines than the male.
- The pointed jaw was found to be a mistake that was made when two pieces were put together from two different specimens.
- Scientists realised that the thickened enamel was not a sign that *Ramapithecus* was a human ancestor.

By reanalysing the fossil evidence, scientists realised that the relationships were more likely to be the one shown in Figure 1b.

Sivapithecus

A few other fossils were found that were classified as *Sivapithecus*. These also came from India and Pakistan. The remains were very similar to those of *Ramapithecus*, although the animal had a larger body size and larger canines. For a long time it was thought that while *Ramapithecus* was an early hominid, *Sivapithecus* evolved into the modern orang-utan. This is because its face and teeth are similar to the orang-utan. Three species of *Sivapithecus* are currently recognised, all dating from between 8 and 13 million years ago.

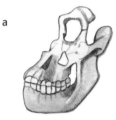

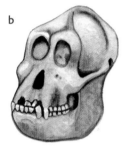

Figure 2 *Fossil skulls of Sivapithecus: (a) female, (b) male*

Changing ideas

In the 1970s, more complete specimens of *Ramapithecus* were found. These showed it was less like a human than had been thought previously. Scientists realised that it looked very similar to *Sivapithecus*. In fact, it was possible that *Ramapithecus* was just the female form of *Sivapithecus*. In many modern apes, such as gorillas and orang-utans, the male is much larger than the female and has larger canines. It was certainly clear that both these fossils belonged to the same genus. Therefore, *Ramapithecus* was re classified as *Sivapithecus*. You can see two fossil skulls of *Sivapithecus* in Figure 2. The larger skull is male and the smaller one is female.

Studying these specimens also showed that they were probably ancestors of the orang-utan, but not of chimpanzees, gorillas and humans. They seemed to date from a time after the orang-utan line had split from the chimpanzee, gorilla and human line. However, we have not yet found an ancestor for gorillas, chimpanzees and humans.

Summary questions

1 Suggest why the males of many apes, including *Sivapithecus*, have large canines while females do not.

2 If scientists were able to find DNA from former *Ramapithecus* and *Sivapithecus* fossils, they might be able to investigate further whether they belong to the same species. Explain how.

1 (a) Three human ancestors are *Australopithecus afarensis, Homo erectus* and *Homo habilis.* Explain what information their Latin names give about their relationships to each other. *(2 marks)*

(b) Copy and complete the table to show the classification of *Australopithecus afarensis.*

	Animalia
	Chordata
	Mammalia
	Primates
	Hominidae
Genus	
Species	

(2 marks)

(c) Explain how evidence from DNA could be used to investigate the evolutionary relationship between *Australopithecus afarensis* and modern *Homo sapiens.* *(3 marks)*

2 Neanderthals lived in Europe about 50 000 years ago. They walked upright, were about 1.65 m tall and had a brain volume of approximately 1500 cm^3. They were robust, muscular hunter-gatherers with a diet which included plant material and meat. They lived in caves and huts, used animal skins for clothing and shelter, and made specialised stone tools.

(a) Explain how fossil remains provide evidence for an upright posture *(3 marks)*

(b) **Figure 1** shows the skulls of a Neanderthal and an early modern human living at the same time.

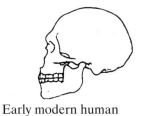 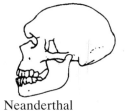

Early modern human   Neanderthal

Figure 1

How does the skull of a Neanderthal differ from that of an early modern human? *(3 marks)*

(c) **Figure 2** shows some of the tools used by Neanderthals.

Figure 2

Suggest how these stone tools would have been made and used. *(4 marks)*

AQA, 2001

3   **Figure 3** shows front and side views of the skull of an Australopithecine.

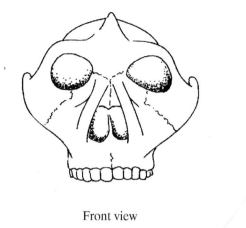

Front view

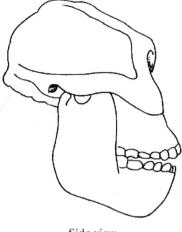

Side view

Figure 3

(a) (i)   Describe how investigation of this skull could give evidence about the posture, brain size and diet of this Australopithecine.

    (ii) What conclusions are likely to have been drawn about the posture, brain size and diet of this Australopithecine? *(6 marks)*

(b) (i)   Outline **one** method by which it would be possible to determine how long ago this Australopithecine lived.

    (ii) Describe **one** assumption that must be made using this method of dating. *(3 marks)*

AQA, 1995

4   The drawings in **Figure 4** show some stone tools. **A** and **B** were found in Olduvai Gorge in Tanzania. **C** and **D** were found at Le Moustier in France.

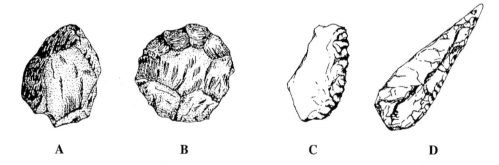

A   B   C   D

Figure 4

(a) (i)   Give **one** piece of evidence to suggest that tools **A** and **B** are older than tools **C** and **D**.

    (ii) Suggest **two** possible uses of tools such as **A** and **B**. *(3 marks)*

(b)   Describe how tools **C** and **D** might have been made. *(2 marks)*

AQA, 1997

5   (a) *Homo erectus* had a larger brain and was taller than *Homo habilis*. Scientists believe that *Homo erectus* evolved from *Homo habilis.* Suggest how this might have happened. *(4 marks)*

(b) Scientists believe that *Homo erectus* was able to use fire. Suggest and explain **two** ways in which this might have increased the chances of survival of *Homo erectus*. *(4 marks)*

10.1 Successful reproduction

Learning objectives:

■ How do humans ensure
that their offspring reach
adulthood and can reproduce
themselves?

Specification reference: 3.2.4

Humans have adaptations to their environment and way of life. These adaptations increase the probability of survival and successful ongoing reproduction.

Extended childhood

Many mammals give birth to young that are only dependent on their mother for a short period of time. These animals develop quickly, and are born with innate behaviour patterns that help them survive. For example, newborn deer are able to walk and even run with the herd within hours of birth. However, primates have evolved a different strategy to ensure survival of their young. Primate babies are much more dependent on their mothers than other mammals.

Primate mothers hold their babies as they move through the trees. This means that most primates have single births, as it would be difficult to care for many young in this environment. As primates have evolved, there has been a trend towards bigger-brained infants. In order for the brain to grow, more nutrients are needed. A single foetus can obtain more nutrients from its mother, so a bigger-brained infant can be born. With a smaller number of young, the mother can invest more time and energy in the infant, so it is able to learn more complex behaviour. Although the primate baby is very helpless, it is in close contact with its mother so it is likely to survive. It is born with some innate behaviour patterns to help its survival, but its survival ultimately depends on its mother.

Early humans also developed the culture of food sharing. This would have improved the survival of humans, and made it easier to raise big-brained offspring. Another advantage of food sharing is that it cements social relationships.

The trend towards bigger-brained infants is mirrored by a longer period of dependency on the mother. This means that the infant can learn more complex skills from its mother, and is therefore better able to survive in the long term. Humans have the biggest brains among the primates, and the longest period of dependency on the mother. This enables human infants to learn complex skills such as language and tool use.

Young primates also engage in play. This is an activity in which they can practise adult skills such as fighting, finding food and interacting with others. This enables young primates to learn the skills they will need as an adult. Therefore, once a young primate is past infancy it is learning from other members of the social group.

■ Delayed puberty

As humans evolved a longer childhood, this meant that the development of sexual maturity was delayed. Look at Figure 1.

You can see that the brain is highly developed at birth, and grows to its adult size fairly soon after birth. This allows the human infant to learn complex skills needed for survival. However, the reproductive organs do not grow significantly until puberty. This means that the human infant has a long period of dependency on its parents. It also ensures that humans cannot reproduce until they have reached social maturity themselves – caring for a highly dependent infant requires considerable skills in the parent.

The extended childhood of humans was very important in the intellectual and cultural development of our species. This is summarised in Figure 2.

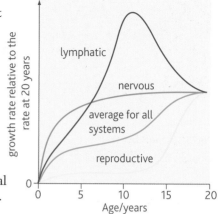

Figure 1 *Relative growth rates of different organs in humans*

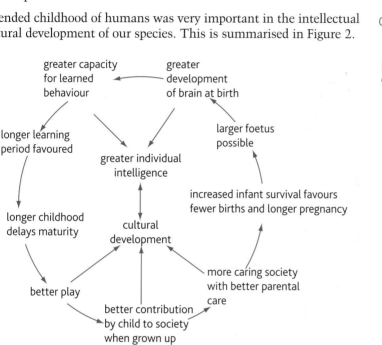

Figure 2 *The importance of extended childhood in the intellectual and cultural development of humans. Source: Steven Tomkins,* The Origins of Mankind, *1984, Cambridge University Press.*

The way that different parts of the body grow at different rates is shown in Figure 3.

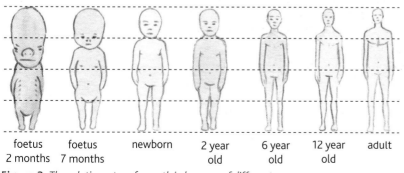

foetus 2 months · foetus 7 months · newborn · 2 year old · 6 year old · 12 year old · adult

Figure 3 *The relative rates of growth in humans of different ages*

■ Application and How science works

Stages of development of early hominids

Some scientists have examined fossil bones and teeth of hominids that died before reaching adulthood. They concluded that early hominids, like modern apes, had three stages of development:

■ infancy, when the infant is mainly dependent on the mother

■ juvenile, when the young animal is learning by social interactions with others but is not yet sexually mature

■ adult, when the animal is sexually mature and reproduces.

They claim that two more stages developed in *Homo erectus*:

■ childhood, when the young animal is cared for by other members of the social group and learns through play

■ adolescence, when the reproductive organs of the animal have developed, but the animal is not yet fertile and capable of reproducing.

Figure 4 shows the results of their research.

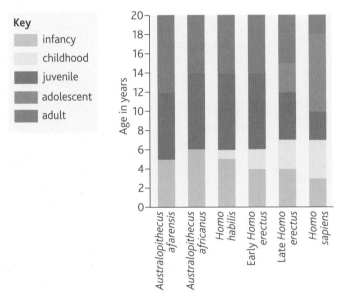

Figure 4 *Stages in the development of different hominid groups.*
Source: Bogin and Smith, American Journal of Human Biology, *Vol 8, 1996, pp 703–716. © John Wiley & Sons, Inc. 1996. Reprinted with permission of Wiley-Liss, Inc.*

1 What are the problems in carrying out an investigation of this kind?

2 Use your knowledge of these hominids to suggest the importance of a progressively later adulthood.

3 Assuming these data are reliable, suggest the advantage to *Homo sapiens* of:

a having a shorter infancy than earlier hominids

b having an adolescence phase in the life cycle.

4 It is thought that female hominids rarely lived beyond the age of about 40–50. At this age, females reach the menopause and are no longer fertile. However, female *Homo sapiens* often live for many years after they have reached the menopause. Suggest the advantage that this may have had for early *Homo sapiens*.

Summary questions

1 Australopithecines probably did not share food. However, later hominids lived in food-sharing social groups. Use your knowledge of hominid evolution to explain the importance of food-sharing.

2 Look at Figure 3. Explain the significance of:

a a foetus having a relatively large brain compared to the adult

b a newborn infant having relatively short legs compared to a 6 year old.

10.2 Adaptations of human behaviour

Learning objectives:

- How is an extended childhood an advantageous adaptation?

- What advantage does language give humans over other animals?

- Why is it advantageous that language develops during childhood?

- Why is communication by facial expression important?

Specification reference: 3.2.4

Extended childhood

In Topic 10.1 you learned that humans have an extended childhood compared to other primate groups. This means that humans have a longer period before they reach puberty and are capable of reproducing compared with other animals. This allows humans to learn more complex skills before they reach adulthood. One of the most important skills that they learn is language. They also learn problem solving and can explore different behaviours and activities through play.

Because humans rely much more on complex learned behaviour than other animals, they are born with fewer innate (or inborn) behaviours. You will have seen wildlife films in which young animals, like deer, are able to run and follow their mother within a very short time of being born. Young humans are much more helpless than this. They need to be carried by their mothers and protected from the many dangers that could harm them. However, being so dependent on their mothers and the other adults around them means that young humans have the opportunity to learn more complex skills that will lead them to become very intelligent adults.

Developing language

Language is an extremely important skill. No other primate uses language, although there have been studies showing that some great apes are able to use sign language in a simple way if they are taught by humans.

Language must have been a very important development in human evolution. It would have allowed early humans to tell each other what had happened to them during the day, and where the best hunting sites were. Older humans would have been able to pass on information about things that had happened to them in the past, such as where they found water to drink the previous time that there was a drought. It would also have helped to develop culture. It is likely that early humans would have sat around the fire in the evenings, telling stories to entertain and educate each other. Sharing a culture would have been important in forming social groups. It would also mean that older people, who might have injuries or diseases that made them dependent on others, would have been valued nevertheless because of their accumulated wisdom that could be passed on.

The fact that language develops early in childhood is important for the learning of complex skills and ideas. Humans use language not only for naming things, but to convey abstract ideas and emotions. We use language to think. Developing language early means that children can think in more complex ways, as well as communicating ideas and feelings. For example, they can tell their parents that they need something, or that a particular thing has upset them.

Language is also important in learning skills. Imagine that you are trying to show a friend how to do something, like doing a three-point turn in a car, or bandaging a sprained ankle. It would be much harder to do this without having language. With language, you can explain how an action should be done, or pass on tips that make it easier.

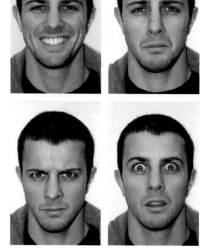

Figure 1 *Chimpanzee facial expressions*

Figure 2 *Four of the six basic human facial expressions. Clockwise from top left: happiness, sadness, surprise and anger (disgust and fear not shown).*

■ Communication using facial expressions

While humans are the only animals that can use language, communicating by facial expression is found widely among higher primates. For example, chimpanzees have a number of facial expressions that are often accompanied by vocalisations. You can see some of these in Figure 1.

When humans developed language, they did not lose their ability to communicate by facial expressions as well. Across all human cultures, scientists have identified six basic facial expressions. Four of these are shown in Figure 2. They involve coordinated movements of muscles in the face.

These basic facial expressions are seen in people from different social and cultural backgrounds, and even in people who have been born deaf and blind. Further expressions are also widely seen, including the eyebrow flash that people use when greeting each other, yawning, and the facial expressions used to express shyness or embarrassment and shame.

Facial expressions are clearly important in signalling to other members in a social group. They benefit both the signaller and the receiver. They allow people to communicate even when they speak different languages, and they can convey feelings. For example, smiling indicates that you are not a threat to a stranger, while scowling warns a stranger not to approach.

One situation that scientists have studied closely is the interaction between a human infant and its parent. Human infants use facial expression to encourage their carers to pay attention to them. Carers usually smile or speak to the infant in response. You can see this kind of interaction in Figure 3.

Figure 3 *A human infant interacting with its mother*

Infants from just a few weeks old can engage their carers in smiling and talking to them by using facial expressions in this way. This activity of the infant is very important for its survival. By interacting with its carer in this way, the baby forms a close attachment bond.

■ Summary questions

1 What evidence is there in this section that humans' ability to recognise basic facial expressions, such as fear or joy, are innate or inborn, rather than learned?

2 Suggest how natural selection may have led to the development of an extended childhood in humans.

10.3 Adaptations of human anatomy

Learning objectives:

- What are the advantages of anatomical adaptations of humans (bipedalism, opposable thumb, skin colour, surface area to volume ratio)?

Specification reference: 3.2.4

There are several adaptations to human anatomy that increase survival.

Bipedalism

You learned in Chapter 9 that humans evolved from an ape-like ancestor. Our earliest ancestors became **bipedal**. This means that they walked on two legs.

Our ape-like ancestors would have lived in trees. However, about 5 or 6 million years ago there were climate changes in East Africa. Instead of dense forest, large areas became covered with what we call 'treed savannah'. This means grassland with trees, but the trees are very spread out.

In these conditions, our ape-like ancestors would have been forced to survive in the open. Natural selection would have favoured individuals who were more adapted to these conditions. Bipedalism has a number of advantages:

- It enables the animal to look over tall vegetation to spot predators, sources of food, etc.
- Bipedal animals can fight more effectively, as they can wing their arms, etc.
- The arms can be used to communicate and make signals.
- The arms can be used to throw things.
- The arms can be used to carry things such as tools. Humans even make containers such as baskets so that they can carry more.
- Fine manipulative skills can be developed, e.g. tool use, writing.

Opposable thumb

Humans have an opposable thumb on their hands. This means they have a very mobile joint at the base of the thumb so that they can hold an object between their thumb and any one of the fingers. Other primates have an opposable thumb that is not quite so flexible, as their hands are adapted for grasping. The human thumb is relatively broad and long at the end. Look at Figure 1. This shows a human hand and the hands of some other primates.

You learned in Topic 9.8 that human hands have two kinds of grip: the power grip, as in grasping a tennis racquet, and the precision grip, as in holding a pencil. Human hands are very well adapted to making and using tools. This ability to use tools was very important in human evolution.

Skin colour

As you already know, when animals die, the soft parts of the body are rarely preserved. We do not have any remains of the skin of human ancestors. However, it is very likely that our early ancestors had black skin. This is because they evolved in Africa. Modern humans who are native to Africa also have black skin because their skin contains a large amount of a black skin pigment, melanin. You will remember from Topic 8.3 that ultraviolet radiation can penetrate the skin, damaging DNA and

tarsier   **orang-utan**

gorilla   **human**

Figure 1 *Primate hands*

causing skin cancer. In tropical areas where people are exposed to strong sunlight, melanin in the skin protects them from absorbing too much ultraviolet radiation.

However, when *Homo erectus* migrated out of Africa about a million years ago, humans were living in more temperate regions. Another effect of ultraviolet radiation on the skin is that it produces vitamin D. You will remember from Topic 1.3 that vitamin D is needed for teeth and bones. People without enough vitamin D develop rickets. Dark-skinned people in Africa have skin that makes enough vitamin D because there is so much ultraviolet radiation. However, when they moved to more temperate regions, the melanin in their skin would have stopped them absorbing enough ultraviolet radiation.

By chance, some of these *Homo erectus* people would have had alleles that gave them slightly less pigmentation in their skin. These individuals would have absorbed more ultraviolet radiation, and would have had a better supply of vitamin D. They would be less likely to develop rickets so would have survived, reproduced more, and passed on their alleles to their children. Mutations causing less melanin in the skin would have been a selective advantage. As a result, people living in more temperate regions, such as Europe, would have evolved paler skins.

Surface area to volume ratios

Climate has not only affected skin colour. Human body shape is also an adaptation to climate.

Look at Figure 2. You can see a Masai man, who is adapted to living in hot, tropical conditions, and an Inuk, who is adapted to living in very cold conditions. The Masai has a large surface area to volume ratio, so that body heat can be lost easily. The Inuk has a shorter, broader body with layers of insulating fat. This helps to conserve heat in the arctic regions.

Summary questions

1 Suggest how natural selection could result in the development of a human hand with a mobile, fully opposable thumb.

2 Rickets makes bones softer and misshapen. Women with rickets are more likely to have difficulties in childbirth. Explain why.

3 Negroes have woolly hair. People from colder regions tend to have straight hair. Suggest an advantage of woolly hair to Negroes.

Figure 2 *A Masai warrior and an Inuk*

10.4　Breathing faster

Link

You should reread the sections in Chapter 3 to remind yourself about breathing and gas exchange.

Humans have physiological adaptations that equip them for vigorous exercise. One of these is the ability to breathe faster. This is an adaptation to a way of life. For instance, when hunting, humans would have had periods of intense physical activity either chasing prey or being chased by predators.

Normal breathing

Our breathing is mainly involuntary. This means that it is a reflex action that we do not need to think about. It is controlled by a **breathing centre** in the medulla of the brain. There are two parts to the breathing centre: an **inspiratory centre** and an **expiratory centre**.

The inspiratory centre stimulates breathing in. It does this by sending impulses along the phrenic nerve to the diaphragm, and along the intercostal nerves to the intercostal muscles. As a result, the diaphragm and intercostal muscles contract, causing inspiration.

As the lungs inflate, the alveoli fill with air. Stretch receptors in the walls of the alveoli and bronchioles are stimulated as the alveoli fill. These stretch receptors send impulses to the expiratory centre of the medulla. This inhibits inspiration and stimulates expiration. No more impulses pass along the phrenic nerve and the intercostal nerves, so the diaphragm and intercostal muscles relax. This causes expiration. Now that the stretch receptors are no longer stimulated, the expiratory centre is no longer stimulated so the inspiratory centre causes inspiration again and the cycle continues. You can see this in Figure 1.

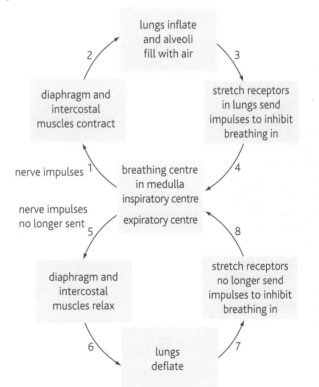

Figure 1 *The control of breathing*

⚠ 💡 The effects of exercise on breathing

When you exercise, your cells respire more. This means that they produce more carbon dioxide. However, the respiring cells also need more oxygen. Therefore when you exercise, your breathing rate increases so that more oxygen is delivered to the body cells that need it.

The main stimulus that controls the breathing rate is the concentration of carbon dioxide in the blood. Carbon dioxide is slightly acidic. It dissolves in blood plasma to form weak carbonic acid. Carbonic acid then dissociates into hydrogen ions and hydrogencarbonate ions:

$$CO_2 + H_2O \rightleftharpoons H_2CO_3 \rightleftharpoons H^+ + HCO_3^-$$

The higher the concentration of hydrogen ions, the more acidic the plasma becomes. In other words, the pH falls.

This fall in pH is detected by special cells called **chemoreceptors**. These are found in:

■ the **carotid bodies** in the carotid artery, which carries oxygenated blood to the brain

■ the **aortic bodies** in the aorta, which carries oxygenated blood away from the heart

■ the medulla of the brain.

If the chemoreceptors detect a fall in pH, they send impulses to the inspiratory centre of the medulla. The medulla then sends impulses along the phrenic nerve to the diaphragm and along the intercostal nerves to the intercostal muscles, causing the rate and depth of breathing to increase.

Figure 2 shows the effect of increased carbon dioxide (i.e a fall in pH) on ventilation rate.

Summary questions

1 Some people have panic attacks, during which time they breathe very rapidly. This is called hyperventilating. One treatment for this is to get the person to breathe in and out into a paper bag. Suggest what effect this will have.

2 Under circumstances where there is an increase in concentration of carbon dioxide in the atmosphere, what would you expect to happen to the breathing rate? Explain why this would happen.

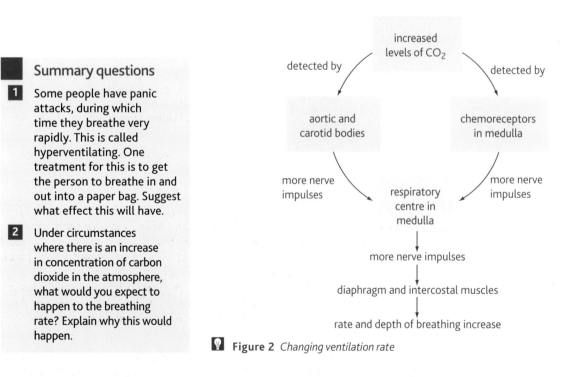

💡 **Figure 2** *Changing ventilation rate*

10.5 Beating faster

Learning objectives:

- How does the human heart beat faster during vigorous exercise?

Specification reference: 3.2.4

You have already seen in Topic 10.4 that your respiring cells need more oxygen when you exercise, and in response to this the rate and depth of breathing increase. However, this is not the only change that happens. When you start to exercise, your heart beats faster too.

Controlling the heart rate

You will remember from Topic 6.2 that the heart muscle is **myogenic**. This means that it does not need stimulation by a nerve to make it contract. You will also remember that the cardiac cycle starts when impulses are generated by the sinoatrial node (SAN) in the wall of the right atrium. However, the nervous system can change the rate at which the heart beats.

The medulla of the brain contains a region called the **cardiovascular centre**. This receives impulses from various receptors in the body, and as a result, it can bring about changes in heart rate. Figure 1 shows some of the nerves connecting the heart to the cardiovascular centre in the medulla.

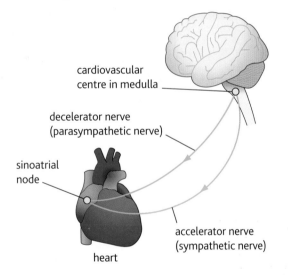

Figure 1 *Nerves connecting the heart to the cardiovascular centre in the medulla*

Carbon dioxide

The heart rate is increased when there is a build-up of carbon dioxide. When you exercise, muscle cells respire more and produce more carbon dioxide. This lowers the pH. The fall in pH is detected by chemoreceptors in the medulla, carotid body and the aortic bodies in the wall of the aorta. These send impulses along sensory nerves to the cardiovascular centre in the medulla of the brain. As a result, more impulses are passed along the sympathetic nerve from the cardiovascular centre to the SAN of the heart. This stimulates the SAN to send out more frequent impulses, increasing the heart rate.

When carbon dioxide levels fall, the chemoreceptors detect this and send impulses to the cardiovascular centre in the medulla. As a result, more impulses are sent along the parasympathetic nerve to the SAN, slowing the heart rate.

Blood pressure

When the body is exercising actively, body muscles contract strongly. This increases the rate at which deoxygenated blood returns to the heart in the venae cavae. The walls of the venae cavae are stretched by this increase in blood flow, and this causes the heart rate to increase. The increased volume of blood stretches the heart muscle. As a result, the heart muscle contracts more strongly during systole, pumping out more blood each time it contracts.

The volume of blood pumped out by the heart during one beat is called the **stroke volume**. The volume of blood pumped out by the heart in one minute is called the **cardiac output**.

$$\text{cardiac output} = \text{stroke volume} \times \text{heart rate}$$

The increased stroke volume stretches the walls of the aorta and carotid arteries. Pressure receptors in the wall of the aorta, and in the carotid sinus in the carotid artery detect the stretching and send impulses to the cardiovascular centre in the medulla. As a result, the cardiovascular centre sends more impulses along the parasympathetic nerve to the SAN, slowing the heart rate.

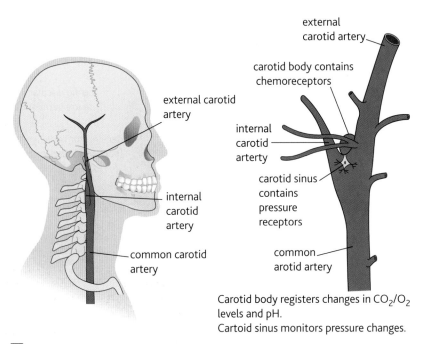

Carotid body registers changes in CO_2/O_2 levels and pH.
Cartoid sinus monitors pressure changes.

💡 **Figure 2** *The carotid body and the carotid sinus*

> ## AQA Examiner's tip
>
> Be careful you don't confuse the carotid body and the carotid sinus. Look at Figure 2. You can see the carotid body contains the chemoreceptors that monitor blood pH, while the carotid sinus contains pressure receptors that respond to changes in blood pressure.

Summary questions

1. A person's heart rate increases if they have lost a lot of blood, for example as the result of an accident. Suggest what causes this to happen.

2. A trained athlete has a lower resting heart rate than a non-athlete. Suggest why.

3. A person has a heart rate of 70 beats per minute and a cardiac output of 4900 cm³. Calculate this person's stroke volume.

4. A person has a cardiac output of 6000 cm³ and a stroke volume of 110 cm³. Calculate this person's heart rate.

10.6 Energy sources

Learning objectives:

- What are the sources of energy used by muscles during exercise?

- How do aerobic and anaerobic respiration compare in terms of providing energy (ATP) for muscle contraction?

- What is the role of haemoglobin in carrying oxygen?

- How do people adapt to living at high altitude (lower oxygen concentration in air) in terms of their red blood cells and haemoglobin?

Specification reference: 3.2.4

You will remember from GCSE that cells obtain their energy from respiration. Respiration is when molecules from our food, such as glucose, are broken down to release energy. However, the energy released in respiration is used to form a molecule called **ATP** (**adenosine triphosphate**). You can see the structure of ATP in Figure 1. It has three phosphate groups. In cellular respiration, the energy released is used to add a phosphate group to **ADP** (**adenosine diphosphate**), to form ATP.

When one of the phosphate groups splits off the ATP molecule, energy is released. This energy can be used for active transport, muscle contraction and other energy-requiring activities in the body.

The energy from respiring a molecule like glucose is converted into ATP for several reasons. ATP is a relatively small and simple molecule. It can diffuse easily where it is needed, for example, muscle fibres. It delivers energy in small, convenient amounts.

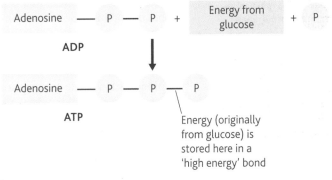

Figure 1 *ATP and ADP*

Sources of energy

Glucose is the normal source of energy for our cells. This glucose comes from carbohydrates in our food. You will remember from Topic 1.7 that glucose is a carbohydrate monomer. When we eat a meal that contains carbohydrates, the carbohydrates are digested to glucose so that they can be absorbed into the bloodstream. However, much of this glucose is then stored as the polysaccharide glycogen in liver and muscle cells. When the glucose in our blood is used for cellular respiration, glycogen is broken down to release more glucose to be used for respiration.

Triglycerides can also be used as a source of energy. Most triglycerides are stored in adipose (fat-storage) tissue. Triglycerides cannot be broken down as quickly as glycogen, so they are no good for short-term exercise. However, for long-term exercise, such as long-distance jogging, triglycerides are a useful energy source.

Aerobic and anaerobic respiration

Aerobic respiration is respiration that uses oxygen. When glucose and triglycerides are respired aerobically, they can be broken down completely to carbon dioxide and water. This means that as much energy as possible is released from them. In other words, we obtain the maximum yield of ATP from aerobic respiration. Potentially, 38 ATP molecules can be made from the aerobic respiration of one molecule of glucose.

However, when oxygen is not available, another respiration pathway is available. This is called anaerobic respiration. When a molecule of glucose is respired anaerobically it is not broken down completely. Instead lactate is produced, with a yield of only two molecules of ATP. Triglycerides cannot be respired anaerobically.

Lactate is acidic, and lowers the pH of the blood. It builds up in muscles during exercise, and causes painful muscle fatigue if it reaches high levels. The lactate that builds up diffuses into the blood. Several different things can happen to this lactate after exercise:

- Most of the lactate is oxidised to carbon dioxide and water. This requires additional oxygen and is called the **oxygen debt**.
- A smaller amount of the lactate is converted into glycogen.
- Small amounts of the lactate are converted into glucose and into protein.
- Trace amounts of lactate are excreted in urine and in sweat.

Haemoglobin

Haemoglobin is a protein that is present inside red blood cells. It is a large, globular protein made of four sub-units. You can see its quaternary structure in Figure 2.

You will notice that each protein chain has a non-protein haem group attached to it. This haem group contains an iron ion. Each iron ion can combine with a single oxygen molecule, which means that a haemoglobin molecule can carry four oxygen molecules altogether. Haemoglobin with oxygen attached is called oxyhaemoglobin, and it is bright red in colour. When the haemoglobin is deoxygenated it becomes slightly darker in colour.

The oxygen concentration in the air decreases at higher altitudes. This means that people moving to a higher altitude have to breathe in and out more often to take in enough oxygen to combine with the haemoglobin in their red blood cells. People who try to climb very high mountains without preparation can find themselves short of breath. In extreme cases they may suffer from altitude sickness, which can be fatal.

Scientists have studied humans who live permanently at high altitudes (3.5 km and more above sea level), such as those who live in the Andes of South America. They have found that these people have a higher concentration of haemoglobin in their blood than people who live at lower altitudes. This is because they have a greater concentration of red blood cells in their blood.

Some athletes have tried to take advantage of this effect. They do this by training at high altitudes in the hope it will raise haemoglobin levels in their blood and boost performance.

four polypeptide chains make up the haemoglobin molecule. Each molecule contains 574 amino acids

each chain is attached to a haem group that can combine with oxygen

Figure 2 *The structure of haemoglobin*

Summary questions

1 Explain why anaerobic respiration of glucose produces less ATP than aerobic respiration.

2 Athletes sometimes train at high altitude to increase the haemoglobin concentration in their blood. Explain why this might help them to perform better.

3 Anaemia is a condition in which a person lacks haemoglobin in their blood.

a Suggest the symptoms of anaemia.

b Anaemia is often treated by giving the patient iron tablets. Suggest the reason for this.

10.7 Adaptations of parasites

Learning objectives:

■ How have parasites adapted to their environment?

■ What are their principal adaptations?

Specification reference: 3.2.4

Parasites are organisms that live in or on another living organism, called their **host**. They feed on the organism and cause it harm. Many parasites eventually cause the death of the host.

Parasites are very well adapted to features in their environment (the body of their host). This is a difficult environment to invade and survive in, but there are very many successful parasites. There are more parasites that live on the outside of the host, or in the gut, than live inside the blood and tissues. This is partly because parasites living in the blood and tissues have to escape the host's immune system. It is also because it is harder to get eggs to the outside from a site inside the host.

Although parasites cause harm to their hosts, it is not in their interests to kill their host. This is because the host is their source of food, and parasites usually die when their host dies. Natural selection has acted on parasites over a long period of time, resulting in some very specialised adaptations that allow them to survive in the very hostile environment inside the host, without causing it immediate serious harm.

Structural adaptations

■ Many parasites are large compared with their free-living relatives. This is thought to be because they need to produce so many eggs.

■ Most parasites are dorso-ventrally flattened (back to front) because they need to cling on to the host. However, fleas are laterally flattened (sideways) because they need to slip between body hairs.

■ Many parasites show loss of locomotory organs (limbs).

■ Most parasites have organs of attachment. These include hooks and suckers, although fleas have special comb organs.

■ Many parasites show a reduction in the nervous system and sense organs.

■ Many parasites that live inside the host have a reduced gut, and absorb nutrients through the whole body surface.

■ Parasites that live inside the host but do not absorb nutrients through the body surface usually have a thick cuticle.

■ Many parasites have highly developed reproductive organs, so that they can produce enormous numbers of gametes.

Adaptations of the life cycle

Parasites usually produce many more offspring than their free-living relatives. Life cycle adaptations may include hermaphroditism, where one individual has both male and female sex organs, or parthenogenesis, where one individual can produce offspring without fertilisation taking place. Parasites usually reach sexual maturity quickly, and many parasites incorporate asexual reproduction in part of their life cycle, which increases the reproductive potential considerably.

Parasites usually infect more than one host. These other hosts are called secondary hosts. This has certain advantages:

■ increased reproductive potential, since asexual reproduction can take place in the secondary host,

■ the parasite can spread into different environments, for example, it may infect one host that lives on the land and another host that lives in water,

■ the parasite can survive periods when one host is temporarily scarce,

■ the secondary host is often a means of infecting the primary host. This is often because the primary host eats the secondary host, and in doing so, becomes infected with the parasite.

Many parasites do not have adaptations for infecting new hosts except for producing large numbers of eggs or larvae. However, the infective stages of many parasites often show adaptations that help to increase their chances of infecting a host. These include:

■ behavioural responses to locate favourable environments,

■ responding to chemical stimuli from their host,

■ changing the behaviour of the infected intermediate host to increase the chances of them being eaten by the final host. For example, mice infected with *Toxoplasma* are attracted to cat urine and show less fear of cats than uninfected mice. This increases the chances that the mouse will be eaten, thereby helping the *Toxoplasma* to find a new host.

■ Adaptations to avoid the host's immune system

In mammals it takes approximately nine days for the immune response to become fully effective, so any parasite that lives inside a mammalian host for longer than this must have some mechanism for avoiding the host's immune response. These include changing their antigens, living in a part of the body where the immune system does not operate, e.g. the gut, or coating itself in host antigens.

■ Biochemical adaptations

Parasites living inside the host's body need to be adapted for anaerobic respiration as there is little or no oxygen available inside the body. Parasites living in the host's gut need to be adapted to resist their host's digestive enzymes. They absorb their host's soluble digested food products through their body surface.

How science works

Can a parasite carried by cats change your personality?

Cats carry an infectious parasite called *Toxoplasma gondii*, which is a single-celled organism. Scientists think that it could change personality. It could also affect intelligence and it has been linked to schizophrenia. Some studies suggest it can even raise your chances of being knocked down by a car.

Toxoplasma gondii can infect all mammals, so it is unfair to blame cats. In the UK, the biggest risk of catching it is probably from eating an undercooked burger or bacon sandwich. At least a third of British people are already unwitting carriers (rising to about 80% in France and Germany).

People shouldn't panic, because in the vast majority of cases – 99% of people or above – the changes will be very subtle. There is also no means of getting rid of the infection. However, for those that are interested, a simple blood test for antibodies raised against the parasite can tell you whether you're infected or not.

The possible risks of *Toxoplasma gondii* to unborn children have been known for some time, hence pregnant women are urged not to clean out cat litter trays, for example. More recently, scientists have begun to unpick its effects on behaviour, discovering that infected rats lose their aversion to cats and so are more likely to be eaten. This allows the parasite to complete its life cycle. There are fewer experiments in humans, but results from studies of students and conscript soldiers in the Czech Republic in the mid-1990s highlighted the fact that infected people showed different personality traits to non-infected people – and that the differences depended on gender. Infected men were more likely to become aggressive, jealous and suspicious, while women became more outgoing and showed signs of higher intelligence. Another study showed that *Toxoplasma* infection and subsequent delayed reaction times were linked to a greater risk of traffic accidents.

True or not, scientists are now trying to work out how the parasite might affect people's behaviour. In rats, the infection has been shown to affect the brain chemical dopamine, and new results from a study in humans show that it may do the same thing in human brains.

Questionnaires designed to probe personality types, given to a thousand soldiers, found that those infected exhibited altered levels of novelty seeking, which is a common psychological marker for high dopamine levels.

Adapted from an article in the Guardian *25 September 2003 by David Adam. © Guardian News & Media Ltd. 2003.*

Application and How science works

Bed bugs

The bed bug (*Cimex lectularius*) has been a parasite of humans for thousands of years. It is so well adapted to humans that its bite is rarely felt until well after the bug leaves its victim. Until insecticides were widely available in the 1940s and 1950s, this was a widespread pest. Because they feed on human blood, they were more hated than cockroaches. Even now, bed bugs are occasionally found in homeless shelters, and even smart hotels and houses.

Bed bugs feed on the blood of animals including people and pets. They can survive for up to 18 months without feeding. This means they can wait for humans to visit camp cabins, apartments and temporary housing. It also helps them survive transportation.

Bed bugs are wingless, only about 5 mm long, and flattened dorso-ventrally to fit in cracks and crevices where they hide by day. They live in mattresses, curtains, bed frames, behind skirting boards, floorboards and peeling wallpaper. Female bed bugs lay five eggs a day. The bug's mouthparts painlessly bite its victim, inject saliva and suck up the host's blood. During the 3 to 5 minutes it takes to complete feeding, the bug elongates and becomes reddish brown. It then retreats to its hiding place for a few days to digest the meal.

Most people who are bitten do not usually realise it until the body reacts with inflammation and swelling around the bite, along with intense itching. However, bed bugs do not transmit diseases to humans when they bite.

1 Using the information and photograph, list some of the bed bug's parasitic adaptations.

Figure 1 *Bed bugs*

AQA Examiner's tip

You don't need to know details about bed bugs, but you should be able to apply the principles you have learned about parasites to any example that you are given.

Summary questions

1 Use your knowledge of natural selection to explain how parasites have developed adaptations that mean they rarely kill their hosts quickly.

10.8 *Toxocara*

Learning objectives:

■ How is *Toxocara* adapted to life as a human parasite?

Specification reference: 3.2.5

💡 How does Toxocara infect animals?

One example of a parasite that can infect humans is *Toxocara canis*. This is a roundworm that lives in the gut of dogs, but it can sometimes infect humans. Figure 1 shows the life cycle of *Toxocara canis*.

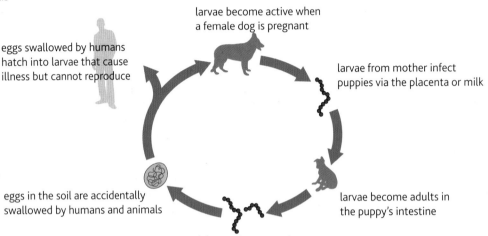

larvae become active when a female dog is pregnant

larvae from mother infect puppies via the placenta or milk

eggs swallowed by humans hatch into larvae that cause illness but cannot reproduce

larvae become adults in the puppy's intestine

eggs in the soil are accidentally swallowed by humans and animals

adults produce eggs that are released in the puppy's faces

💡 **Figure 1** *The life cycle of Toxocara canis*

Toxocara eggs are present in the faeces of infected dogs. Another dog may ingest these eggs in their food or by licking their coat. The eggs hatch into larvae in the dog's intestine, from where they migrate into various organs in the dog. They do not develop any further in adult dogs. However, when a female dog becomes pregnant, these larvae become reactivated. They migrate back to the intestines where they develop into adult worms. Larvae also migrate to the placenta where they can infect the foetal puppies, and the mammary glands where they can infect the young puppies in the milk.

If puppies become infected, the larvae migrate from the intestine via the blood system to the lungs. Here, the larvae migrate through the bronchi, bronchioles and trachea to the oesophagus. The larvae are swallowed and they return to the intestine, where they develop into adult worms.

Toxocara cati is a closely related roundworm parasite found in cats. It has a very similar life cycle to *Toxocara canis*.

Toxocara eggs in dog or cat faeces can also be passed on to other species, such as rats, mice, birds, etc. In these animals, the eggs hatch into larvae in the intestine, and then migrate to the tissues, where they do not develop further. However, if a dog or cat kills or eats an infected animal, the larvae become active in the intestines and infect the dog or cat that has eaten them.

Humans can also become infected with *Toxocara*. The usual source of infection is dog faeces, as cats tend to bury their faeces or use cat litter trays. Soil invertebrates, such as earthworms, may also carry *Toxocara* eggs. Children are most vulnerable to infection. They can become infected when they ingest soil contaminated with eggs, or even ingest soil invertebrates. Children can also pick up the infection from stroking a dog that has eggs in its hair, or by letting an infected dog lick their face. The larvae hatch in the intestine, and migrate via the bloodstream to other organs. You can see this in Figure 2.

5 Occasionally the larvae migrate to organs such as the eye, where they can cause pain and problems with vision. Other organs that may be infected include the lungs, heart, brain, liver and kidney.

4 Larvae enter the systemic circulation and may travel to any organ. These larvae usually do not develop further.

3 The larvae enter the blood vessels and travel to the liver. Some larvae are trapped in the liver.

1 Fertile egg eaten, usually when a child eats soil or something contaminated with *Toxocara* eggs.

2 The larvae hatch in the small intestine and burrow into the lining of the intestine.

Figure 2 *Toxocara infections in humans*

In many cases they cause no further harm. However, the larvae can invade many parts of the body, such as the liver, brain, muscle, heart and lungs. They can cause various symptoms including fever, loss of appetite and weight loss, wheezing and coughing, skin rashes, and enlargement of the liver and spleen. The infected organs can be damaged, and in rare cases the infection may be fatal. Sometimes the larvae migrate to the eyes, where they can cause damage to the retina that occasionally results in blindness. About 2% of adults in the UK have antibodies against *Toxocara*, showing that they have been exposed to infection. However, these people rarely show symptoms of infection.

💡 Adaptations of Toxocara

Toxocara has many adaptations that make it a successful parasite. These include the following:

- Mature eggs are very sticky so they can attach to animals' fur or birds' beaks. This increases the chances that they will infect a new host.
- The worm has hooks to hold it in place in the intestine.
- The worm does not have highly developed locomotory structures, as it stays in the host's intestine.
- The worm has a poorly developed nervous system as its environment is relatively stable.
- The worm has a thick, resistant cuticle so that it is resistant to the enzymes in its host's gut.
- The reproductive organs are highly developed, so that the worm can produce enormous numbers of fertilised eggs. This is necessary to ensure that at least some of the eggs reach a new host.
- The ability of the worm to infect other hosts, such as rats and mice, helps to ensure that the parasite reaches new hosts.
- The worm can respire in low oxygen conditions in the intestine.
- The worm can produce anti-enzymes to reduce the damage that might be caused by the host's enzymes.
- The larvae form cysts of fibrous tissue around them when they are in the host's tissues. This means that the cells of the immune system are less able to reach them. It also means that the parasite's antigens are less likely to be detected.
- The larva sheds its cuticle regularly and replaces it. This means that antibodies and white blood cells that attach to the worm are also shed, thus reducing the damage that is done to the larva.

Summary questions

1 Children sometimes become infected with *Toxocara*. Use the information on this page to suggest ways of reducing the infection rate in children.

2 Suggest the advantages to *Toxocara* of living in the intestines of a cat or dog.

3 Use your knowledge of natural selection to explain how *Toxocara* has developed the ability to produce anti-enzymes.

1   **Figure 1** shows the way in which breathing is controlled.

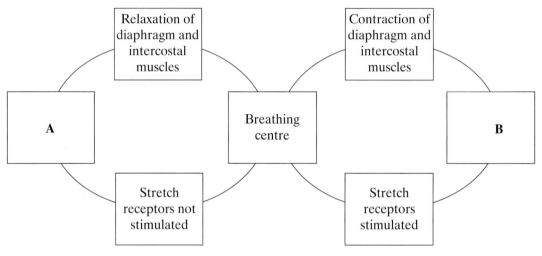

Figure 1

(a) (i) Box **B** describes what happens to the lungs. What should be written in box **B**?

   (ii) Copy the diagram and mark an **X** to show a stage in which nerve impulses travel to the breathing centre.   *(2 marks)*

(b) Explain **two** ways in which changes in the contraction of the diaphragm muscle affect pulmonary ventilation.   *(4 marks)*

AQA, 2006

2   The rate of blood flow to different parts of the body changes during exercise. The bar chart in **Figure 2** shows the blood flow to different organs and tissues, at rest and during strenuous exercise.

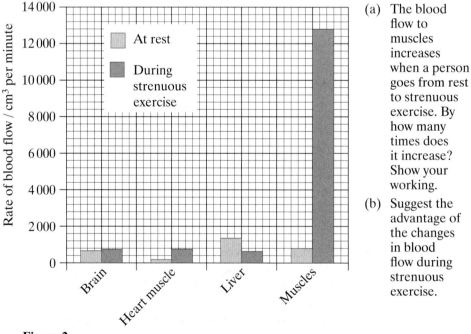

(a) The blood flow to muscles increases when a person goes from rest to strenuous exercise. By how many times does it increase? Show your working.   *(2 marks)*

(b) Suggest the advantage of the changes in blood flow during strenuous exercise.   *(4 marks)*

Figure 2

AQA, 2007

3 Heart rate increases during exercise. Describe the part played by chemoreceptors and the medulla in increasing heart rate. *(5 marks)*

AQA, 2004

4 (a) Describe the role of stretch receptors in the process of breathing. *(2 marks)*

(b) The graph in **Figure 3** shows the effect of changing the concentration of carbon dioxide in inhaled air on the ventilation rate.

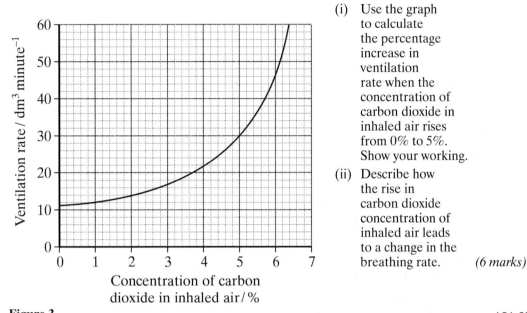

(i) Use the graph to calculate the percentage increase in ventilation rate when the concentration of carbon dioxide in inhaled air rises from 0% to 5%. Show your working.

(ii) Describe how the rise in carbon dioxide concentration of inhaled air leads to a change in the breathing rate. *(6 marks)*

Figure 3

AQA, 2004

5 Scientists investigated the ability of people with bipolar disorder to identify facial expressions. Eleven people with bipolar disorder were shown photographs of faces displaying happiness, sadness, anger or fear. They were asked to identify the emotion the person in the photograph was feeling. The same photographs were also shown to 25 healthy subjects of similar age and intelligence. The results of the investigation are shown in the graph in **Figure 4**.

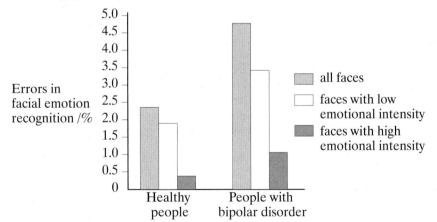

Figure 4

(a) (i) Describe the results shown in **Figure 4**.

(ii) People with bipolar disorder were more likely to misidentify faces as angry. Suggest how this could lead to difficulties in social interactions. *(4 marks)*

(b) (i) Explain why the photographs were also shown to healthy people.

(ii) Give **one** reason why the results of this investigation may not be reliable. *(3 marks)*

(c) Explain how the ability to recognise emotions from facial expressions may have improved the chances of survival among early humans. *(3 marks)*

Change in the way we live and our environment

11.1 Early farming

Learning objectives:

- How has farming contributed to our society?

- What is the evidence for early farming?

Specification reference: 3.2.5

As we have already seen, early humans were hunter-gatherers. This meant that they moved around from time to time, feeding on plant foods that they gathered, and animals that they were able to hunt or trap. Modern hunter-gatherer tribes have been studied, and these show that it is an agreeable way of life. These tribes rarely suffer food shortages and have plenty of leisure time.

Farming involves purposely breeding animals or sowing seeds. The resulting animals and plants are then cared for, and later harvested. However, a certain proportion of the animals or seeds are carefully chosen to breed from the next year.

Early farmers must have been able to plan ahead, as farming involves a considerable investment in effort before any benefits are seen. Furthermore, the first farmers would have needed to feed themselves by hunting and gathering until their first harvests were available. Even then, there were risks that the crops might fail despite all their hard work. They would also need to stay settled in one place. Scientists have tried to explain why early humans decided to take up farming. There seem to be three reasons:

- Farming allowed communities to settle and villages to grow. Once this happened, people could become specialised in trades and a more advanced culture could develop.
- Farming can support a larger population.
- Farming allowed people to settle in areas where there was not a plentiful supply of food.

The first farmers probably moved around every few years. It is likely that they used 'slash and burn' methods. They would choose an area of forest, which would have a soil rich in humus from fallen leaves and remains of animals and plants, as a result of natural recycling. They would have first killed the trees by 'ringing' them with axes, then they would have chopped them down and burned them. The stumps would gradually rot. Crops could then be grown among the dead roots. However, after about 20 years the soil fertility would have been lost, and they would move on to a new area.

Early farmers would have had to clear the land and grow crops using only stone tools and antlers. It would have been very hard work. After a period of time, however, they would have returned to previously cleared areas. This would have been the beginning of permanent fields. Once they learned the skills of crop rotation, and using manure and compost, their settlements would have become permanent. Eventually, these farmers were able to produce surplus food. This would have led to the beginnings of trade.

Early farming communities

The first farming communities developed between 7000 and 10000 years ago in the Near East. Most communities were no larger than a hundred people or so, although the largest settlements may have housed several hundred people.

Animals such as goats, sheep and cattle were domesticated and cereal crops were cultivated. However, other animals were often hunted as well.

Remains of early settlements show that they consisted of round buildings with reed roofs. Pottery containers, stone bowls, mortars and querns (millstones) have been found showing that the people processed their food and stored it. Later, however, larger rectangular buildings are found with hearths and separate areas for storage and making crafts. There is evidence that there was some trading with other settlements.

Figure 1 *Mehrgarh, in Iraq, dating from almost 7000 years ago*

Evidence for farming

When scientists find the remains of animal bones, they need to find out whether the animals were hunted or farmed. There are several ways in which they can do this.

- Animals killed by hunting can be any age, but hunters tend to be able to catch weaker animals more easily. This means that there will be many older animals and younger animals amongst those caught. When animals are farmed, they tend to be killed as soon as they have reached adult size. This is because the young adult animal will not grow any more, but it will still need to be fed. If the remains of animal bones show that most of the animals are adult, we can be reasonably sure that they were farmed.

- Domesticated animals differ in skeletal structure from wild animals. This is because early farmers would have chosen animals with particular traits, and were selectively breeding the animals. You will read more about this in Topic 11.2.

- The bones of farmed animals have an altered mineral crystal structure. This means that the minerals in their bones would be deposited in a different way, so that microscopic analysis of the bones can be made to determine the differences.

- Pollen analysis can show where crops were grown for food. When crop plants are grown, pollen analysis shows that most of the pollen is of the same type. Also, the pollen found will come mainly from crop species such as wheat and other cereals, rather than weed species or woody plants.

- A key factor in working out whether animals were hunted or farmed is the age at which the animals died. Scientists usually conclude that animals were kept for milk production if they find evidence that many animals were killed young, and only a small number of older individuals were kept. This is because unwanted calves would have been killed at an early age so that the milk could be used for human consumption. On the other hand, if animals are kept mainly for meat production, many of them will be killed as soon as they are fully grown.

How science works

Calculating the age at which an animal died

There are various ways of identifying age at death. One method is based on teeth. Animals, like humans, have two sets of teeth in their life. Young animals have a set of deciduous (milk) teeth, and later develop their permanent adult teeth. Scientists estimate the ages at which these deciduous and adult teeth erupt in different species, and then use this information to work out the ages of animals found on an archaeological site. Also, during an animal's life its teeth gradually wear down. This leaves patterns on their teeth which can be examined under a microscope. These patterns can also be used to calculate an animal's age when it died.

Limb bones are another indicator of an animal's age. All infant animals (including humans) are born with the ends of the limb bones detached from the main shaft. This allows the bone to grow in length, and the bones only fuse together when the animal is fully grown. This bone fusion takes place at a specific age for any particular animal. By studying the state of fusion of the bones, scientists can determine the age at death of an animal.

Summary questions

1. Make a list of advantages and disadvantages of farming compared to the hunter-gatherer lifestyle.

2. Suggest how scientists can find the age of early settlements such as Mehrgarh in Iraq.

11.2 Domesticating animals and plants

Humans have not only changed their environment by farming, but they have been able to change the characteristics of some kinds of animals and plants. They have achieved this through **selective breeding**.

Cereals

The most important plant foods grown by early farmers were cereal grasses. This is because the seed grain is rich in starch and can be stored when dry. Look at Figure 1. You can see that wild grasses have much smaller seed grains than modern cereals. Wild cereal grasses were clearly a source of food in Israel 13 000 years ago.

In time, people started to save seeds and grow them the following year. Wild grasses have small seed grains, and a rachis that is easily broken. This means that the seed will fall from the plant as soon as it is ripe. However, when early farmers gathered grain from wild grasses, any grains attached to a fragile rachis would fall to the ground. This meant that the grain would not be gathered, and so the seed would not be sown the following year. They were only able to gather grains from plants that had a strong rachis. In this way, selective breeding of grain occurred, although it was probably accidental.

However, once the early farmers were growing cereal grasses, they would notice if some plants produced bigger or better grains than others. In this way, they could choose the best grain to be used as seed for next year's crop. The less useful grain would be eaten.

Einkorn, *Triticum monococcum*, was the first domesticated wheat, grown about 9000 years ago. However, it did not produce a high yield. Another early wheat was Emmer wheat, *Triticum dicoccum*. This was a hybrid of Einkorn which had developed accidentally, and was being grown in parts of Israel. About 7500 years ago, Emmer formed a hybrid with another wild grass to form *Triticum aestivum*, common wheat. This was the kind of wheat that was grown in the civilisations of Mesopotamia and Ancient Egypt.

For thousands of years, humans selected strains of wheat with tall, strong stems. Tall stems were preferred because the wheat was harvested by hand, using a sickle, and tall strains of wheat were therefore easier to harvest. The stalks also needed to be strong because tall wheat with weak stems was more likely to be blown over by wind and rain. This is called **lodging**. Lodging meant that the crop was usually spoiled.

However, in the last 60 or so years, harvesting wheat has become more mechanised. Wheat is harvested using machinery such as combine harvesters, rather than by hand. This means that plant breeders have developed strains of wheat that are high-yielding, but have much shorter stems because machinery can harvest these easily. Furthermore, short stems are less prone to lodging. A further advantage of short stems is that more of the energy from sunlight that the plant harvests in photosynthesis can go towards growth of the grain, rather than growth of the stem.

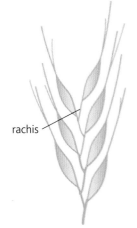

rachis

Figure 1 *Early wheat*

Domestication of cattle

Modern cattle, *Bos tauros*, have developed from the wild aurochs, *Bos primigenius*, shown in Figure 2. These were first domesticated about 8500 years ago.

Aurochs were fierce and strong animals with long horns, and they would not have been easy to domesticate. Early farmers chose to domesticate ruminants such as cattle for the following reasons:

- Ruminants eat grass, which means they digest cellulose. This is a food source that cannot be used by humans directly, so they were not competing with humans for the same food sources.
- Ruminants have a herding instinct, which makes them easier to manage because they can be rounded up together.

Figure 2 *The aurochs*

These animals were artificially selected so that they had shorter horns, were smaller in size, and with a more docile temperament. Cattle were important for meat and milk, but their carcass was used for other things, too. Their horns were used to make tools, and the hide to make clothing. Also, cattle could be used to pull things along, such as primitive ploughs.

Since the 19th century, farmers in the UK and northern Europe have recognised several different breeds of cattle. However, for many centuries before this, cattle with specialised characteristics had been bred. Today there are more than 270 different breeds, with many other varieties and types in addition. Modern cattle can be divided into two main categories:

- Dairy cattle have been bred mainly to produce milk. They are usually lean, with fairly fine bones and large udders. They have strong feet to walk to and from the milking parlour, which may include walking along roads. They also need to be capable of breeding regularly. In addition, there are some breeds which produce large volumes of milk, such as Holstein-Friesians. However, other breeds produce a lower volume of milk, but with a higher fat content, such as the Jersey.
- Beef cattle have been bred mainly for the production of meat. Beef breeds have a great deal of muscle tissue, especially around the loins and hindquarters, where the most expensive cuts of meat are found. Because they have so much muscle, these breeds have strong bones and large frames. It is also important that they are able to convert the food they eat into muscle efficiently. Important breeds of beef cattle in the UK include Herefords, Aberdeen Angus and Charolais.

Figure 3 *Examples of Friesian (left) and Hereford cattle*

Figure 4 *A wolf*

Domesticating dogs

It is thought that dogs, *Canis familiaris*, were the first animals to be domesticated by humans. We know that humans kept domesticated dogs 14 000 years ago, but it may have been much earlier than that. As soon as humans formed settlements, it is likely that dogs would have gathered around the settlement, attracted by the remains of food. Studies of DNA show that dogs were domesticated from the wolf, *Canis lupus*, but it seems that dogs were domesticated several times.

Dogs themselves may have played a part in this. Those that were fierce or attacked children would have been killed or chased away, while those that were friendlier would have been tolerated. Pups may have been reared by humans as companions. It seems that humans have artificially selected juvenile features in dogs. For example, barking is hardly ever seen in adult wild dogs. However, early humans may have decided that barking was a desirable characteristic, as it frightened off predators and helped them to act as watchdogs. Therefore, they would have chosen to breed only from dogs that barked as adults. Humans also selected for characteristics that made them look friendlier.

Dogs would have been valuable to early humans. Not only would they act as watchdogs, and frighten off predators, but they could also be trained to retrieve carcasses when hunting and follow animal scent trails.

Over the last few centuries, different breeds of dogs have been produced by selective breeding. Some have been bred as working dogs to assist with hunting, with rounding up sheep and cattle, to pull sledges or carts, to follow scent trails, and all kinds of other roles. However, others have been bred simply to make good companion animals, and features such as ear shape, fur colour and temperament have been selected for.

Figure 5 *Modern breeds of dog*

Summary questions

1. Suggest how DNA studies could show that domestic dogs have been bred from wolves.

2. Suggest how early farmers could use selective breeding to produce cattle that are smaller and more docile than the wild auroch.

3. Scientists find the bones of dogs in early human settlements. Suggest how they can tell whether these were domesticated dogs, or wolves that were hunted and killed for food.

11.3 Changing the landscape

Learning objectives:

- How has farming changed the UK landscape?
- What happens when farmed land is not cultivated or grazed anymore?
- What is the effect of draining wetlands?

Specification reference: 3.2.5

The landscape and ecosystems that are present in the UK today are largely a result of human activities.

The effect of farming

Scientists can use pollen analysis to work out what the vegetation of Britain was like over the centuries. When the Neolithic period started about 5000 years ago, most of lowland Britain was covered with mixed forest, predominated by oak.

The first farmers would have used the foliage of trees, particularly elm, to provide food for their animals. Neolithic farmers cleared these forests for the first time to provide grazing land for their animals, and sometimes to provide fields for growing Emmer wheat. The main areas that were cleared were the chalk areas on the South Downs and the limestone areas in the Cotswolds. These are drier, upland areas.

By Roman times, there were still many areas of mixed oak forest in Britain, for example in the Midlands. Many animals lived in these forests, including deer, wolves, bears and lynxes. Higher land and areas with poorer soil were covered with pine and birch woods. Forest trees were useful. Oak trees provided timber for building and ships, and oak bark was used for tanning. Beech trees were used to make furniture.

At the end of the Romano-British period, much of lowland Britain was still covered with forest. The Angles and Saxons settled in the lowlands, and large areas of the lowland forests were cleared. This provided fields with more fertile, easily worked soil.

Application and How science works

Pollen analysis

In pollen analysis, or palynology, microscopes are used to analyse the range of plant pollens present in a sample. Scientists can take a sample of soil from different layers, and look at the pollen present. This can tell us what crops or vegetation may have been present when that soil layer was deposited. Pollen is part of the reproductive system of plants. Pollen grains are tiny structures containing the male gametes. They may be blown by the wind or carried by insects to female plants. Particularly in the summer time, the air is filled with pollen. Each kind of pollen grain has a very distinctive appearance when seen under the microscope, enabling scientists to identify them.

Pollen from soil that has been excavated or removed from the ground is analysed. Each layer of soil is analysed separately. Radiocarbon dating is usually used to date these layers so that the changing pollen composition over time can be measured.

The soil is mixed with water and placed in a centrifuge (a machine that spins it very fast). This separates the lighter pollen from the denser soil. Individual grains are then identified and counted. A graph may be made showing the types of pollen present at any particular time. Scientists can distinguish between grass, weed, tree or cereal pollens. This can tell us whether forest clearance has happened; whether farming was taking place; or whether settlements were abandoned.

Succession

Early Neolithic farmers, as you learned in Topic 11.1, would have moved on after some years, so they were responsible for deforestation in large areas of Britain. When fields are abandoned, they undergo a process called **succession**. Seeds are blown in by the wind, so that grasses and small herbaceous plants start to grow on the bare earth. After a while, small woody plants and young trees appear, forming scrub. These plants grow taller than the grasses and herbaceous plants, and compete with them for sunlight. This means that the smaller plants start to die out. If the abandoned field is left for many years, the young trees grow even taller. They compete with the shrubs and smaller plants for light, and eventually, after a hundred or more years, the land is covered with forest. This is called a **climax community**. A climax community remains stable unless there is a change in the environment. Mixed forest is the natural climax community over most of Britain. As succession progresses, there are more species of both plants and animals. The more different species that are present, the greater the **biodiversity**. As more plant species are present in an area, there will be more animals. This is because there is a greater variety of food supply and also more habitats.

Farming reduces biodiversity, because farmers grow just one or a few crops in an area. They remove other plants that will compete with their crops (weeds) and they try to get rid of animal pests that will eat their crops. Modern farming has an even greater impact on diversity, as the same crop may be grown over enormous areas. This is called **monoculture**.

Grassland with small flowering plants, like daises.

as grazing is reduced

Taller herbaceous plants grow, and compete with lower plants for light. Tree seedlings start to grow. There are more animal species present as there are more different plant species for them to feed on.

Bushes and shrubs start to grow. Most of the smaller herbaceous plants die as they are unable to compete with the bushes and shrubs for resources such as light. More animal species are present as there are more sources of food, etc.

Fast growing trees start to grow, forming a forest. Many of the smaller plants die as they are unable to compete with the trees for resources such as light. Even more animal species are present, as there are more sources of food and more habitats.

Larger, slower growing trees, such as oak, grow. These grow taller than most other trees, so they compete successfully for light. This forms the climax community. A large number of different animal species are able to grow here, as there are many different plant species to feed on, and more habitats.

Figure 1 *Succession in an abandoned field*

The New Forest

The New Forest is in the South of England near to the English Channel. It is an area that was formed by King William I in 1079 to provide him with forest where he could hunt deer. He described the area as 'waste'. It is likely that the land was partly natural forest that was being heavily grazed by animals such as cattle and pigs, and partly abandoned fields that were slowly reverting to scrubland. King William passed laws to

New Forest

Figure 2 *The New Forest*

restrict the rights of local people to use the land to graze their animals. As a result, trees could grow and herds of deer could flourish.

For centuries after this, the forest was used as a source of timber, mainly to build ships for the British navy. By the 17th century, the forest was being managed to provide timber for ship-building. In an effort to produce more timber, deer were removed from the forest. However, by the late 19th century, there was a reduced demand for timber for ship-building. Local people were given rights to the forest again, instead of the Crown. People started to realise the ecological value of the New Forest. The special landscapes found there are a result of these human activities.

Figure 3 *The New Forest*

Since the 1960s, fences have been put in alongside many of the roads, to reduce the number of deer killed by cars. Cattle grids have also been installed. The Forest was made a National Park so that it could be preserved.

Draining wetlands

Britain contains a number of marshy wetland areas. One of these is the Fens, an area of 750 000 acres in the east of England. The original fenland was very flat, with plants such as sedges and willow. The area is very wet and prone to flooding because it contains many rivers, and is only very slightly above sea level. The rate of flow of water in the rivers is therefore slow, and over the years a great deal of silt has been deposited. Plants, even trees, grew here in the drier areas. Periodic flooding caused more silt to be deposited, and dead vegetation was turned into peat. This must have happened several times as there are numerous layers of silt and peat.

The Romans attempted to drain the fenland for farming. They even built a few roads across the Fens. However, by Anglo-Saxon times the area had become marshy again, either from natural causes or because people had allowed Roman work to decay. In the 15th century a river was cut in an attempt to drain the Fens, but nothing significant happened until 1630. This was when a Dutch engineer, Cornelius Vermuyden, was given a contract to drain the Fens. He built many drainage channels and put in windmills to pump water from one level to another. A further drainage improvement project was completed in the 1960s. As a result of draining this land, it is highly fertile and very useful for agriculture. Vegetables, fruit and wheat are the main crops.

Figure 4 *Fenland location*

However, there are now plans to restore some of this area to traditional wetland. People have realised that a special and rare habitat is being lost, leading to the extinction of many species. The Great Fen project has been awarded lottery funding to buy land that connects two existing nature reserves, to create an area where wildlife can flourish. Land that is currently used for agriculture will be allowed to return to its natural, wetter condition.

Conservationists hope that the area will provide a habitat for rare species such as fen violets, fen wood-rush and fen ragwort. Animals such as otters and water voles should thrive in the area, as well as many species of beetles and a rare dragonfly. Many bird species, such as nightingales and long-eared owls, live in wetland habitats. It is hoped that other rare species of bird such as bitterns, spoonbills, purple herons and cranes, will eventually colonise the area, increasing biodiversity. Another benefit of restoring some of these wetlands is that it provides an area to hold flood water, reducing urban flooding.

Figure 5 *Fenland*

Summary questions

1 Explain why there is very little biodiversity in a farmer's field.

2 List some arguments for and against the Great Fen project.

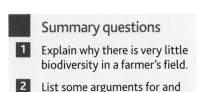

AQA Examination-style questions

1 Between 8000 and 12 000 years ago humans began the cultivation of wheat and the domestication of cattle.

(a) Describe **two** pieces of archaeological evidence that early settled communities began cultivating crops and keeping domesticated cattle. *(2 marks)*

(b) Explain how the cultivation of plants and the domestication of animals influenced the development of human societies. *(4 marks)*

AQA, 2001

2 **Figure 1** shows wild 'einkorn' wheat first cultivated about 12 000 years ago and a modern type of bread wheat, both drawn to the same scale.

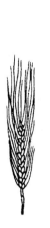

Einkorn Modern bread wheat

Figure 1

(a) (i) Give **two** differences between 'einkorn' and modern bread wheat.

(ii) Archaeologists excavating sites in the Middle East showed that wheat changed considerably over its first 5000 years of cultivation. Suggest how the activities of early farmers led to these changes. *(5 marks)*

(b) Cultivation of grain enabled early farmers to produce a surplus. Explain the effects this would have had on human societies. *(3 marks)*

AQA, 1997

3 Cattle are thought to have been one of the first animals to have been domesticated, about 8500 years ago.

(a) In addition to providing milk, suggest **one** characteristic of cattle which made them particularly suitable for domestication. *(1 mark)*

(b) Give **two** pieces of archaeological evidence that cattle were domesticated by early humans. *(2 marks)*

AQA, 1996

4   **Table 1** shows the number of different animal remains found at two sites of different ages in the same region of the Middle East.

Table 1

Age of site/ years	Number of remains			
	Goat	Cattle	Gazelle	Fox
8000	22	30	294	130
7000	380	97	110	60

What evidence in **Table 1** would suggest that farming started in this region between these two dates?   *(4 marks)*

5   Describe **four** ways in which communities changed when farming started.   *(4 marks)*

6   Read the following passage:

A plan to create one of the country's biggest conservation areas has moved a step closer after the acquisition of 1294 hectares of land that has been used for farming. The Great Fen Project in Cambridgeshire aims to eventually connect Woodwalton Fen and Holme Fen nature reserves. The conservation scheme aims to provide a haven for a wide variety of wildlife once common in the Fens. Organisers have already started to turn some fields back into wild wetlands, and   5
believe recent sightings of marsh harriers and more skylarks are signs of success. About 10 000 years ago eastern England, like most of Britain, was covered in woodland. Over millennia, trees grew in warm, dry periods then decayed into peat during cooler, wetter times. By the 1600s, the Fens was one of the most prosperous areas of the country. They were full of wildlife habitats and abundant species, and the people living in the fens were making their living from that   10
– cutting reeds, shooting enormous numbers of wildfowl, taking huge numbers of fish out of the rivers and grazing animals. Woodwalton Fen alone is thought to have been home to more than 900 species of moth and 850 invertebrates over the years.

Use the information in the passage and your own knowledge to answer the following questions.

(a)   Describe how succession would result in eastern England being covered in woodland 10 000 years ago (line 7).   *(6 marks)*

(b)   Evaluate the benefits of the Great Fen project.   *(6 marks)*

Unit 2 questions: Humans – their origins and adaptations

1   (a)   Describe and explain how the structure of DNA results in accurate replication.   *(4 marks)*

      (b)   Describe how the behaviour of chromosomes during mitosis and explain how this behaviour results in the production of two genetically identical cells.   *(7 marks)*

      (c)   A cancerous tumour is formed by uncontrolled mitotic division. This results in a mass of cells with an inadequate blood supply. Drugs are being developed which only kill cells in a low oxygen environment. Suggest how these drugs could be useful in the treatment of cancer.   *(2 marks)*

AQA, 2006

2   Geographical distribution of body shape and size is thought to be an adaptation to climate. The drawings in **Figure 1** show different human forms found in the savannah and tropical rain forest. They are drawn to the same scale.

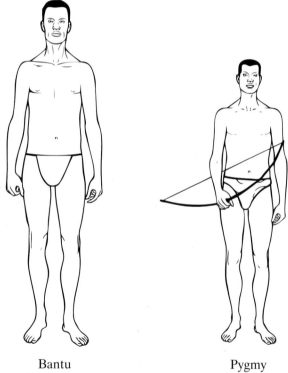

Bantu
(savannah)

Pygmy
(tropical rain forest)

Figure 1

      (a)   (i)   How is body size and shape affected by climate?

           (ii)   Suggest an evolutionary advantage for this.   *(2 marks)*

      (b)   Skin pigmentation is another feature which shows geographical variation. Suggest an evolutionary advantage for darker skin pigmentation in people living close to the equator in Africa.   *(2 marks)*

AEB, 1987

3 **Figure 2** shows how a tumour is produced from a single normal body cell.

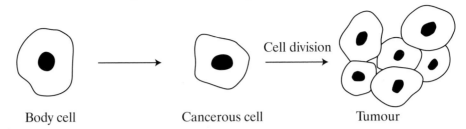

Body cell   Cancerous cell   Tumour

Figure 2

(a) (i) What type of cell division occurs when a cancerous cell develops into a tumour?

    (ii) Give **two** characteristics that would indicate that a group of cells is a tumour.   *(3 marks)*

(b) (i) Vincristine is a drug that interferes with spindle formation in mitosis. Vincristine is useful in treating cancer. Explain how.

    (ii) Vincristine may have side effects such as hair loss and reduced red blood cell numbers. Suggest why.   *(4 marks)*

AQA, 2000

4 The graph in **Figure 3** shows the mean number of cigarettes smoked per person per year from 1911 until 1991. **Table 1** shows the number of deaths from lung cancer during the same time period.

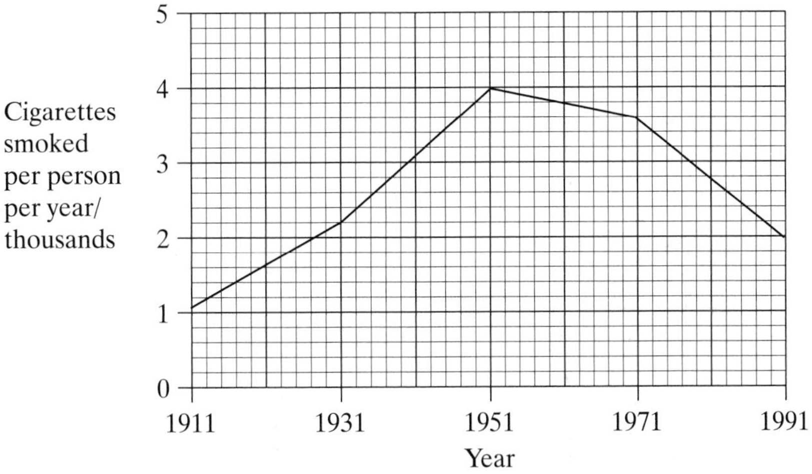

Cigarettes smoked per person per year/ thousands

Year

Figure 3

Table 1

Year	Deaths per year from lung cancer
1911	600
1931	1 500
1951	14 000
1971	23 000
1911	25 000

(a) (i) Describe the relationship between the data on the graph and the figures given in **Table 1**.

    (ii) Suggest an explanation for the relationship betweeen the data on the graph and the figures given in **Table 1**.   *(2 marks)*

(b) Radon is a radioactive gas formed by the breakdown of radium. Suggest how inhaling radon may lead to the development of lung cancer.   *(3 marks)*

AQA, 2000

5   (a) Explain how the following adaptations would have increased the chances of
         survival of early humans:
         (ii) bipedalism,
         (ii) an opposable thumb.   *(4 marks)*

    (b) It is thought that dogs were the first animals to be domesticated by humans. It is
         thought that domestic dogs were selectively bred from the wolf. Wolves are
         very fierce.
         (i)   Suggest how humans may have used selective breeding to develop domestic
               dogs that were more docile.
         (ii) Suggest how domestic dogs may have been useful to early humans.   *(5 marks)*

6   (a) Explain the advantages of farming to early humans.   *(3 marks)*

    (b) Early farmers probably cleared an area of forest to produce farmland. However,
         after a few years, the soil would lose its fertility and the farmers would move on to
         another area. The cleared area would gradually return to becoming forest again.
         Explain how.   *(4 marks)*

7   An investigator observed a cell during part of one cell cycle. The graph in **Figure 4**
         shows the mean distance between the sister chromatids.

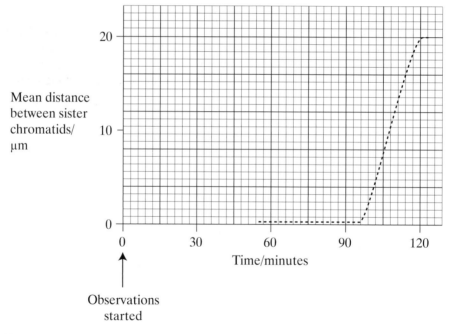

         Figure 4

    (a) (i)   At what time did anaphase start?
         (ii) Explain the evidence from the graph that supports your answer.   *(3 marks)*

    (b) The investigator was not able to obtain measurements between 0 and 60 minutes.
         Use your knowledge of the cell cycle to explain why.   *(2 marks)*

(c) **Figure 5** summarises gamete formation and fertilisation in humans.

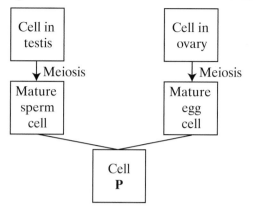

Figure 5

(i) Name cell **P**.

(ii) Meiosis halves the chromosome number. Explain why this is important. *(2 marks)*

AQA, 2007

8 Scientists extracted DNA from two different species of animals, A and B. Each sample of DNA was heated so that it became single-stranded.

In one tube, the single-stranded DNA from species A was cooled so that it could re-form into double-stranded DNA (A/A).

In the other tube, single-stranded DNA from species A was mixed with single-stranded DNA from species B, and cooled so that it re-formed double-stranded DNA (A/B).

Samples of DNA from each tube were heated separately. The temperature was raised slowly. The temperature at which 50% of the double-stranded DNA had become single-stranded ($T_{50}H$) was recorded for each tube. The results are shown in **Figure 6**.

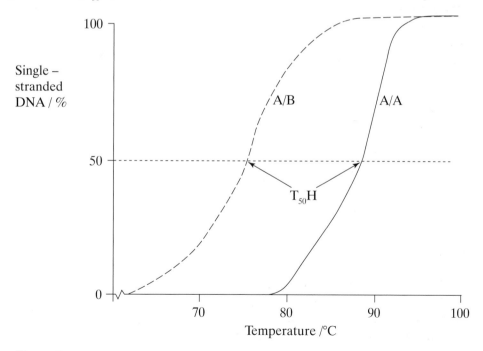

Figure 6

(a) Explain why $T_{50}H$ is lower when species A DNA is mixed with species B DNA. *(3 marks)*

(b) Explain how this technique might be useful in comparing evolutionary relationships between species. *(2 marks)*

Glossary

A

Acheulian culture: The techniques used for tool-making by *Homo erectus*. These tools had slimmer and straighter cutting edges (called bifaces) than the earlier Oldowan tools.

activation energy: The energy needed for a reaction to occur.

active immunity: This is when the body produces its own memory cells, either as the result of infection or as the result of vaccination.

active site: The specific part of an enzyme's structure into which the substrate fits.

active transport: The movement of a substance across a membrane against its concentration gradient. A carrier protein is required for this, as well as energy from ATP.

allele: An alternative form of a gene. For example, the gene coding for eye colour may have alleles coding for blue or brown eyes.

alveoli: (Singular = alveolus) Air sacs in the lungs where gas exchange takes place.

anaphase: The stage in mitosis when the daughter chromatids separate and move to opposite poles of the cell.

aneurysm: The ballooning out of a weakened the wall of an artery caused by an atheroma. The artery may rupture as a result, causing a haemorrhage.

angina: Severe chest pains caused by a lack of oxygen and glucose to the heart muscle. This is caused by atheroma narrowing the coronary arteries.

angioplasty: A treatment for blocked coronary arteries. A catheter is inserted into the blood vessel, carrying a balloon. When the catheter is in the right place, the balloon is inflated, pushing the artery wall outwards and making the artery wider.

antibiotic: A substance produced by a microorganism that kills or inhibits bacteria.

antibody: A protein produced by B-lymphocytes. It has a specific shape that is complementary to one specific antigen.

antigen: A large molecule, usually a protein or polysaccharide that stimulates an immune response. They may be 'free' molecules, such as toxins, or on the surface of a microorganism.

aortic bodies: A small cluster of chemoreceptors and supporting cells located in the wall of the aorta.

arteriole: A blood vessel that connects an artery to the capillaries.

artery: A blood vessel with a muscular wall that carries blood away from the heart.

atheroma: A fatty deposit that builds up inside the wall of an artery.

ATP: Adenosine triphosphate. This is an energy storage molecule made in respiration. When ATP breaks down to form ADP (adenosine diphosphate), energy is released that can be used for processes in the cell.

atrial systole: The stage of the cardiac cycle when the atria are contracting, forcing blood into the ventricles.

atrioventricular node (AVN): A small mass of specialised cardiac muscle fibres between the atria and the ventricles. It receives impulses from the walls of the atria, and conducts impulses down the bundle of His.

atrioventricular (AV) valves: The valves between the atria of the heart and the ventricles

attenuated vaccine: A vaccine containing a live microorganism that has been repeatedly sub-cultured so that it no longer causes the disease.

Australopithecines: Early hominids that evolved in Africa about 5 million years ago, and became extinct about a million years ago. They walked upright, had small brains, and ate a largely plant-based diet.

B

bacteriophage: A virus that infects bacteria.

basal metabolic rate: The energy you need to stay alive, when you are at rest but not asleep.

BCG vaccine: Bacille Calmette-Guerin. A vaccine containing attenuated *Mycobacterium bovis* that protects people against TB.

benign tumour: A tumour that does not spread to other organs or destroy the tissue it is in. A benign tumour is not cancerous.

beta-blockers: Drugs used to treat hypertension. They fit into receptors on the heart muscle, stopping noradrenalin fitting into them, as a result, heart rate is slowed.

bilayer: A double layer. Phospholipids in a cell membrane form two layers called a 'bilayer'.

binomial system: A system whereby living organisms are given two names based on Latin. The first name is the genus, and the second name the species.

biodiversity: The variety of living organisms in a particular area.

bipedal: The ability to walk on two legs.

body mass index: Body mass index (BMI) = body mass in kilograms divided by (height in metres)^2

bronchi: (Singular = bronchus) Tubes leading from the trachea, bringing air into each lung.

bronchioles: Highly branched tubes leading from the bronchi, carrying air to the air sacs or alveoli.

bundle of His: Specialised cardiac muscle fibres that conduct impulses from the atrioventricular node to the bottom of the septum.

C

capillary: A thin-walled blood vessel that allows exchange of substances between the blood and the tissues.

capsid: The protein coat that surrounds a virus particle.

capsomere: One of the protein units that makes up the capsid of a virus.

carbon dating: A method of dating preserved remains of artefacts up to 50 000 years old. It measures the ratio of ^{14}C to ^{12}C in a sample.

carcinogens: Chemicals that can cause cancer, such as chemicals in cigarette smoke.

cardiac cycle: The sequence of events that results in the heart pumping blood round the body.

cardiac muscle: The type of muscle that makes up the wall of the heart. It is different from other kinds of muscle in the body because it contracts and relaxes continuously throughout life, and does not need stimulation by the nervous system.

cardiac output: The volume of blood pumped by the heart in one minute.

cardiovascular centre: The cardiovascular centre is a part of the medulla in the brain. It is responsible for the regulation of the rate at which the heart beats.

carotid bodies: A small cluster of chemoreceptors and supporting cells located in the wall of the carotid artery.

carrier proteins: Specifically shaped proteins in the cell membrane that carry particular molecules or ions across the membrane.

cellulose: A polysaccharide found in plant cell walls. It is a polymer of beta-glucose, not alpha-glucose as in starch. This means that the bonds linking the glucose units together are a different shape from those found in starch, so human enzymes cannot digest it.

centriole: A small, hollow cylinder found inside a cell that organises the microtubules that form the spindle fibres.

CFTR: Cystic fibrosis transmembrane regulator. It is a protein in the cell membrane that transports chloride ions out of the cell. In cystic fibrosis, this protein is faulty and does not work properly.

chemoreceptors: Receptor cells that detect changes in blood pH.

cholesterol: This is an important molecule in cell surface membranes, where it helps to keep the membrane fluid. It is also a precursor of many hormones.

chromatid: Either of the two daughter strands of a replicated chromosome that are joined by a single centromere and separate during cell division to become individual chromosomes.

chromatin: The DNA present in the nucleus of a cell when it is not dividing. During this stage the DNA is spread out. It is only organised into chromosomes when the cell is dividing.

chromosome: One of the thread-like structures found in the nucleus of a cell. A chromosome consists of a tightly coiled length of DNA, closely associated with proteins including histones.

cilia: (Singular = cilium) Tiny hair-like organelles found on the surface of certain cells. The cilia beat in a rhythmic, coordinated way.

climax community: A stable community of plants and animals that will remain unchanged unless the environment changes. It results from the process of succession.

clonal selection: This is the process by which a B-cell with a receptor complementary to a specific antigen is stimulated to divide.

clone: A cell, group of cells, or organism that is genetically identical to a single common ancestor, such as another cell or organism. In the case of eukaryotic cells, clones are produced by mitosis.

complementary base-pairing: A term used to describe the specific pairing mechanism in DNA, in which the base adenine will only pair with thymine, and cytosine will only pair with guanine. The bases that pair together are said to be complementary.

condensation: A chemical reaction in which two molecules are joined together and a molecule of water is removed.

contact isolation: A method of reducing the spread of MRSA in hospitals. It involves medical staff washing their hands very carefully before and after touching each patient, and keeping a patient with MRSA in a separate room.

coronary arteries: Blood vessels that branch off the aorta and supply the heart muscle with glucose and oxygen.

coronary heart disease: The collective name for diseases of the heart and blood vessels, e.g. angina, aneurysm and myocardial infarction.

cranial capacity: The volume inside the skull. It can be estimated by pouring dry sand into the skull. This gives an estimate of the volume of brain that was inside the skull.

cristae: The folded inner membranes of a mitochondrion. It is here that ATP is produced in aerobic respiration.

cytochrome c: A protein found in mitochondria, that is needed in respiration. It is useful in studying evolutionary relationships between organisms.

D

deep vein thrombosis (DVT): A blood clot that forms in a deep vein in the body, usually the lower leg.

deficiency disease: A disease caused by a lack of certain vitamins or mineral salts.

denaturation: A change in shape of a protein molecule, usually as a result of high temperatures or a change in pH.

diaphragm: A dome-shaped sheet of muscle that lies across the bottom of the thorax, below the lungs.

diastole : The stage of the cardiac cycle when the heart muscle is relaxed, and the heart is filling with blood.

dietary fibre: Polysaccharides that cannot be broken down in the human gut, such as cellulose from plant cell walls.

diploid: A cell, nucleus or organism in which the nuclei contain two copies of each chromosome.

disaccharides: Sugars composed of two monosaccharides joined together, e.g. maltose is made of two glucose units joined together.

DNA polymerase: An enzyme that joins DNA nucleotides together to form a strand of DNA.

Down's syndrome: A condition in which the individual has three copies of chromosome 21 instead of two. It results from non-disjunction.

droplet infection: An infection transmitted from one individual to another when a person breathes in droplets of moisture expelled from the upper respiratory tract through sneezing or coughing.

E

elastic recoil: This results from the elastic tissue in the walls of arteries. When blood is forced into the arteries under high pressure, the elastic tissue stretches, and then it contracts back again. This helps to even out blood flow and keep the blood under high pressure.

embolus: A piece of a thrombus that breaks off. It travels in the blood until it gets to a place where the artery is narrowed.

emphysema: A respiratory disease in which the walls of the alveoli break down. This results in larger air sacs with a much smaller surface area for gas exchange.

endothelium : Thin, flattened cells that form lining tissues, for example, the lining of veins and arteries.

endotoxin: A toxin found inside a bacterial cell. It is only released after the bacterium has died.

epithelium: Outside layer of cells that covers all the open surfaces of the body including the skin, and mucous membranes that communicate with the outside of the body. For example, ciliated epithelium lines the respiratory tract.

eukaryotic cells: Cells containing a membrane-bound nucleus, and membrane-bound organelles, such as mitochondria, e.g. animal cells and plant cells.

extrinsic protein: A protein present in only one of the two phospholipid layers in the cell surface membrane.

F

flagellum (bacterial): A long, thin hair-like structure on the surface of a bacterium that enables it to move.

fluid-mosaic: The fluid-mosaic model describes the way in which molecules are thought to be arranged in a cell surface membrane. A double layer of phospholipids has proteins floating in it, which are able to change their positions.

foramen magnum: A hole in the skull where the backbone meets with the skull.

fossil: Any form of preserved remains from a living organism, e.g. imprints in stone, preserved bones.

G

gamete: A sex cell, such as an egg or sperm, containing the haploid number of chromosomes.

gene: A length of DNA that occurs at a specific locus on a chromosome. Usually, a gene codes for a particular protein or polypeptide.

geographical isolation: The isolation of populations of a species by a geographical barrier, such as a river, so that they no longer interbreed.

glycaemic index: A measure of the effect of 50 g of a food on blood glucose level, and how quickly blood glucose is raised, compared to 50 g of pure glucose. It is given as a figure out of 100; 50 g of glucose has the highest possible glycaemic index, which is 100.

glycaemic load: A measure of the effect of a portion of food on blood glucose level.
Glycaemic load = carbohydrate content of food (g) × GI of food/100

glycogen: A polysaccharide found in animal cells. It is a polymer made up of many glucose molecules. It is similar to starch, but it is more branched.

glycolipid: A lipid with a carbohydrate molecule attached. Glycolipids are found in cell surface membranes and have similar functions to glycoproteins.

glycoprotein: A protein with a carbohydrate molecule attached. Glycoproteins are found in cell surface membranes. They help cells to join together and can also act as antigens.

Golgi body: A series of flattened sacs in a cell, made of membranes. It modifies proteins made on the rough endoplasmic reticulum and packages them in vesicles for secretion.

growth factor: A polypeptide hormone that can stimulate cell division.

guideline daily amounts (GDAs): A guide to the amount of energy, sugar, fat, saturated fat and salt a typical adult should eat in a day.

H

haploid: A nucleus, cell or organism in which the nuclei contain just one set of chromosomes.

helper T cells: A type of T cell which produces chemicals that stimulate phagocytosis by macrophages, stimulate antibody production by B cells, and activate killer T cells.

heparin: A drug that inhibits blood clotting, and is often used to treat deep vein thrombosis.

hierarchy: A system in which big groups are subdivided into smaller groups with no overlap.

histone: A type of protein that is found with DNA in chromosomes. It is important in packaging DNA to form chromosomes. However, bacterial DNA does not contain histones.

HIV positive: A person is said to be HIV positive when they are infected with HIV and contain antibodies against HIV, but do not have symptoms.

hominid: A member of the family Hominidae. At one time, humans were considered to be the only living members of this family, but many scientists now include the great apes in this family as well, because of their close similarities to humans.

homologous chromosomes: A pair of chromosomes which have the same genes but different alleles.

host: An organism that a parasite lives in or on, feeding from it and causing it harm.

hydrolysis: The splitting of a molecule into smaller molecules by adding a molecule of water.

hydrophilic: This means 'water-liking'. A hydrophilic molecule associates closely with water.

hydrophobic: This means 'water-hating'. A hydrophobic molecule will not mix with water.

hypertension: High blood pressure.

hypertonic: A solution is hypertonic to another if it has a lower water potential. If a cell is placed in a hypertonic solution, water will leave the cell by osmosis.

hypotonic: A solution is hypotonic to another if it has a higher water potential. If a cell is placed in a hypotonic solution, water will enter the cell by osmosis.

I

induced fit theory: This theory suggests that the enzyme has a flexible basic shape. When the substrate collides with the enzyme, the active site changes shape to become a close fit for the substrate.

intercostal muscles: Muscles between the ribs, that contract and relax to bring about breathing movements.

interphase: The stage in the cell cycle when a cell is not dividing. During this period proteins are made, cell organelles are replicated, respiration occurs and DNA is replicated.

intrinsic protein: A protein that passes through both phospholipid layers in the cell surface membrane.

isotonic: Two solutions are isotonic if they have the same water potential. If a cell is placed in an isotonic solution, it will remain at equilibrium. The same amount of water will enter the cell and leave the cell, so there will be no net osmotic movement.

K

killer T cells: A type of T cell that binds to cells carrying a specific antigen and destroys them.

kingdom: One of the major groups used in classification. Currently, biologists usually divide living organisms into five Kingdoms: Animalia, Plantae, Fungi, Prokaryotae and Protoctista.

L

lactose intolerant: This is when a person is unable to digest the lactose in the food they eat because they do not produce enough lactase enzyme. The undigested lactose causes growth of certain bacteria, and leads to stomach cramps and diarrhoea. [this definition was given as part of the entry for pancreatitis; I have added 'lactose intolerant' as an entry and put it here; please check with author. Mitch]

lock and key theory: A theory to explain how an enzyme works. According to this theory, the substrate fits into the enzyme's active site, reducing the activation energy for the reaction to occur.

locus: The position of a gene on a chromosome.

lodging: The ability of cereal grain crops to be blown over by the wind and rain.

lymph: A fluid similar in composition to tissue fluid, but with less oxygen and nutrients in it.

lymph vessels: Blunt-ended vessels that carry lymph back to the blood system.

M

malignant tumour: A cancerous tumour that destroys the surrounding tissues. Cells from it may spread through the body via the blood or lymphatic systems and cause secondary tumours elsewhere.

Mantoux test: A test for TB. It involves injecting a protein called tuberculin from *Mycobacterium* into the skin. The area will become red and swollen if the person has had contact with TB.

matrix: The fluid-filled area inside the mitochondrion. It contains enzymes used in aerobic respiration.

meiosis: A type of cell division that results in the formation of four haploid cells (or gametes) from one diploid cell. The daughter nuclei are all genetically different.

memory B cells: B cells that remain in the blood for a long time after an infection has been combated. If the same antigen is encountered a second time, the B-cells will divide and produce large numbers of specific antibodies very quickly.

metaphase: The stage in mitosis when the chromosomes are arranged around the equator of the spindle.

metastasis: The process by which a cell can break off a primary tumour and travel in the blood or lymph system to start off a secondary tumour elsewhere in the body. Another name for the secondary tumour is a metastasis.

microtubule: Any of the slender, tubular structures composed chiefly of tubulin, found in the cytoplasm of nearly all cells. They are involved in maintenance of cell shape and in the movements of organelles, and form the spindle fibres of mitosis.

microwear: Microscopic scratch marks found on bones and teeth. Microwear on teeth can give an indication of the kind of food eaten by an organism.

mitochondria: A cell organelle where the reactions of aerobic respiration take place.

mitosis: A process of cell division in which a parent cell divides to form two genetically identical daughter cells.

monoclonal antibodies: Identical antibodies against one specific antigen, produced by a single clone of plasma cells.

monoculture: Growing the same kind of crop over a large area.

monomer: One of the smaller molecules that are linked together to form a polymer.

monosaccharides: These are the simplest kind of carbohydrate. They consist of single sugar units, such as glucose.

monounsaturated fatty acid: A fatty acid with just one double bond between carbon atoms.

Mousterian culture: The techniques used for tool-making by Neanderthals. These were tools made from stone flakes, refined by using a softer hammer of bone, wood or stone.

multi-drug resistant: This term describes bacteria that have developed resistance to several different antibiotics.

mutation: A change in the base sequence of DNA.

myocardial infarction: The scientific name for a heart attack, which happens when one of the coronary arteries becomes blocked by atheroma or by a thrombus, cutting off the oxygen supply to some of the heart muscle cells. This means that some of the heart muscle cells die.

myogenic: This term is applied to cardiac muscle because it contracts on its own without any stimulation by the nervous system.

N

natural selection: The process by which the best-adapted organisms in a population survive, reproduce and pass on their alleles to their offspring.

non-disjunction: The failure of chromosomes to separate properly during meiosis. It results in gametes containing the wrong number of chromosomes.

non-virulent: A term meaning 'does not cause disease'.

nucleotide : The monomer from which polynucleotides are made. A nucleotide contains a five-carbon sugar, a phosphate group and an organic base.

O

obese: People with a body mass index over 30.

oedema : The medical term for a swelling in the tissues caused by a build-up of tissue fluid.

oestrus: The time in the reproductive cycle of a female mammal when ovulation occurs, and the female is receptive to mating.

Oldowan culture: The techniques used for tool-making by early humans, i.e. *Homo habilis*. The tools were made by hitting one rock against another to make sharp flakes. The flakes were used to cut up meat, leaving a sharp-edged chopper that could be held in the hand.

oncogene: A mutated proto-oncogene that causes uncontrolled cell division, or cancer.

opportunistic disease: An infection by a microorganism that normally does not cause disease but becomes pathogenic when the body's immune system is impaired and unable to fight off infection, as in AIDS and certain other diseases.

opposable thumb: A mobile thumb that can grip objects against any of the other fingers, like that of modern humans.

oral rehydration therapy: A method of controlling diarrhoea. A person is given a balanced solution of salts and glucose which stimulates the mechanism leading to the reabsorption of water.

oxygen debt: The additional oxygen required by a person after exercise to oxidise the lactate that has built up as a result of anaerobic respiration.

P

pancreatitis: An inflammation of the pancreas, caused when enzymes become active inside the pancreas and start to break down the tissue of the pancreas.

partially permeable: A membrane that only allows small molecules, such as water, to pass through it.

passive : A process is passive if it does not require additional energy for it to happen.

passive immunity: This is when a person receives ready-made antibodies, e.g. an unborn baby receiving antibodies from its mother across the placenta.

pathogen: A microorganism that causes a disease.

pentadactyl limb: A limb consisting of five digits, such as the human leg or arm.

peptidoglycan: A polymer found in the cell walls of prokaryotes that consists of polysaccharide and peptide chains in a strong molecular network.

phagocyte: A white blood cell that engulfs large particles such as bacteria.

phagocytosis : The process by which certain kinds of white blood cell engulf bacteria. The bacterium is engulfed by the cell so that it becomes enclosed in a vacuole in the cytoplasm. Enzymes are released into the vacuole so that the bacterium is digested.

phenotype: The characteristics of an organism resulting from its alleles.

phospholipids: A type of lipid made of a glycerol molecule with two fatty acids and a phosphate group attached to it.

phylogenetic: A term that describes a system of classification which groups organisms with other organisms that have close evolutionary relationships with them.

plasma cells: A kind of B-cell that produces specific antibodies.

plasmid: A circle of DNA often found in bacterial cells. It carries genes additional to those in the main piece of DNA.

plasmolysis: The shrinking of the cell membrane away from the cell wall in a plant cell because of the loss of water. This happens when the cell is placed in a hypertonic solution.

polymer: A large molecule made up of many similar smaller molecules, or monomers, joined together.

polynucleotide: : A polymer made up of many nucleotides.

polysaccharides: A carbohydrate made of many sugar units joined together, e.g. starch and glycogen which are both made of many glucose units joined together.

polyunsaturated fatty acid: A fatty acid with more than one double bond between carbon atoms

potassium–argon dating: A method of dating volcanic rocks, based on the fact that ^{40}K decays into ^{40}Ar at a known rate.

power grip: The type of grip that the human hand uses when gripping a tennis racquet.

precision grip: The type of grip that the human hand uses when holding a pencil.

primary response: The activation of a B-cell so that plasma cells are produced, resulting in the production of antibodies.

primary tumour: A tumour that is still in one place. If it is removed, it is very likely that it will not return.

probiotic bacteria: Bacteria that live in the human gut, and are believed to have a beneficial effect on human health.

prokaryotic cells: These are bacterial cells. They are much smaller than eukaryotic cells, and have a different structure. They do not have a membrane-bound nucleus or membrane-bound organelles, such as mitochondria.

proto-oncogene: These are genes that stop a cell dividing too often. They work by coding for receptor proteins that control cell division, or by coding for a specific growth factor.

prophase: The stage in mitosis when the chromosomes condense out.

pulmonary artery: An artery carrying deoxygenated blood from the right ventricle to the lungs.

pulmonary embolism: The obstruction of a blood vessel in the lungs by a blood clot.

pulmonary vein: A vein bringing oxygenated blood from the lungs to the left atrium of the heart.

Purkyne fibres: Specialised cardiac muscle fibres in the walls of the ventricles that carry electrical impulses that cause the ventricles to contract.

R

receptor protein: A protein in a cell membrane that has the complementary shape to a particular molecule.

reproductive isolation: The inability of two populations to interbreed because of changes in their reproduction, e.g. one population may produce gametes at a different time of year from the other group.

retrovirus: A virus that contains RNA and an enzyme called reverse transcriptase. This means that the virus can make a DNA copy of its RNA that it can insert into the chromosomes of the host cell. HIV is an example of a retrovirus.

R_f value: A means of identifying substances separated by chromatography. The R_f value can be calculated using the equation: R_f = distance travelled by the spot/distance travelled by the solvent

ribosomes: A very small organelle which synthesises proteins in a cell.

rough endoplasmic reticulum: A network of membranes found in the cytoplasm of a cell. The outside surface is covered with ribosomes that produce proteins which are transported through the membranes.

S

saturated fatty acid: A fatty acid in which all the C–C bonds are single.

secondary response: The encounter of an antigen for a second or subsequent time. Memory B-cells are present, which means that specific antibodies are produced very quickly and in large numbers, so the pathogen is destroyed before the person experiences any symptoms.

secondary tumour: A tumour in a part of the body that was started by a cell breaking off a primary tumour. It is also called a metastasis.

selective advantage: A variation that gives one organism an advantage over another organism, making it more likely that it will survive and reproduce.

selective breeding: The intentional breeding of organisms with desirable traits in an attempt to produce offspring with similar desirable characteristics or with improved traits.

semi-conservative replication: The means by which DNA replicates. It results in each daughter DNA molecule containing one old strand and one newly made strand.

semi-lunar valves: These are the valves in the pulmonary artery and the aorta, that close to prevent backflow into the ventricles.

sino-atrial node (SAN): A group of cells in the wall of the right atrium that start off the electrical activity that produces the cardiac cycle.

smooth endoplasmic reticulum: A network of membranes found in the cytoplasm of a cell. The outside surface does not have any ribosomes. Its main function is the production and transport of lipids.

speciation: The process by which new species develop.

species: A group of similar organisms that can interbreed to produce fertile offspring.

spindle: A system of protein fibres or microtubules that is involved in organising chromosomes during cell division.

starch: A polysaccharide found in plant cells. It is a polymer made up of many glucose molecules linked together.

stratigraphy: The study of layers in rocks. Generally, older rocks lie below newer ones, so this enables rock layers to be dated.

stroke volume: The volume of blood pumped out by the heart in one beat.

succession: Changes in the community of plants and animals living in an area over a period of time.

surfactant: A substance which lowers the surface tension of a liquid. It is present in the fluid surrounding the alveoli to stop the surfaces of the alveoli sticking together.

systole: A stage of the cardiac cycle when the heart muscle is contracting to pump blood into the arteries.[I have added this entry; delete if not needed. Mitch]

T

telophase: The stage in mitosis when the daughter chromosomes unwind, becoming shorter and thinner. The spindle fibres break down and a new nuclear membrane forms around each group of chromosomes.

thorax: The chest cavity, which is surrounded by the rib cage and the diaphragm.

thrombus: A blood clot that forms in an artery as the result of atheroma formation.

thrombosis: The blockage of an artery by a thrombus, or blood clot. The blood supply is cut off, reducing the supply of glucose and oxygen to the tissues. A thrombosis occurring in a coronary artery is called a coronary thrombosis.

tissue fluid: A watery fluid formed from blood plasma that carries nutrients, such as glucose, and oxygen to body cells.

trachea: The windpipe. A tube that brings air into and out of the lungs. It is lined with rings of cartilage.

triglyceride: A fat or oil, made of a molecule of glycerol with three fatty acids attached to it

tubercle: A mass of dead lung tissue surrounding *Mycobacterium* bacteria. These form in people infected with tuberculosis.

tumour: A mass of abnormal cells that keep multiplying in an abnormal way.

tumour suppressor gene: A gene that codes for a protein that stops cells dividing.

turgid: A turgid plant cell is full of water. This means that the cell membrane is pressing against the cell wall. This happens when the cell is placed in a hypotonic solution.

U

ultrastructure: The fine structure of cells and tissues visible only by the use of electron microscopy.

unsaturated fatty acid: A fatty acid containing some double bonds between carbon atoms.

V

vaccine: An injection of antigens that cause a person to produce memory B-cells against that specific antigen. This means that the person will produce large numbers of specific antibodies in a secondary response, should they ever encounter the pathogen that carries the specific antigen.

variation: The differences that exist between living organisms.

vein: A blood vessel that carries blood back to the heart. It contains blood under low pressure.

ventilation: The mechanism by which the air in contact with a gas exchange surface is changed. Oxygen and carbon dioxide diffuse across the gas exchange surface. Ventilation makes sure that the difference in concentration of gases across the exchange surface is kept as high as possible.

ventricular systole: The stage of the cardiac cycle when the ventricles are contracting, forcing blood towards the lungs and around the body.

venule: A blood vessel that connects the capillaries to a vein.

virulent: A term meaning 'disease-causing'.

vitamins: Organic molecules needed by the body in very small amounts.

W

water potential: A measure of the pressure that water molecules exert in a solution, and their ability to move freely. The more water there is, the higher the water potential and the more freely the molecules can move. It is measured in kilopascals. Pure water has the highest possible water potential, which is 0.

Z

zygote: A cell formed by the fusion of two gametes in the process of sexual reproduction.

Answers

1.1

1. orange squash, cola drink, biscuit
2. It takes time to break the bonds between the glucose units, so it takes longer to be absorbed into the bloodstream.

Basal metabolic rate

1. The man has a higher ratio of muscle tissue, and muscle has a high metabolic rate.
2. The foetus has a high rate of respiration because it is growing and developing, and it gets its energy needs from the mother.

Anorexia nervosa

1. In starvation, body tissues are broken down and these cannot be replaced. For example, if the intestines are broken down, the person will not be able to digest or absorb the food they are given.

1.2

1. a GI tells you how much glucose a food contains and how quickly it will be released.
   b GL measures the effect that a portion of food will have on blood glucose levels.
2. GL = GI/100 × grams of carbohydrate in portion. Therefore the GL of 50 g glucose = 50.
3. Strawberries contain sugars that are absorbed quickly, so they raise blood glucose. However, they contain a lot of water, and also contain quite a lot of fibre. This means the glucose is absorbed more slowly.
4. Brown rice contains more fibre, and fibre means that carbohydrates are digested and absorbed more slowly.
5. Boiling spaghetti hydrolyses some of the bonds in the starch molecules, so it is digested and absorbed more quickly.

1.3

1. Macronutrients are needed in larger amounts than micronutrients, but both are essential for health.

Should we take vitamin and mineral supplements?

1. rickets (vitamin D deficiency) and night blindness (vitamin A deficiency)
2. Pregnant women need extra vitamins to provide for the growing foetus. Elderly people may have a poor appetite, preventing them from consuming enough vitamins and mineral salts. Also, vitamins and mineral salts are not absorbed from the gut so efficiently in older people.
3. A variety of responses are acceptable here. Students should consider the fact that some vitamins are harmful if taken in excess. Also, it is better to eat a healthy balanced diet that contains all the vitamins and minerals that are required, than to eat an unhealthy diet and take supplements.

1.4

1. A population of different bacteria which do not cause disease, and may contribute to health by releasing useful compounds and competing with harmful bacteria that get into the gut.
2. It is used by the liver to make thrombin, an enzyme needed in blood clotting.
3. A range of possible answers can be credited here. For: value of bacteria in binding mutagens; competing with harmful bacteria; producing useful compounds; etc. Against: if you eat a good balanced diet, these bacteria are likely to be present anyway; bacteria grow in the gut, so there should be no need to consume them every day; there are no studies yet that actually prove these drinks are beneficial to health.

Research on vitamin K and *E. coli*

1. It shows that bacteria in the gut make vitamin K but the concentrations of vitamin K are not measured. Therefore we cannot be sure whether this extra vitamin K is essential. Also, we do not know whether it was *E. coli* that produced the most vitamin K as there were other bacteria present in the gut. Antibiotics kill many kinds of bacteria and not just *E. coli*.
2. The studies show that they may be important in producing vitamins but it does not show that they are important for health. The first study is about mice so we do not know how applicable this is to humans. We also do not know whether having more vitamin K as a result of gut bacteria makes people healthier. There could be other effects of these bacteria on human health that were not measured in these studies. The humans who had died had taken the antibiotics because of an infection. We do not know whether this infection has affected their vitamin K level and not the gut bacteria.

Probiotic bacteria

1. This is a difficult study to carry out and there are various approaches that could be taken. Students should consider how they will define 'health' and measure it – e.g. number of illnesses suffered in a year, days off work, blood pressure, etc. There should be two groups of people, one taking a probiotic drink every day and another group taking the same kind of drink every day but without the probiotic bacteria. The members of each group should be picked at random, and ideally they should be limited in age, for example, all aged 16–20 years. Some measurement of health should take place at the beginning of the study and then this should be measured during and after the study. Students should suggest a time-frame for the study, e.g. one year or even five years. They may wish to control other variables, e.g. excluding smokers from the study. The study should also be double-blind, ie neither the participants nor the investigators should know which people are consuming which kind of drink.

2 Difficulties include defining health and controlling other variables that affect health, e.g. other foods eaten; amount of exercise; obesity; smoking; and alcohol intake.

1.5

1 Any three from: sweating; breathing out; urine; faeces.

2 These drinks contain caffeine, which is diuretic. This means they increase the amount of water you lose in your urine.

3 This is a drink with the same water potential as blood plasma. It contains salts, water and sugar.

4 It would have a lower (more negative) water potential than your blood plasma. (Remember that adding solutes lowers the water potential, and adding water raises the water potential.)

1.6

1 Any two from: increased alcohol consumption (alcohol contains energy but has little nutritional value); increased stress levels so people eat more convenience foods and/or turn to 'comfort eating'; warmer homes and workplaces, so the body expends less energy in keeping warm; living in towns and cities so people do not have to walk far to get to amenities; fear of crime means people are less likely to let their children play or cycle out of doors and women or older people may be reluctant to walk or jog, especially at night.

2 Any three sensible suggestions, including educating people about the dangers of obesity and how to eat properly; passing legislation to make food labelling clearer to people; passing legislation to reduce the amount of salt, trans-fatty acids and other harmful ingredients in convenience foods; encouraging schemes that improve the amount of exercise people get, e.g. introducing cycle lanes that are safe to use so more people cycle to work.

3 The answer you give is not important, but you need to think of sound reasons for your answer. If you think the government should do something, you may link this to the cost of treating obesity-related diseases and the cost of days off work. You may also think that the government has a duty to raise public awareness, and that the National Curriculum should include more information on the benefits of exercise and healthy eating. The provision of public spaces in which people can exercise safely is also a government responsibility. On the other hand, you may feel that if the government is involved in raising public awareness of obesity, those who are obese may feel stigmatised. You may feel that obesity is a matter for the individual and there is nothing that other people can do about it.

Food labelling

1 This will depend on your point of view. The system in Figure 1 is easier to use, because it just relies on colour, but it does not give such detailed information. People may not be sure whether a food with amber on it is good or bad for them. The system in Figure 2 gives more detail but it takes more time to read and understand it, so may not be useful if a person is in a hurry. The recommended daily amounts only apply to a typical adult, so do not apply to children and may not apply to the person actually buying the food.

Food additives

1 It has passed safety tests and has been approved for use throughout the European Union.

2 Any three from: improve colour/texture; prevent 'off' flavour developing; inhibit microbial growth.

3 The answer here will depend on your point of view. You may argue that the additives are tested for safety, and make food safer by inhibiting microbial growth and increasing shelf-life. Alternatively, you may say that these additives may not be safe if we eat a lot of processed food, and that many of them would be unnecessary of we ate more fresh food and better quality ingredients were used.

1.7

1 Joining two molecules together by removing a molecule of water.

2 a A sugar made of two single sugars/monosaccharides joined together.

b A polymer of many monosaccharides joined together.

3 The bonds between glucose units in cellulose cannot be broken down in the body, so it remains in the intestines and cannot be absorbed.

Dietary fibre and colon cancer

1 It allows comparison as there may not be the same number of people in each group.

2 It shows that eating large amounts of red meat increases the risk of colon cancer. However, if a person eats a high fibre diet as well as red meat, this reduces the risk of colon cancer.

3 We do not know anything about other aspects of the person's diet, e.g. alcohol or fat consumption; we do not know anything about their lifestyle, e.g. whether they are obese or smoke cigarettes; the people responded by questionnaire and may not have accurately reported their fibre and red meat consumption.

1.8

1 They have different side-chains or R-groups.

2 Because she needs amino acids/proteins not only for repair, but also for her growing tissues and the foetus's growing tissues.

1.9

1 A molecule of glycerol with three fatty acids attached by condensation reactions.

2 In a saturated fat, all the carbon–carbon bonds are single. In an unsaturated fat, some of the carbon–carbon bonds are double.

3 Fat is very high in energy, so it can lead to obesity. Also saturated fats are thought to give an increased risk of coronary heart disease.

4 Any three suitable ideas, e.g. the study has to be carried out over a long period of time; there may be other items in the person's diet that affect the person's health; other factors affect health, such as exercise, smoking or drinking alcohol.

Fish oil supplements

1 The more omega-3 fatty acids in the blood, the lower the risk of sudden cardiac death.

2 Various possible answers including how much exercise the men took, the components of their diet, whether they smoked or drank alcohol, etc.

3 It shows that this is likely because there is a clear correlation between omega-3 fatty acids in the blood and the risk of sudden cardiac death. However, this is a correlation and does not prove that omega-3 fatty acids protect against heart disease as there may be another factor involved.

1.10

1 Proteins are made up of many amino acids joined together, and polysaccharides are made of many monosaccharides joined together. Lipids are made of glycerol and three fatty acids, so they are not made of many smaller molecules linked together.

2

Food molecule	Composed of
proteins	amino acids
polysaccharides	monosaccharides/glucose
lipids	glycerol and fatty acids

3 When two molecules are split by adding a molecule of water.

4 So that they become soluble, and can be absorbed into the blood.

1.11

1 Ink might dissolve in the solvent.

2 $R_f = \dfrac{\text{distance moved by spot}}{\text{distance moved by solvent}}$

3 $25\,\text{mm} \div 50\,\text{mm} = 0.5$.

2.1

1 a Only the correct substrate has the right shape to fit into the enzyme's active site.

  b When the substrate(s) fit into the enzyme's active site, this makes the reaction much more likely to occur. This lowers the activation energy needed.

2 disulphide bridges and hydrogen bonds

3 The induced fit theory suggests that the enzyme's active site changes when the substrate is present, but the lock and key theory suggests that the active site is always the same shape.

4 The bonds in cellulose are a different shape from those in starch, so they will not fit into the active site of the starch-digesting enzyme.

2.2

1 a This slows down enzyme activity, because the molecules have less kinetic energy. Therefore there are fewer collisions between the enzyme and substrate molecules.

  b Heating denatures enzymes, so that they cannot work.

  c Vinegar has a low pH, so it denatures enzymes. This means the enzymes cannot work.

2 This keeps the pH the same, so that there is only one variable, i.e. temperature. This means that any change in rate of reaction must be the result of the change in temperature, and not any other factor.

2.3

1 At these temperatures, the enzyme is very stable. If it is exposed to higher temperatures, the enzyme might denature. Its active site would change shape and it would not work.

2 Only glucose can fit into the active site of the glucose oxidase enzyme.

3 When glucose is detected by glucose oxidase, gluconic acid and hydrogen peroxide are produced, but they cannot be seen. The second enzyme and chromagen are needed to produce a colour change that can be detected.

2.4

1 Digestive enzymes do not leave the pancreas effeciently and start to break down the tissue of the pancreas.

2 Digestive enzymes are secreted into the intestines, and they are not broken down.

3 They can carry out paper chromatography on the milk. Next to the origin with the milk on, they can place a sample of pure lactose. They can then check that there is no spot on the milk chromatogram that corresponds to the known lactose spot.

3.1

1 trachea, bronchus, bronchiole, alveolus

2 Holds the tubes open, and prevents them collapsing when the pressure inside them falls.

3 Allows stretching as the neck moves/provides flexibility in the neck/ provides flexibility when food moves down the oesophagus (which is next to it).

4 The mucus will not be moved out of the lungs, so the smoker will have to cough to remove mucus from the air passages. Also, the smoker will be more likely to have lung infections, as bacteria will be carried into the lungs.

3.2

1 a pulmonary artery, b pulmonary vein

2 Stops the alveoli sticking together during ventilation.

3 large surface area, thin permeable surface, large concentration gradient

4 Any three from: there are millions of tiny alveoli in each lung; each alveolus is folded, giving an even greater surface area; the epithelium of the alveolus is made of very thin, flattened cells; the wall of the capillary is also made of very thin, flat cells; the capillary walls are in close contact with the alveolus walls; ventilation brings air high in oxygen and low in carbon dioxide into the alveoli, and takes away air high in carbon dioxide and low in oxygen; the capillaries constantly bring deoxygenated blood to the alveoli, and remove oxygenated blood; red blood cells are slowed down as they flow through the capillaries, allowing more time for diffusion.

3.3

1 Composed of a glycerol and phosphate 'head' with two fatty acid chains as a 'tail'.

2 The 'heads' are hydrophilic, so arrange themselves on the outside of the bilayer, towards the water that is inside and outside the cell. The hydrophobic 'tails' are on the inside of the bilayer, away from the water.

3 Any three from: carriers; receptors; antigens; enzymes; add stability.

4 The phospholipids can move around within the layer they are in. Proteins are scattered among them, giving a mosaic appearance.

3.4

1 The net movement of molecules from a region of high concentration to a region of low concentration.

2 Similarity – any one from: both involve the molecule moving from a region of high concentration to a region of lower concentration; neither uses additional energy. Difference: simple diffusion occurs across the phospholipid bilayer, while facilitated diffusion uses protein channels or protein carriers.

3 A small, lipid-soluble molecule would diffuse across the membrane more quickly, because it can dissolve in the phospholipid bilayer.

3.5

1 The movement of substances into or out of a cell, against their concentration gradient. It uses ATP energy.

2

Process	Moves molecules against a concentration gradient	Uses ATP energy	Uses protein carrier molecules
diffusion	✗	✗	✗
facilitated diffusion	✗	✗	✓
active transport	✓	✓	✓

Interpreting data about active transport

1 a They both enter the plant cell against a concentration gradient (there are more sodium and potassium ions inside the cell than outside).

    b More potassium ions enter the cell than sodium ions.

2 X enters the cell by active transport. This is because it reaches a higher concentration inside the cell than the concentration outside the cell, so it must be entering against a concentration gradient. Y enters the cell by diffusion. This is because it enters the cell only until a concentration of 4 mg dm^{-3} is reached, which is the same as the concentration of Y outside the cell. At this point equilibrium is reached.

3.6

1 a Osmosis is the movement of water molecules from a region of higher water potential to a region of lower water potential across a partially permeable membrane.

    b Water potential is a measurement of the energy of water molecules in a solution, and their ability to move freely.

2 It uses only the kinetic energy of the water molecules. There is no additional energy needed.

3 Arrows showing water moving from A to B and from B to C.

4 From B to C, because the water potential gradient is bigger.

5 cell A

6 If the blood plasma became hypertonic to the cells, cells would lose water by osmosis and shrivel up. If the blood plasma became hypotonic, cells would take in water by osmosis and burst.

3.7

1 Normal CFTR actively transports chloride ions out of the epithelial cells into the mucus. This lowers the water potential of the mucus, so water enters the mucus from the intercellular fluid. The presence of more water in the mucus makes it thinner than the mucus of a person with CF.

2 a they have frequent lung infections and have to clear their airways of mucus

    b thick mucus carries bacteria and viruses into the lungs

    c mucus blocks the airways, preventing air from ventilating all the alveoli

3 Advantages – any one from: treatment can be started as soon as possible; early treatment reduces the chances of lung damage developing. Disadvantages – any one from: expensive to screen, when most children will prove negative; possibility of false positives or negatives.

3.8

1 Light microscope and electron microscope. The electron microscope is best for viewing a cell's ultrastructure.

2 a synthesising proteins,

    b transporting proteins round the cell,

    c synthesising steroids /phospholipids/ fats,

    d modifying proteins/lipids made by the ER and packaging them into vesicles for secretion.

3 Producing ATP in aerobic respiration.

4 ATP is needed for muscle contraction.

5 ribosome, RER, Golgi body, vesicle, membrane

6 This enables the mucus to be moved. If they all beat randomly, there would be no net movement of the mucus.

7 Any two from: protein synthesis; active transport; contraction of cilia.

3.9

1 Mucus blocks the bronchi and bronchioles, reducing the surface area available for gas exchange. It also carries bacteria into the lungs which can cause infections.

2 This makes the trachea, bronchi and bronchioles wider, so more air can get into and out of the alveoli.

Smoking and emphysema

1 Fewer capillaries around the alveoli, therefore reduced gas exchange. The alveoli are larger, and fewer in number, therefore there is a smaller surface area for gas exchange. Loss of elasticity makes ventilation more difficult, which will also affect gas exchange as the concentration gradient between the blood and the air in the lungs will be reduced.

4.1

1 Any three from: mitochondrion; endoplasmic reticulum; nucleus; Golgi body.

2

Prokaryotic cell	Human cell
no true nucleus with a nuclear membrane	has a true nucleus with a nuclear membrane
has a circular piece of DNA	DNA in the form of chromosomes inside the nucleus. These chromosomes are linear.
Flagella (if present) are rigid and corkscrew-shaped. They rotate from the base.	Flagella (if present) can beat and move from side to side.
no membrane-bound organelles	contains many membrane-bound organelles, e.g. mitochondria, endoplasmic reticulum and Golgi body
ribosomes are smaller	ribosomes are larger
sometimes has a capsule	does not have a capsule

4.2

1 The symptoms are caused by the endotoxin which is released when the bacteria die. There is a time delay while the bacteria get to the small intestine, invade the cells and multiply inside them, and then die.

2 Antibiotics would kill most of the bacteria in the intestine. Many of these bacteria are harmless or even beneficial, and will 'compete' with the Salmonella bacteria, reducing their numbers. Also, doctors will not prescribe antibiotics unless strictly necessary, to avoid bacteria becoming antibiotic resistant.

3

Food hygiene rule	Reason for the rule
Do not re-freeze frozen food that has thawed out.	When the food thaws out, any bacteria in the food will multiply. This means that the next time the food is thawed, there may be very large numbers of bacteria present.
Store raw meat at the bottom of the refrigerator, and cooked food, or food that is to be eaten raw, at the top.	This is so that juices from the meat, which may contain Salmonella, do not drip onto food that is not going to be cooked before it is eaten.
Boil dishcloths regularly, or use disposable ones.	Dishcloths can contain food remains and moisture, providing a moist, nutrient-rich environment for bacteria to grow. Wiping a surface with a contaminated dishcloth can spread bacteria.
Do not use a board or knife that has been used to prepare raw meat for any other food preparation, until it has been thoroughly washed.	Any Salmonella bacteria from the meat that is present on the knife or the board can be transferred to other foods.
Keep food you have prepared, such as ham sandwiches, in a refrigerator until it is ready to be eaten.	This is so that any food poisoning bacteria that might be present in the food are not able to multiply. Usually, large numbers of bacteria are needed to cause disease.

4 The frozen chicken should not have been stored above the ham. It is possible that juices from the chicken, containing Salmonella, dripped on to the cooked ham. When the sandwiches were made, they were not stored in the refrigerator, so the bacteria were able to multiply. Covering the sandwiches in cling film would have kept the sandwiches moist and ideal for bacteria to multiply.

4.3

1 It is spread by droplet infection, so people who live in overcrowded conditions are more likely to breathe in droplets of mucus containing the bacteria that another person has coughed out.

2 These symptoms result from the damage to the lungs and the breakdown of lung tissue.

3 People who live on the streets are more likely to have a poor state of health, so their immune system will not be able to contain the infection as well as a person living in good conditions.

4.4

1 Penicillin does not harm human cells because they do not have cell walls. Tetracycline does not harm human cells because eukaryotic ribosomes are larger than prokaryotic ribosomes.

2 The water potential inside the bacterial cell is lower than that in the solution outside the cell. Therefore water enters the cell by osmosis, down a water potential gradient. This makes the cell swell up so it presses against the weak cell wall, causing it to burst.

3 a Cover the surface of several sterile Petri dishes with a lawn of bacteria. Add lichen extract to each Petri dish. Incubate the dishes and examine them. If there is a clear area around the lichen extract, then the lichen extract does contain an antibiotic. The investigation should be repeated many times, using several different kinds of bacteria.

    b You would need to check that the antibiotic is not toxic or harmful when given to humans. You would also need to check whether it is an antibiotic that is already being produced from another source, and whether it is broken down when taken into the human body.

    c It may stop them being eaten by animals and it may stop bacteria infecting them.

4 a Antibiotic A. Reason: it has the largest inhibition zone.

    b It may be too expensive; it may interfere with drugs the patient is already taking; it may be broken down inside the body; it may have unpleasant side-effects or be toxic.

4.5

1 The person may cough or sneeze droplets of mucus that contain the MRSA bacterium.

2 When you have surgery, the skin is broken open. This makes it easier for the MRSA bacterium to get into the body.

3 An enzyme is a protein, so it will be made at the ribosome.

MRSA infections

1 To allow comparison because some people stay in hospital for a longer period than others.

2 The infection rate varies but it tends to be higher in Jan–March and lower in the summer months. Accept any sensible suggestion, e.g. more respiratory infections Jan–March, e.g. colds and flu, so MRSA may spread from one person to another in droplets. These people with MRSA in their noses may then be taken into hospital for another reason.

4.6

1 Viruses do not show any signs of life outside a living host cell, such as respiration, growth, reproduction etc. In other words, they have no metabolism of their own.

2 When a person is HIV positive, they have antibodies against the virus because they have been infected, but the virus is latent and the person shows few or no symptoms of disease. When a person has full-blown AIDS, HIV is multiplying rapidly and destroying T cells, resulting in various diseases.

3 Suggestions include: limiting the number of sexual partners; using condoms during sexual intercourse; screening blood transfusions; giving intravenous drug abusers sterile needles; encouraging HIV positive mothers not to breast-feed their babies.

4 Antibiotics interfere with bacterial metabolism, e.g. by preventing proteins being made or by inhibiting cell wall synthesis. Viruses do not have any metabolism of their own, nor do they have a cell structure so they do not have cell walls or ribosomes. Therefore, antibiotics are not effective against viruses.

5.1

1 amino acids

2 hydrolysis

3 ribosomes (A better answer is to say they are made by enzymes on the endoplasmic reticulum, then packaged into lysosomes at the Golgi Body.)

5.2

1 Antibodies are specific to one antigen. The antigen on the *Salmonella* bacterium is a different shape from the antigens on *Mycobacterium*. This means that the antibodies against *Salmonella* will be the wrong shape to fit on to *Mycobacterium*.

2 Once a person has had measles, there will be memory B-cells present. If a person ever becomes infected with the measles virus again, these B-cells will produce specific antibodies very quickly. These will destroy the measles virus before the person can become ill.

3 The cold virus keeps changing its antigens. This means that although you may have antibodies to protect you against one strain of the cold virus, you will not have antibodies against a different strain.

4 Any two from: ribosomes; rough endoplasmic reticulum; Golgi body.

5.3

1 On the membrane surrounding the virus, if there is one. Otherwise it will be on the capsid.

2 People with HIV have fewer helper T-cells. This means that killer T-cells will not be activated; there will be less antibody production by B-cells; and there will be less phagocytosis by macrophages. As this reduces the activity of the immune system, the person is more likely to suffer from infections.

3 These cells are all identical because they all have the same shape of surface receptor and they all respond to the same specific antigen.

5.4

1

	Natural immunity	~~Passive immunity~~ Artificial
Passive	Antibodies passed from the mother to the fetus via the placenta	
	Antibodies passed from a mother to a baby in breast milk	Antibodies produced by another organism are injected into a person
Active	Antibodies are produced by plasma cells as a result of infection by a pathogen. As a result of this infection, memory B-cells are produced which become active if the person becomes infected by the same pathogen on a later occasion.	Antibodies are produced by plasma cells as a result of antigens being introduced to the body by a vaccination. As a result of the vaccination, memory B-cells are produced which become active if the person become infected by the same antigen on a later occasion.

2 Memory B-cells are not produced, so the baby does not produce its own antibodies.

3 The horse antibodies destroy the venom, but they are also seen as 'foreign' by the body. They act as antigens, and the body's immune system responds by making antibodies against the horse antibodies. Memory B-cells will also be produced. If the same person receives a later injection of the same antibodies, the memory B-cells will produce a very fast secondary response, which will destroy the horse antibodies very quickly.

Mass vaccination – risks and benefits

1 Tuberculin is only an extract from the bacterium. It does not have all the components of the bacterium such as the DNA.

2 Cells and tissues have been damaged by the needle. The damaged cells release a chemical that makes the capillaries become more 'leaky' which causes the redness and swelling. As a result of this, phagocytic white blood cells engulf the tuberculin.

3 These people may be infected with active TB. A chest X-ray will show whether this is the case. If the person does have active TB, they will need treatment.

4 Attenuated means 'weakened'. An attenuated microorganism has been repeatedly subcultures so that it no longer causes the disease.

5 The antigens of *Mycobacterium bovis* are similar in shape to those of *Mycobacterium tuberculosis*, so antibodies against *Mycobacterium bovis* will be effective against *Mycobacterium tuberculosis*.

6 No, the incidence of TB had declined rapidly well before the BCG vaccine was introduced.

7 Improved housing, e.g. less overcrowding, and better ventilation. Also, fewer people were malnourished, making them more resistant to infection.

8 a There was economic decline in the country at this time, meaning that more people were living in overcrowded conditions and there was more malnutrition.

   b Immigration into the UK of people who were already infected with TB because of poor conditions in their country of origin; development of antibiotic-resistant TB; decline in number of people being vaccinated.

9 Students may decide yes or no. If 'yes', reasons may include: measles is a serious disease that can kill children; measles can also have unpleasant side-effects such as brain damage; mumps can lead to hearing impairment; rubella causes serious harm to a foetus, so vaccinating children protects pregnant women from the risk of catching the disease by ensuring that most of the population are immune; serious reactions to MMR vaccine are extremely rare. If 'no', reasons may include that measles does not often kill children and most do not suffer side effects; mumps rarely kills children and the side-effects are very rare; rubella is not dangerous to children, only to pregnant women; MMR can cause slight side-effects but there is no need to put the child at risk.

10 This is to reduce the pool of infection. If most of the population are immune to rubella, pregnant women are very unlikely to contact the disease.

11 The number of people with autism rises following the introduction of MMR, supporting Dr Wakefield's theory.

12 The number of cases of autism was slowly rising before MMR was introduced. It does not prove that MMR causes autism because another factor could be responsible for this. The data do not show that it is children who have received MMR that develop autism.

13 No, they do not. The number of cases of autism is rising when MMR is introduced. Shortly after this, there is a fall in cases of autism. Although the number of cases of autism does rise over the period when MMR is being used, this increases even more after MMR is stopped. The data do not show that it is children who have received MMR that develop autism.

14 People are better at diagnosing autism and more aware of what it is, so it is being diagnosed earlier and more often. Also, this only shows cases of autism diagnosed by age 7: it does not show overall increases in the incidence of autism.

15 Students will form a point of view based on many of the arguments already listed in the answers to previous questions.

Cervical cancer

1 For: protects girls/women against a type of cancer that could otherwise kill them. Against: some people think it may encourage promiscuity; girls who never have a sexual partner, or who only ever have one or two sexual partners are not at high risk, so there is no need to give them the vaccination.

2 For: it reduces the chances of HPV being passed on during sexual intercourse if males are immune to it. Against: the vaccine presents no advantage to men, and there is always a slight risk of side-effects; it is expensive to vaccinate men when they will not gain any personal benefit.

5.5

1 The antibody binds specifically to one antigen. Some kinds of breast cancer cells may have a different antigen on their surface, so herceptin will not bind.

2

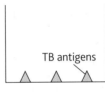
well in test dish
TB antigens

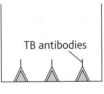
Sample of blood is added. If TB antibodies are present they bind to the antigens.
TB antibodies

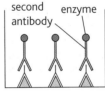
second antibody   enzyme
The well is washed to remove unbound antibodies. Next an antibody is added that attaches to the first antibody. The second antibody has an enzyme attached.

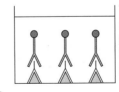
The well is washed again to remove unbound antibody. A colourless solution is added. This changes colour due to the enzyme, indicating a positive test for TB antibodies.

3 a This causes a colour change, so that a positive result can be seen.

   b There would be no colour change. This is because the antigen would not attach to the antibodies in the well in stage 1. This means that the secondary antibody would not stick to the antigen in stage 2. Without the enzyme on the secondary antibody being present, there will be no colour change.

   c This removes any antibodies that are not stuck to the antigen. If some unbound antibodies were left behind, they could react with the dye in stage 3 and produce a colour change, even though PSA would not be present.

6.1

1

	Diastole	Atrial systole	Ventricular systole
AV valves	open	open	closed
semilunar valves	closed	closed	open

2 The left ventricle has thicker muscular wall to generate a higher pressure to pump blood to the body, whereas the right ventricle has thinner walls as less pressure is used to pump blood to the lungs.

3 The blood is not oxygenated at the lungs of a foetus, so there is no need for all the blood to pass through the lungs. The hole in the heart means that both the left and right ventricles can pump blood round the body of the foetus.

4 Oxygenated and deoxygenated blood will mix. This means that blood which is not fully oxygenated is pumped around the body. A person with this condition is likely to get tired easily and become breathless when they exercise.

6.2

1 a $\frac{60}{0.6}$ = 100 beats per minute,

b The pressure changes in the right atrium would be very similar to those in the left atrium, because both atria only have to pump blood to the ventricle. The pressure changes in the right ventricle would be different. The pressure would be the same as the left ventricle at 0.12 seconds when the AV valve closes, and the same at about 0.4 seconds when the AV valve opens. In between these times the pattern would be the same as the left ventricle, i.e. rising to a peak then falling, but the peak would be considerably lower than the left ventricle. This is because the right ventricle only has to pump blood as far as the lungs.

2 a If the fibrous tissue was not there, waves of electrical activity would pass straight from the atria to the top of the ventricles and the ventricles would contract from the top down. As the blood vessels leading from the ventricles are at the top, this would not be efficient at causing the ventricles to empty completely.

b This allows the atria to empty completely before the ventricles start to contract.

c This means the ventricles contract from the bottom up, which is the most efficient way for them to empty.

6.3

1

Feature	Artery	Vein	Capillary
lumen	narrower than vein	wider than artery	very thin so blood cells flow through one at a time
endothelium layer	present	present	present
elastic fibres	relatively thick	relatively thin	none present
collagen fibres	present	present	none present
valves	none present	present	none present

2 renal vein – vena cava – right atrium – right ventricle – pulmonary artery – lungs – pulmonary vein – left atrium – left ventricle – aorta – hepatic artery

3 This allows more antibodies and white blood cells to leave the capillary and destroy any pathogens present. The white blood cells will engulf the pathogens by phagocytosis.

4 In the body, a vein is circular in cross-section because it is filled with blood. When you prepare a section for microscopy, the relatively thin wall of the vein collapses and makes it appear oval. The artery wall is much thicker so it is less likely to collapse when a section is made.

6.4

1 When you exercise, your heart beats faster. This means the heart muscle cells are respiring more, and need more oxygen. As blood flow is restricted along the coronary artery because of the angina, the heart muscle cells cannot get enough oxygen. This causes pain.

2 Atheroma means that some of the muscle and elastic fibres in the artery wall die, and fibrous tissue builds up. The artery wall is less elastic. This makes the artery wall weaker, and more likely to stretch under pressure of the blood passing through the artery.

3 A thrombosis is a blood clot in an artery, so this stops blood reaching some cells in the brain. As a result, these cells lack glucose and oxygen for their respiration, and they die. A ruptured aneurysm causes a haemorrhage in the brain. As a result, blood is not passing along the artery to the brain cells. The cells lack glucose and oxygen needed for their respiration, so they die.

6.5

1 Salt in the blood lowers the water potential of the blood. This means that more water enters the blood by osmosis. This increases the volume of blood in the blood vessels, so it increases blood pressure.

2 The more cholesterol present in the blood, the more cholesterol will be engulfed by macrophages and deposited inside the artery walls.

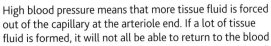

3 If nicotine narrows blood vessels, this means the same amount of blood will flow through a smaller space. This increases blood pressure.

Coronary heart disease and ethnicity

1 The populations of each country are different. This ratio allows different countries to be compared.

2 12

3 They may be more likely to smoke, or to eat a high fat, high salt diet. They may also be more likely to be overweight or lack exercise.

4 This is not a reliable conclusion because the sample size is very small (1 person born in China and 3 born in Hong Kong).

6.6

1 Protein receptors in cell membranes have a specific tertiary structure so that only the 'right' molecule can fit. If beta-blockers have a similar shape to noradrenalin, this means they will be able to fit into the specific receptors. This stops noradrenalin from binding.

2 A vein from another person would have different proteins on the cell membranes, which would act as antigens. The body would undergo an immune response and produce antibodies against the new vein. Eventually this would destroy the new vein. Using a vein from the patient means that it would not be seen as 'foreign' and there would be no foreign antigens present.

Beta-blockers and coronary heart disease

1 This was a control group that was treated in exactly the same way as the other groups except for the medication. It allows doctors to tell whether the medication has any effect on reducing deaths from CHD.

2 So that there would not be any bias.

3 This allows the groups to be compared. There are different numbers of people in each group.

4 Yes, because it reduces patient-deaths better than the low dose. However, the doctor would also need to consider other factors such as side-effects of a larger dose, or interaction with other drugs the patient may be taking.

6.7

1 The valves in the leg veins are damaged. This means they do not prevent backflow efficiently, and blood will accumulate in the lower leg.

2 Enzymes are highly specific. Their active site is exactly the right shape for only one substrate. This means that they can break down the proteins in a blood clot, but not the proteins in a blood cell.

3 Streptokinase is a protein. It acts as an antigen. It is recognised by B-cells which divide to produce a clone of plasma cells that make specific antibodies against the enzyme.

6.8

1 Large surface area – arterioles branch into many capillaries, each with a narrow lumen. Thin permeable surface – capillary wall consists of a single layer of thin, flattened cells with small spaces between them. Large diffusion gradient – tissue fluid is high in oxygen and nutrients, while body tissues are low in nutrients and oxygen as they are using them up all the time. Similarly, cells constantly produce waste products such as carbon dioxide, while tissue fluid is low in waste products.

2 High blood pressure means that more tissue fluid is forced out of the capillary at the arteriole end. If a lot of tissue fluid is formed, it will not all be able to return to the blood via the lymph system and capillaries, so oedema will result.

3 If a person does not have enough plasma proteins, the blood at the venule end of the capillary will have a relatively high water potential. This means that the water potential gradient between the tissue fluid and the blood in the capillary will be small, so very little water from the tissue fluid will be absorbed into the capillary by osmosis. The excess tissue fluid causes oedema.

4 This is because fluid is more likely to accumulate in the feet and legs because of gravity. The excess fluid needs to enter lymph vessels in the leg and travel upwards, against gravity.

7.1

1 70%

2

	Base composition/%			
Source of DNA	A	T	C	G
human	30.1	30.1	69.9	69.9
sea urchin	82.5	82.5	17.5	17.5

7.2

Hammerling's experiments

1 To show that when *Acetabularia* is cut in half and the halves are rejoined, the cell is unchanged.

2 The nucleus of the cell must contain the information that controls the shape of the cell.

The work of Fred Griffith

1 He needed to show that the live S-strain bacteria kills the mice, but live R-strain does not. He needed to use dead S-strain bacteria alone to show that they really were dead, and therefore unable to cause disease. The fourth investigation with dead S-strain and live R-strain bacteria showed that the dead S-strain must be causing the live R-strain bacteria to transform into a type that can cause disease and kill the mice.

2 He could put a sample of the dead bacteria on an agar plate and incubate them. If no bacterial colonies grew, he could show they were dead.

Avery, MacLeod and McCarty

1 Because they wanted to tell whether DNA or protein was the hereditary material.

2 The digested DNA could not produce the whole piece of RNA that is needed to make proteins.

Hershey and Chase

1 This shows that only the DNA from the virus enters the bacterial cells, so it must be DNA that causes the production of new 'phages.

2 To show that only DNA enters the bacterial cells, and not protein.

3 In the centrifugation process, small pieces of bacterial cells may remain in the supernatant, and some of the 'phage coats may still have remained attached to bacterial cells in the pellet.

Erwin Chargaff

1 Paper chromatography would allow him to separate the four nucleotides. He could then cut out each spot from the chromatogram, dissolve the nucleotides in a known amount of solute, and calculate the concentration of each nucleotide present.

2 **a** Watson and Crick would have concluded that the organic bases do not pair with each other, or possibly that T pairs with C and A.

   b The DNA in this virus is single stranded.

7.3

1 Diagram as Figure 1 in Topic 7.1 (page 118) except that the five-carbon sugar should be labelled 'ribose'

2 300

3 Both are polynucleotides/polymers of nucleotides/nucleic acids; both have phosphate groups/sugar-phosphate backbone; both contain adenine, guanine and cytosine.

The RNA world hypothesis

1 It has four different bases in it that can carry the code to make a protein. Base-pairing rules mean that it could replicate itself, and it is compact.

2 Uracil and cytosine are both present in RNA.

3 It is double-stranded, so it is more stable and less likely to undergo changes in the base sequence.

4 It is impossible to re-create the exact conditions that were present on the early Earth, and the evolution of life would have happened gradually over an extremely long period of time. Even if we managed to prove that life based on RNA can exist, this would not prove that this is actually what happened early in the evolution of life.

7.4

1 A gene is a section of DNA that codes for a protein/carries coded information that controls a characteristic of an organism. Alleles are different forms of the gene.

2 The allele that causes alkaptonuria has a different DNA base sequence from the normal allele. This means that it codes for a protein with a different sequence of amino acids. Therefore, the protein has a different tertiary structure. As a result, the enzyme's active site will be a different shape, and homogentisic acid will not be able to fit in it.

Genetic diseases

1 Phenylalanine and tyrosine are converted to hydroxyphenylpyruvic acid and homogentisic acid, but they lack the enzyme to break down the homogentisic acid so this accumulates.

2 Normal people have an enzyme that converts it to maleylacetoacetate then carbon dioxide and water.

3 To show that normal people can break down phenylalanine and tyrosine, even when they consume more of it. Therefore people with alkaptonuria were shown to have different metabolism.

4 They lack pigment in their skin and other parts of the body, e.g. the back of the eye and the hair. They would be very pale in appearance and would get sunburnt even in modest light intensities.

5 Phenylalanine cannot be broken down, because they have a faulty enzyme, so it accumulates. However, they can break down all the other amino acids including tyrosine. The accumulation of phenylalanine leads to mental retardation, so avoiding it in the diet means it cannot build up.

7.5

1 The nitrogen atoms are found in the nitrogenous bases, A, C, T and G.

2 In generation 3 there is twice as much DNA as in generation 2. All the new molecules formed since generation 1 will contain 'light' nitrogen, so three-quarters of the DNA present will be 'light'.

3 **a** If DNA replication had been conservative, there would be no mid-way bands at all. In generation 1, there would be a 'heavy' band and a 'light' band. This would be the same in generations 2 and 3, although the 'light' band would get increasingly dense as the proportion of 'light' to 'heavy' DNA increased.

   b If DNA replication was dispersive, a 'midway' band would be formed in generation 1. In generations 2 and 3 there would also be a single band but it would be higher up, as the proportion of 'light' nucleotides increased. The bands would be rather wider than the one shown in the Meselson-Stahl experiment, since the dispersive method implies that 'new' and 'old' nucleotides are used randomly.

4 It is easier to extract DNA from a bacterial cell because it is not contained inside a nucleus.

8.1

1 A chromosome is a structure made of DNA and protein that contains genetic information. A chromatid is a replicated chromosome.

2 This is because the DNA in the chromosome is 'unwound' forming very long, thin threads that cannot be seen as separate structures.

3 Some genes are not active in a particular cell. For example, the gene that codes for mucus production might be 'switched on' in a cell lining the respiratory tract but 'switched off' in a nerve cell.

8.2

1 **a** interphase/S phase,

   b C,

   c Cytoplasm is dividing/two new cells being formed.

2 B, F, C, A, D, E

8.3

1 Benign tumours are usually slow-growing whereas malignant tumours are often fast-growing. Benign tumours usually stay in one tissue and do not spread, but malignant tumours spread. Benign tumours do not always cause damage and do not grow back when they are removed. Malignant tumours are life-threatening unless treated at an early stage.

2 They may have another allele that does not predispose to breast cancer; there may be an environmental factor that is needed for breast cancer to develop, and so the allele does not cause cancer.

3 It is less likely to have spread to another tissue.

Cervical cancer vaccine for girls aged 12

1 This would give two secondary responses. A secondary response results in more memory cells being produced, which produce specific antibodies against HPV.

2 This is so that they receive the vaccine before they become sexually active. The vaccine is not effective if the person already has the virus.

3 Because cancer takes many years to develop. There will be people who were not vaccinated who go on to develop cervical cancer.

4 To screen for cancer in women who have not been vaccinated; cancer takes many years to develop; the vaccine is only effective against certain strains of HPV and there may be other strains of HPV that also cause cervical cancer; some kinds of cervical cancer are not caused by HPV.

5 They may feel that HPV is sexually transmitted, and vaccinating against HPV encourages promiscuity. People who never have sex, or have only one sexual partner, are at very low risk of getting cervical cancer. People may think that for people like this, the very small risk of side effects from the vaccine is greater than the risk of ever developing cervical cancer.

6 If boys were vaccinated, they would be unable to pass HPV on to women.

Evaluating the causes of cancer

1 The rise in cigarette smoking is followed by an almost identically-shaped line showing a rise in the incidence of lung cancer.

2 This allows comparison as the overall population size may have changed during the time of the study.

3 This is a correlation, not proof of cause and effect. There could be another factor that caused the lung cancer. Also, it shows average number of cigarettes smoked and incidence of lung cancer. It does not show the risk for non-smokers, or the risk according to the number of cigarettes smoked.

Colorectal cancer

4 Various suggestions are possible, including men may eat a higher fat diet than women; men may be less likely to eat food high in antioxidants; men may be more overweight; men may be more likely to smoke than women.

5 The graphs show that in 2001 compared to 1971 the mortality rate for those aged 70+ had dropped significantly, and had dropped more modestly for those under 70. However, over the same time period the incidence of colorectal cancer has increased, showing that people with colorectal cancer have a better chance of surviving in 2001.

8.4

1 Haploid means the cell has one set of chromosomes. Diploid means that the cell has two sets of chromosomes, i.e. the chromosomes are in homologous pairs.

2 Homologous chromosomes have the same genes because a gene is always at the same place (locus) on the same chromosome. However, the alleles, or the form of the gene, may be different on the two chromosomes. For example, both chromosomes may have a gene for eye colour, but one may have the allele for blue eyes and the other may have the allele for brown eyes.

3 9.6 units – this is the diploid cell that is about to divide by meiosis. Its DNA has replicated during interphase. 4.8 units – this is the haploid cell at the end of the first meiotic division. Although it has the haploid number of chromosomes, each chromosome consists of two chromatids. (This could also be a diploid cell that will undergo meiosis but the DNA has not yet replicated.) 2.4 units – this is a gamete (sperm) formed at the end of the second meiotic division.

9.1

1

Kingdom	Animalia
Phylum	Chordata
Class	Mammalia
Order	Carnivora
Family	Felidae
Genus	*Panthera*
Species	*tigris*

2 The tiger and the lion are members of the same genus (Panthera). This means they are more closely related to each other than either of them is to the cheetah which has a different genus. However, they are all members of the same family so all three species have many features in common.

9.2

1 The cytochrome c of a penguin differs from human cytochrome c by 11 amino acids. Rabbit cytochrome c differs by only 9 amino acids.

2 hydrogen bonds between the organic bases

3 The more similar the base sequence of DNA from two different organisms, the more complementary base-pairs can form. This means that there will be more hydrogen bonds formed, and so more heat will be needed to break these hydrogen bonds.

4 The more similarities in the base sequence of DNA between two organisms, the more closely related they will be.

5 It takes time for clonal selection/specific antibodies to be made.

9.3

1 Lamarck would suggest that ancestral ducks continually spread their toes when swimming, which stretched the skin between them. These ducks would pass on their stretched toes and skin to their offspring. Eventually the feet became webbed. Darwin would suggest that ancestral ducks showed variation in their feet. By chance, some ducks had toes that were more spread and had more skin between them. These ducks were able to swim faster so they could get more food and escape predators. As a result, these ducks survived and passed on their alleles to their offspring.

2 There are alleles coding for these features in the pigeon population. However, pigeons with these features are not as successful in the environment as other pigeons. Therefore they do not breed as often, and pass on their alleles.

The germ plasm theory

1 This is evidence that Lamarck was wrong, because none of the newborn mice had tails. However, the mice lost their tails by mutilation, and the experiment only lasted 22 generations.

9.4

1 Bacteria populations show variation. By chance, a mutation occurred that gave some bacteria an allele that produced penicillinase. The bacteria with the new allele were not killed by penicillin, so they survived and reproduced. Their offspring also had the allele for penicillinase. Bacteria without the new allele were killed. This means that the frequency of the penicillinase allele in the population increased so that most bacteria became resistant to penicillin.

2 a The sea is a geographical barrier here, as one population is on the mainland and the other on islands.

b The original populations showed variation. The environment on the mainland was different from the environment on the islands. In each population, those individuals which, by chance, had an advantageous phenotype survived, reproduced, and passed on their alleles. This meant that in each population, the frequency of alleles changed. However, the alleles that conferred an advantage on the mainland were not the same as those that conferred an advantage in the islands. Mutations occurred and further selection occurred. Eventually mutations affecting their reproduction would occur and this would make them separate species.

c There are many changes in their DNA. The scientists may also have interbred the clouded leopards. If they are separate species, they will not produce fertile offspring.

Industrial melanism

1

Site		Non-melanic	Melanic
Dorset 1955 (unpolluted)	released	496	473
	recaptured	62	30
	% recaptured	12.5	6.3
Birmingham 1953 (polluted)	released	137	447
	recaptured	18	123
	% recaptured	13.1	27.5

2 Various suggestions possible, such as use of larger numbers and removing natural moths from the area first.

3 It provides very good evidence for this because it shows that birds eat one kind of moth more than another. This makes it very likely that this is responsible for the change in the frequency of the different kinds of moth. However, there is always a chance that another factor is responsible, so this is not absolute proof.

9.5

1 Fossils are usually found in sedimentary rocks, so we may need to use potassium-argon dating to date the layers above and below the layer the fossil is in. This can only give us a minimum and maximum age for the fossil.

2 After 30 000 years very little ^{14}C is left in the sample so any date would be unreliable.

3 Environmental changes occurred so that the species was no longer well adapted to its environment. Some members of the species with advantageous characteristics survived, and passed on their alleles to their offspring. These individuals, over a long period of time, evolved into a new species better suited to the new environment.

4 There are many similarities between the two species in terms of body size and shape. Both animals have only three well-developed digits. Merychippus has a more developed third digit, and less –developed second and fourth digits. It is much more likely that Merychippus developed from Mesohippus by a process of natural selection than independently.

9.6

1 The population size of early humans was small, and they only lived in a restricted area. They are also likely to have been eaten by scavengers. They were unlikely to die in conditions where fossilisation might occur.

2 This included comparing the amino acid sequences in proteins and hybridising DNA.

9.7

1 Foramen magnum under the skull; twisted femur; fairly broad hip bone.

2 Factual: e.g. height; arm:leg length ratio; bipedal walking; skull shape. Intelligent guesswork: e.g. colour of skin; amount of body hair.

3 Potassium-argon dating. (They were made in volcanic ash.)

9.8

1 Various possible answers, e.g. warning others of danger; allowing cooperation when hunting; passing on information.

2 Australopithecines lived at the same time as *Homo habilis*; australopithecines may have used wooden or bone tools that have not survived; australopithecines may have made and used some of the tools that we find.

3 This cannot prove that *Homo habilis* made and used the tools in this way, but it does show that they might have been made and used in this way, so it is useful evidence.

9.9

1 The bones would show scrape marks and wounds from stone tools, but not teeth marks from scavenging animals.

2 Various answers, including: bonding the group together; everyone gets a share in the food, including the weak and young; there was division of labour, so while some individuals cooked, others hunted, made tools, gathered food or looked after the young. During the meal they may have been able to share experiences and pass on useful knowledge using their language skills, e.g. the location of good places to find food.

3 They could continue activity into the night, e.g. making tools. They could also use their language skills to pass on useful knowledge about places to find food or how to make tools.

9.10

1 They can look at the animal bones found near their shelters.

2 Scientists can compare the DNA base sequences in Neanderthals, early modern humans and present-day humans to see if there are similarities. They can also look at remains of early humans to see if there are bones showing features of Neanderthals as well as modern human features.

9.11

1 They had better and sharper tools, and they could throw spears from a greater distance, perhaps making them more successful in hunting. Other reasons might be: They may have had better clothing, enabling them to survive cold weather. Possibly they were more intelligent (as shown by their ability to produce art), and able to find more food sources and develop survival strategies.

2
  a In australopithecines and great apes, the heavier the body, the greater the tooth area. In humans, the heavier the body, the smaller the tooth area.

  b This suggests that as the different species of *Homo* evolved, the diet became softer and there was less need for large, grinding molars. As *Homo* evolved, they were able to cook their food and soften it.

9.12

1 Populations were very small and confined to a small area in Africa; fossilisation is rare; fossils unlikely to be found; dead animals usually eaten by scavengers or die in situations where fossilisation is unlikely.

2 They shared food so everybody would have had food available. The division of labour meant that more food could be gathered in the same time. Hunting cooperatively in a planned way is more successful than individual efforts.

9.13

1 Canines are used to display aggression. Males use displays of aggression to establish their superiority over other males. Females do not show displays of aggression in the same way.

2 They could examine similarities in the DNA of both organisms. They could do this by finding the base sequences and comparing them, or by making the DNA single stranded and examining the amount of base-pairing that occurs when single-stranded DNA from one organism is mixed with single-stranded DNA from the other organism.

10.1

1 Big-brained infants need more nutrients during pregnancy and after birth. A mother might not be able to supply enough food for the infant on her own.

2
  a The baby is born with a big brain so that it is capable of learning complex skills.

  b The baby is carried by its mother so it does not need to walk, and the ability to move away from the mother might put it in danger. Also, being born with longer legs would require more nutrients. The foetus already consumes a lot of nutrients in developing its big brain.

Stages of development of early hominids

1 Many problems including the fact that we only have fossils of these individuals and we can only make assumptions about their development from their bones, so the data may be unreliable.

2 This allowed a longer period of learning, so that adults had the chance to develop more skills (e.g. tool use) before they became parents themselves.

3
  a This allowed for a longer childhood, when individuals could learn skills by playing with others and interacting with many different individuals in the group.

  b This stage allows individuals to observe and practise adult roles without having the responsibility of children to look after.

4 This allowed older females to share in the care of their grandchildren or other children in the group. These older women would have useful experience and knowledge to share with younger members of the group.

10.2

1 Six basic facial expressions are seen in people from different social and cultural backgrounds, as well as in people born deaf or blind.

2 Ancestral humans had a shorter childhood than modern humans, but it varied in length. Those individuals who had a slightly longer childhood than others would have been able to learn more skills before they became adult themselves, so when they did become parents their children would have a better chance of survival. These children would inherit the alleles for a longer childhood. Gradually, the alleles determining a longer childhood would increase in frequency.

10.3

1 Human ancestors showed variation. By chance, some individuals would have a more flexible thumb that gave them greater mobility. These people would be better at making and using tools. This would make them better at hunting and avoiding predators, so they would be more likely to survive. They would reproduce more and pass on their alleles. Mutations might occur that gave the thumb more mobility. Gradually everybody in the population would have a very mobile thumb.

2 The pelvis might not be wide enough to allow a baby with a large brain to be born. A woman with rickets might die in childbirth.

3 The woolly hair would prevent the heat of the Sun from overheating the brain.

10.4

1 This helps them to focus on their breathing and reduces the panic. Anxious or nervous people start to feel they can't get enough oxygen and breathe too quickly. This lowers the carbon dioxide level in the blood, which can cause symptoms of numbness and tingling of the hands, and dizziness. By re-breathing expired air, they are breathing in air rich in carbon dioxide. Increasing the carbon dioxide level in the air breathed in stimulates the chemoreceptors which control breathing rate. This restores their breathing to normal.

2 The air breathed in is high in carbon dioxide, as well as containing oxygen. This stimulates the chemoreceptors and should help to start breathing again.

10.5

1 One explanation is that the loss of blood means that the concentration of carbon dioxide in the blood increases so the chemoreceptors are stimulated. This increases heart rate.

2 Training results in a larger stroke volume. At rest, an athlete needs roughly the same amount of oxygen as a non-athlete, but the increased stroke volume means that this oxygen can be delivered to body tissues using a lower heart rate.

3 70 cm³

4 55 beats per minute

10.6

1 The glucose is not fully broken down.

2 More haemoglobin and more red blood cells means that their blood can carry more oxygen. This means that they can deliver more oxygen to their tissues when competing, keeping aerobic respiration going for longer.

3 a tiredness and lack of energy

b Iron is needed for the haem group in haemoglobin. One possible cause of anaemia is lack of iron so that haemoglobin cannot be synthesised.

10.7

1 A parasite that causes serious harm to its host, or kills it, is less likely to survive because it needs its host to feed on. In the ancestral population, there was variation. Those parasites which caused serious harm to their host were less likely to survive and pass on their alleles to their offspring. Therefore, over time, the population consisted mainly of parasites that caused less harm to their host.

Bed bugs

1 Answers include: females lay large numbers of eggs; flattened to fit into crevices; bite host painlessly so they are less likely to be noticed; feed at night when host is around.

10.8

1 Some possible answers are: Children should wash their hands after stroking a dog and not put their fingers into their mouth; dogs should be wormed regularly; dog owners should not allow their dogs to foul in areas where children may be playing, eg gardens or parks; disposing of dog faeces into special bins.

2 Good food supply; constant warmth and water supply; easy to release eggs to the environment; avoids exposure to host's immune system.

3 In the ancestral population, a mutation may have occurred that gave a parasite the ability to produce an anti-enzyme. This would have enhanced the ability of that parasite to survive, as it meant it was more resistant to the effects of the host's enzymes. This parasite would have reproduced more and passed on its allele for anti-enzyme to its offspring. Further mutations may have occurred later, and these would be selected for in the same way.

11.1

1 Advantages of farming: Increases the availability of food; allows population growth; allows a settled community to develop; allows division of labour, so some people work on producing food while others take on different roles; enables a surplus to be produced, which leads to trade.

Disadvantages: Farmers have to spend a lot of time looking after their animals and crops; early farmers would have had to rely on hunting and gathering alongside farming to ensure sufficient food in the early years of farming; farming depends on the weather, so crops may still fail.

2 Carbon-dating of animal remains and artefacts found there.

11.2

1 The DNA sequences of modern dogs and modern wolves could be compared. Also, DNA from both modern dogs and modern wolves could be made single-stranded (see Section 9.2) and mixed together. The more base-pairing that occurs, the more closely related the two species are.

2 Larger, fiercer animals would have been killed for meat. Smaller, more docile animals would have been kept for breeding.

3 If they had been hunted and killed for food, there would be signs of injury on the bones where the animal had been killed. There would also be tool marks on the bones showing where the animal had been butchered.

11.3

1 Farmers grow only one kind of crop and get rid of weeds and other plants that grow there. The fact that few plants species are present means that only a few kinds of animal can live there, as they feed on the plants.

2 For: creates a habitat for rare species; allows people to see what the land was like naturally; creates land for recreation that some people think is more attractive to look at than farmland. Against: reduces the land available for food production; some people think that the cost of restoring fenland is not justified by what it achieves.

Index